In the Garden of Our Dreams

In the Garden of Our Dreams

Memoirs of a Marriage

SHIRLEE TAYLOR HAIZLIP

&

HAROLD C. HAIZLIP

KODANSHA INTERNATIONAL

New York • Tokyo • London

Kodansha America, Inc.
114 Fifth Avenue, New York, New York 10011, U.S.A.

Kodansha International Ltd.
17-14 Otowa 1-chome, Bunkyo-ku, Tokyo 112-8652, Japan

Published in 1998 by Kodansha America, Inc.

Library of Congress Cataloging-in-Publication Data
Haizlip, Shirlee Taylor.
    In the garden of our dreams : memoirs of a marriage /
Shirlee Taylor Haizlip & Harold C. Haizlip.
        p.   cm.
    ISBN 1-56836-254-4 (alk. paper)
    1. Haizlip, Shirlee Taylor.   2. Haizlip, Harold C.
3. Afro-Americans—Biography.   4. Spouses—United States
—Biography.   5. Afro-Americans—Marriage.   I. Haizlip,
Harold C.   II. Title.
E185.96.H174   1998
973'.0496073'0092—dc21
[B]   98-20313
                                                                CIP

Book design by Tina Thompson

Manufactured in the United States of America on acid-free paper

98 99 00 01 02   10 9 8 7 6 5 4 3 2 1

To our daughters, Deirdre and Melissa, who have brought shining joy,
profound wisdom, and continuous wonder to our lives.
We hope you will find and cherish
the garden of your dreams.

ACKNOWLEDGMENTS

To our editor, Deborah Baker, we owe deep respect for shining the light on what was really important, and for having the patience and endurance to keep the bulb burning.

To our agent, Faith Childs, we owe the existence of this book. Her support and faith sustained us when we needed it most.

To our parents, Nellie and Allen and Margaret and Julian, we owe the luminous example of constancy.

To our sister, Jewelle, and brother-in-law, Jim, we owe thanks for a road map of a good marriage.

To our sister, Pattee, we owe the joy of remembering her love of her Jim, a love we deeply shared.

To our sisters, Mauryne, Doris, and Vira, and our brother, Julian, we owe thanks for the memories.

To our brother, Allen, and sister-in-law, Elnora, we owe the knowledge that long-term love wears well.

To our friends Helen Andrews, Jonathan Caisse, Libby Clark, Diana Edmonds, Kinderly Haskins, Melody Jackson, David Jackson, DeLois Jacobs, Donna Kline, Kay Malknecht, Phyllis Miriam, Yvonne Peniston, Natalie Sanders, Shahen Zelma Stennis, Althea Tyson, Doris Velasquez, and Bill Young, whose warmth, generosity, and wisdom nourished us, we owe deepest thanks.

To Lucy and William Cromwell, who have found new dreams in old love, we owe renewed commitment.

And kudos to the love that has sustained our friends and family who have been married for more than twenty years: Eva and Johnny Adams; Carol and Glen Battles; Susan and Josi Cazari; Judith and Paul Davis; Bunny and Jeff Dell; Donna and Glenn Dummer; Pat and Lewis Downing; Zaida and Chris Edley; Penny and Greg Edwards; Phyllis and Bill Fields; Ramona and Ralph Gatison; Margo and Tim Gogan; Maureen and Steve Graham; Mayme and Clifton Graves; Dot and John Haizlip; Maisie and Lionel Haizlip; Florence and Bill Harris; Rita and Elmer Henderson; Mary and Tom Herzog; Adelaide and Alec Hixon; Marilyn and Elbert Hudson; Carmen and Bruce Kennedy; Virginia and Bob Lewis; Sue and Richie Lowe; Ronnie and Bill Lytle; Rosie and Paddy Lyske; Fruzina and Rufus Marsh; Patsy and Reggie Mayo; Jean and Joe McAlpine; Verdell and Lloyd McCord; Marguerite and Marcus McCraven; Sandy and Bill Michael; Rae and Tom Minter; Mary and Addie Ottley; Jan and Hank Parker; Barbara and Curtis Patton; Lois and Charles Powell; Marilyn and Hugh Price; Clem and Doug Pugh; Alma and Charlie Rangel; Doris and Wallace Sanders; Carol and Sandy Schreiber; Susan and Skip Sikora; Estelle and Vernon Simpson; Isabel and Donald Stewart; Margo and Reuben Taylor; Penny and Ron Taylor; Teddi and Billy Taylor; Delores and Charles Turner; Earlene and John Turner; Regina and Chuck Warner; Alice and Richard Webster; Dimitri and Earl Williams; and Polly and Chiani Zawadi.

And to Vickie and Dick Bournevanneck; Lucille and Luther Burnett; Limpie and Dante DeCastro; Elaine and Flea Keels; Evelyn and Jose Sprauve; Olivia and Donald Stanford; Easter Mae and Howie Tinney; and Artrelle and Henry Wheatley, whose marriages were gently wrapped in death's curtain, we owe special memories.

Love in the Time of Eisenhower

SHIRLEE: There was no course in courting that was relevant to the way we lived in 1957. Newspaper columnists did not dispense nitty-gritty advice to those who could not get it from their parents or older siblings. Talk shows did not offer up confessionals on what went wrong in relationships or how to walk a smooth path toward lasting matrimony.

Either blithely or with trepidation, we all sailed toward the horizon of Eros, looking for the perfect mate. Some of our friends plunged off the edge, falling pell-mell into a roiling sea. For them, tides of romance and currents of love became tsunamis of betrayal and eddies of disappointment. Others rode smooth waters, sails taut with passion and unwavering commitment.

My father's favorite phrases on the subject of my dating were pithy and few, written in metaphorical granite and hung at eye level: "Respect yourself and respect the Taylor name. Don't call boys, let them call you. If a boy wants to know where he stands with you, tell him on his two feet. No daughter of mine will sit out front of my home in a car with a boy at night. Eleven o'clock is the respectable time for you to be in."

My mother, always sympathetic, gave me more latitude. She sim-

ply said that she knew I would be "a good girl who would go to college." She knew that I knew what "good" meant. It was the "good"
owned and copyrighted by Doris Day.

Lots of boys had hovered around my older sister, Jewelle. And like
a flirtatious Scarlett O'Hara, she kept them all following her bouncing, long skirt. With long eyelashes, long hair, sparkling, dark eyes,
and a sophisticated self-confidence, Jewelle would always be a flower
that attracted many bees.

Since I was four years younger, she did not make me privy to the
inner circle of her romantic adventures. A certain prudishness, characteristic of middle-class black women, was a mainstay of our lives. As
sisters, we did not talk about sex. Part of the reason for that may have
been my age and permanent indentured status as "little sister."

Once my brother showed me a few pornographic cards from a set
that he had just been given. He got embarrassed and quickly put them
away. I had never seen anything like that, but they held no compelling
interest for me. All I could think of was different cuts of colorless
meat in the butcher's window.

The most practical and direct advice was what I heard from the
ladies at my father's church: "Keep your skirt down and your pants
up. A hard head makes a soft behind."

When I was in junior high and high school, our health and hygiene
and home economics teachers periodically showed us short films.
Many featured ponytailed white girls in swirling ankle-length skirts,
twin sweater sets, and white pearls. Their counterparts were crew-
cut white boys in neatly pressed chinos and open-necked dress shirts.
In stilted role playing they acted out some prescribed "good" dating
behavior. It was the documentary version of "Our Town."

In a voice-over, a female whose tone was a cross between Debbie
Reynolds's and Joan Crawford's instructed the somewhat giddy girls
not to wear too much makeup, not to wear tight sweaters, not to have
their bra straps showing, not to talk too loudly, not to be too anxious
when a boy called, and not to stay in a car too long.

One had to listen between the lines to understand what being a
good girl meant and what bad behavior would surely bring. Sex,
though overtly expressed in our dress, our yearnings, and our music,
was not in our daily vocabulary. We were not supposed to talk about

it, and when we did, it was briefly, with a mixture of nervousness, guilt, excitement, and wonder. For girls and young women, life then was full of "not"s and mixed signals.

In the short films, an equally knowing, disembodied male voice advised the boys to be mannerly, to show the girls the same respect they would give their sisters or mothers, to get the girls home on time, and to keep their shirttails and other hanging things tucked in.

There were no black or brown faces in the films. It did not dawn on us to ask where the black students were. As in the commercial movies, they were the black cinematic shadows flickering just behind the silver screen, hoping to make an entrance but never appearing before the lights came up and the seats emptied out.

My classmates and I always laughed when we saw those films, because we knew the behavior was unreal. The coded language did not match our fervid expectations or, for some of us, the forbidden behavior and its consequences. Nonetheless, we all wanted to be the June Allyson/Doris Day girl that men would marry. At the same time we secretly longed to be the Rita Hayworth/Dorothy Lamour woman that men would covet.

In the mid-fifties, when the camera lingered on the exquisite features of the new golden-brown heroine, Dorothy Dandridge, I could see myself as either the prim schoolteacher she portrayed in *Bright Road* or the wanton Dorothy she became in *Carmen Jones*. Carmen held more promise.

CHAPTER 1

❧

That Old Black Magic

𝒮HIRLEE: It was the voice that got to me. I heard it on the other end of the telephone one reddish fall afternoon in 1957. I was a junior then, at Wellesley College. Listening to the latest Nat King Cole album, I was making a desultory effort at studying in my room at Freeman Hall. My roommate answered the phone. I was expecting the call.

One of my classmates, a bright, pretty Jewish girl, had told a friend of her fiancé's about me, one of the Negro girls in her class. My matchmaker assured me that this young man was brilliant, popular, and great looking. What more could I ask?

What serendipity. The voice came through the wire sounding like Nat King Cole. Deep, smooth, buttery sounds. Good diction. Perfect, rounded sentences. Relaxed and self-confident.

The voice, like that of Homer, "sang" his story. He said he did not know all the Negro girls in the area. We both laughed, since there were not too many to know. He was wondering if we could meet for a study date. His suggestion, not mine. I agreed.

A study date was a blind date with a dual purpose. You could study your date and/or your books. If you did not cotton to who showed up, you could actually spend the time reading without insulting your date.

Although I had been going steady with a startlingly handsome fel-

1

low from Boston University for two years, this new voice on the phone wrapped itself around me and drew me close. It was seductive, plain and simple. And I thought seduction was surely the ultimate empyrean, a place of blinding light and intense heat.

I wanted to see his face. I wanted to meet the person who jumped out at me through the phone. Whatever else might happen, the anticipation alone was thrilling. In the meantime, I would keep my date with my Boston University suitor that evening, a local guy from Lexington, Massachusetts, the only son of the only black family in town. Attentive, faithful, he was in love. I thought I was in love, too. There had been much talk about marriage after graduation. But the notion of marriage floated around my head and had not yet settled in my heart. In some deep, deep place I suspected that my great love lay in a land I might never explore.

Harold was from Washington, D.C. He had attended the same high school as my parents, so that made him at least possibly interesting. My father had been one of the school's valedictorians. Above and beyond my dad, my gentleman caller had followed in the footsteps of some of the most brilliant minds of the times.

In those days we interviewed our dates before we met them. What was his major? I asked. The classics! Not to be outdone, I told him that Latin had been my favorite subject in high school and that my favorite Greek name was Mephistopheles. He laughed and then gently corrected my pronunciation.

My embarrassment was fleeting. I was more and more curious. The only other men I knew who were interested in Greek and Latin were my father and some of his closest clergymen friends.

His name gave me pause. "Harold." Such a serious name. Apart from Harold Harefoot, an early king of England, I didn't know any Harolds. Images of someone with thick glasses and protruding teeth came to mind. Did he have another name? I asked. With an easy, deep laugh, he quickly informed me that he did not like "Harry" or "Hal." He allowed his roommates to call him "Haizzy" but barely tolerated that. Intrigued, and tired of the questioning, I agreed to meet this seemingly unstuffy, nonministerial classicist, this forthright Harold, for a Sunday evening study date.

"Who was that? What a voice!" said my normally laconic roommate, Judy. A cornsilk blonde with blue Betty Boop eyes, Judy and I had roomed together for two years. She had come to Wellesley from tiny Chatham, a quintessential New England town on the elbow of Cape Cod. Her curiosity had remained high throughout my phone conversation.

I was already wondering what I should wear. Dressing for a date in the fifties was a big deal. Jeans were not our stock-in-trade. On our campus the casual outfit was Bermuda shorts and a sweater set. But not on a first date. Our options were a dress or skirt and sweater. The Lana Turner college girl look.

I decided on my "killer date" outfit: a royal blue jersey, form-fitting dress with black stripes, and a matching long fringed scarf that I wound dramatically around my neck. My only makeup was red lipstick. I fretted because my hair had not been done recently. It was rough around the edges. There was no salon that catered to colored girls in Wellesley. It was a chore and an expensive journey all the way into Cambridge or Boston to the colored beauty salons. I usually combined such trips with a date, shopping, or a visit to a museum.

For the occasion, I used a goodly supply of Dixie Peach, a popular pomade that was supposed to make your hair shinier and straighter. It did neither for me. Resigned, I brushed my hair back and wore it up in a style somewhere between a teenage ponytail and a spinster's bun.

When I was growing up my mother used to tell me I was pretty. She didn't say it overly much but enough to give me a good sense of myself. I was the middle of three sisters and had an older brother. My father was inordinately proud of his girls and said that all of us were beautiful, but none as beautiful as our mother. I had been a tomboy and a late bloomer. Beauty for the most part was something I saw in my mother or on the movie screen, not in the mirror of the room that I shared with my sister Pattee.

Because ours was a "public" family, my father insisted we give appropriate attention to appearance. He indulged us with a wardrobe of pretty dresses and suits, all of which he personally approved. He always took us shopping, and often he would select the outfits he found "becoming." Once we were old enough, he and my mother gave us free rein. But we always sought his view and blossomed in his assent.

It was not until I was sixteen that I discovered that other people, boys and young men especially, thought I was attractive. When I had to walk across one of the two bridges in our town to catch a bus to go to a summer job in New Haven, there was always a long line of factory workers whistling and catcalling. Having no feminist notions at the time, I secretly enjoyed the experience.

By the time I reached college, I had "come out" as a debutante and dated a number of boys, mostly older than me. One had given me a diamond engagement ring, which I'd accepted for ten minutes and worn for half that time in a closed stall of the girls' bathroom of my high school. Another wanted to elope with me to Maryland. He said he had a set of twins to give me.

In my life then, sex was a secret land behind a veil that would not be lifted until marriage. My goal after high school—and my family's expectation—was not marriage and babies but college and a professional career, and continuing the family role of "uplifting the race." Sex remained the Big Mystery, an important subtext never talked about in polite company. Nor did it cross our lips at home unless someone we knew had "gotten into trouble."

Glamour always hovered around the edges of my life. My mother was a great beauty; my father, handsome. I had had an aunt and an older sister, both stunning, who had been actresses in black films. Much of my family's life had been documented in the black press and magazines. Nonetheless, in the culture of envy, I had a lot of Audrey Hepburn, Marilyn Monroe, and Dorothy Lamour damage. As much as I tried, I knew I could never look like those American prizes. Fortunately, many of my female relatives were my beauty salves.

So when *Mademoiselle* came to Wellesley to interview models for its college issue, I showed up for the sessions. My father had taught me to go after whatever I thought I could do. To me it was not unusual to want to be photographed for one of America's mainstream magazines. What college girl wouldn't want to be in *Mademoiselle*? I didn't even get a nod, much less a callback. In that pristine era, there were no black people on the white pages. Choosing to take a brighter view, I chalked up the rejection to my lack of height. (Years later I finally made *Glamour*. Along with my older daughter, I was photographed in a feature on "Best Moms in America." Not quite the spot I had longed for in years past, but a lovely moment.)

On the November afternoon of the date with Harold, at five-feet-three and 110 pounds I knew I was a well-wrapped package.

Rather than take the elevator down to the lobby and reception area of the dormitory, I walked down, so I could peek at him over the staircase wall without his seeing me. Freeman was the most modern of Wellesley's dorms, and it did not have the grand circular descent of some of the other houses, where you could do your turn on the staircase. (Oh how caught up we were in movie images.) I would have to make it do, though. I did not want to come spilling out of an elevator with a gaggle of other chattering females. I wanted him to focus on and see the singular me. Just the type he would like, I was certain.

What I saw at the bell desk waiting for me was a tall, candy bar–colored young man in a chocolate brown wool sport jacket and black pants. I loved the height. Hated the jacket. He was slender but well formed. I noticed he had large hands. Even from a distance he radiated warmth. I didn't know then it was sex appeal. A few bars of "Some Enchanted Evening" curled around my ears.

As I got closer to him, I don't know why, but I looked at his ears. I thought they were the most peculiarly shaped ears that I had ever seen. They weren't deformed, mind you. Just funny looking. The rest of his face was interesting: open, sunny, good looking. I loved the traces of chubby, pinchable cheeks.

He was comfortably chatting away with the student behind the bell desk. Then he turned and saw me. His move was slight but graceful. He smiled broadly. I could tell he was pleased with what he saw. Practicing moves I had seen many times in the movies, I sidled up beside him, opened my eyes wider, and looked up. I knew my eyes were a good feature. Still gazing upward, I fumbled around until I found and picked up the pen to sign myself out. In those days, Wellesley students had to sign a log if they expected to be out after 10:00 P.M., telling whom they were with, where they were going, and when they expected to return, in time for the 1:00 A.M. college-wide curfew, of course.

Although I was not sure whether we would be out that late, I covered my bases. "How do you spell your name?" I asked.

His eyes twinkled as he said "H-A-I-Z-L-I-P," carefully pronouncing each letter. His spectacular voice had an almost hypnotic effect.

"Well, that's the oddest name I've heard in a long time," I said, a bit smugly and thinking about Harefoot. "Where in the world did it come from?"

"It's Scottish, I've been told," he said simply. The girls at the desk looked at him strangely. He smiled again, broadly. Charm. Charm.

"Now, where do we go around here to study?" he asked casually as he offered me his arm. This was the first time I would notice how both polite and gracious he was. I still notice it.

"Over the hills and beyond the lake," I replied as I folded my hand under his arm and we moved confidently toward the glass doors and the beginning of our life together.

These are the things Harold and I did on our first date. We did not study. Not at all. We began with a stroll along the campus and partly around Lake Waban, talking excitedly all the way.

After our walk, he leaned over in the car, locked my door, and with a big grin opined that I should "move closer so you won't fall out." At that moment I noticed his eyebrows formed almost perfect upside-down vees. Quite attractive.

He took me to dinner at an Italian bistro. During my years in college, I did not drink. Because I wanted him to think I was sophisticated, I suavely drank the red wine he ordered, all the while grimacing inwardly at its bitterness. After one glass and a half hour, I switched to water.

In that silken voice that could have told me anything, he said he had a longtime girlfriend back in Washington and would have to tell her their relationship was over "as of tonight." I was pleased but not surprised. I told him about the boyfriend I had been dating for two years whom I knew I would not see again. It was clear to me that this tall, dark brown man in the long brown jacket was the man I would marry.

Over a red checked tablecloth, with a candlestick in a Chianti bottle, my life had taken a different turn. Unknowingly, I had ventured into that other country, that Shangri-la of my girlhood dreams. I knew that night I would never tire of this man's voice, never be bored by whatever he had to say, never want to leave his presence. We stayed out until curfew.

HAROLD: It's funny how you remember the smells associated with the markers in your life. The day I heard about Shirlee, the lush scent of burning fall leaves competed with the aroma of Mrs. Betancourt's sausage lasagne simmering in the kitchen upstairs. The lasagne won out. Sniffing the air, cocking his head to one side, and rolling his eyes upward, Dan came out of his room to remind me about dinner.

"Haizzy, it's your night to do the honors, right? I'm just checking, because Axel is coming over for dinner with the new Wellesley Wonder that he says he's going to marry. Is there enough tuna for five? Got enough money for the noodles and mushroom soup? And don't forget we need stuff for salad. I'll pick up a bottle of fine wine and some Italian bread. Okay? And if Vitz ever gets out of bed, you'd better remind him about company coming at six-thirty. He'll need to move his shorts off the shower rod in the bathroom and either clean up his room or shut the door. This one's really got Axel googoo-eyed."

"Everything's under control," I said. "Just be sure to bring some white wine that we can drink tonight. Your last 'fine wine' was vinegar before it left the liquor store."

"You thankless bastard. And just when did you become such a wine expert, anyway?"

The front door banged behind him as he bounded down the stairs toward his bike. A lanky six-two brownish-blonde with blue eyes, Dan was off to another day of power politics and intellectual showmanship at Harvard's Graduate School of Russian Studies.

Vitz, Dan, and I had become close friends four years earlier as freshmen at Amherst College. We had joined the same fraternity during our junior and senior years, lived in the frat house together, and, along with several other frat brothers and Amherst friends, had just begun graduate studies in various departments and grad schools at Harvard. Unlike Axel, a business school student who always had rolls of money in his pocket and a fancy private apartment, Vitz, Dan, and I had pooled our meager scholarship monies and rented a semifurnished first-floor apartment, in a distinctly blue-collar area of Cambridge, featuring two- and three-family rowhouses with dozens of unruly, noisy children and countless free-roaming dogs.

At first glance, our Italian landlady, Mrs. Betancourt, didn't know what to make of us. She stared in stunned disbelief as we stood on the small landing outside her second-floor rear entrance asking to see the apartment with the "For Rent" sign in the window downstairs. Having just redone the apartment top to bottom, she wasn't at all sure about renting to three Harvard students. She shook her head, trying to unscramble the issues coming to mind: a lanky blonde, a short red-head, and a tall Negro. What about the sex orgies, loud music, and wild parties with people who don't belong in the neighborhood? Would we destroy the beautiful apartment she had just redecorated?

We waited. She finally called her husband to the door. "What the hell is this?" he shouted, looking directly at us and blowing smoke through the screen door.

We nicknamed the apartment "The Flower Garden." Huge, multi-colored poppies in full bloom on a pale, lime-green background, tied together by pink ribbons, adorned the living room wallpaper. A maroon slipcover festooned with large bouquets of oversized yellow dahlias covered the sagging sofa under two front windows. The stuffed chair opposite the sofa offered a patch of bright red roses and lumi-nescent green thorny stems, also tied together with a satiny ribbon. Double panels of baby-blue billowy satin-sheen curtains, ruffled at the bottom, swagged across the windows and draped to the floor, where they graced the new linoleum Mrs. Betancourt had just laid down, featuring beds of multicolored wildflowers. All the other rooms had been decorated with similar taste and flair. I had never seen anything quite like that arboretum. We took the place.

Mrs. Betancourt gave us explicit rules for cleaning, emptying trash, partying, music, the works. No monkey business.

"How're they hanging, Haizzy?" Vitz asked sleepily while standing behind me, wrapped in a bath towel and reaching over my shoulder for matches to light the cigarette dangling from one corner of his mouth.

"Same place," I mumbled, not looking up from the Herodotus fragment I was decoding.

Short, solid, and stocky, redheaded Vitz had an infectious, broad, toothy smile that sent his freckles flying up both sides of his face, much like a neon sign lighting from the bottom up, in pitch darkness. Majoring in English Lit, he often seemed to be reliving the life of F. Scott Fitzgerald on his own impoverished terms, emerging from his bedroom most Sunday mornings with a new face whose name he'd have to ask before awkwardly introducing her to Dan and me, and politely inquiring about possibilities for breakfast.

"Axel's coming over for dinner with the Wellesley Wonder. Wants to know what we think of her. Remember? It's your turn to do the salad. And, by the way, your shit needs to disappear by show-and-tell time—six-fifteen. Okay?"

"I've already had enough tuna casserole for a lifetime, and I sure as shit don't want to spend hours tonight smiling at Axel's girl. This is the last time, believe you me. When I decide to get married, I'll send you guys a postcard and a photo, that's it. None of this bullshit about you all having to decide whether I've made the right choice."

Barefoot and pissed, Vitz headed for the shower and probably forgot, once again, to put out his cig before jumping in.

"Haizzy and Dan, this is Harriet, my beautiful bride-to-be."

"It's nice to meet you, Harriet," we said in a duet.

Dan headed for the kitchen to pour sherry. Axel and Harriet beamed at each other, taking a seat among the dahlias on the sofa, knees touching.

"Where are you from, Harriet?" I asked, breaking the ice and initiating the third degree. "How and when did you and Axel meet? What year are you? And what's your major? And please don't say you're coming to Harvard after Wellesley, because Axel will never finish the B school. Just look at him. He's wiped already."

"Slow down, Haizzy," Axel warned.

Dan returned with our flea-market stemware glistening halfway with nut-brown sherry, eased to the floor near the coffee table, crisscrossed his long legs, and raised his glass toward Harriet. "To you, Harriet," he toasted. "Did I miss it? Where'd you say you're from? And you're majoring in what?"

"Hey, hey. Cool it, guys," Vitz chimed in. "This isn't the Inquisition. Let Harriet wet her whistle before you have to know her shoe size and her mother's blood type. So which dorm are you in, Harriet, and who's your roommate? I may know her. I'm at Wellesley quite often."

After dinner Harriet turned to me and said, "I have a friend in my class named Shirley Taylor, from Connecticut. She's a beautiful girl, and you and she would make a great pair. I'll tell her all about you. Why don't you give her a call and make a date?"

"Thanks, Harriet," I said awkwardly. "With such a recommendation from you, I'll give it serious consideration."

That was a polite but necessary lie, I admitted later to myself. Rich Wellesley Wonders were not my thing. Probably stuck up, money up the wazzoo, pretentious, looking for a doctor to marry. Not for me. Besides, there was Pam.

During my four years at Amherst, I had regularly dated black women at Mount Holyoke, Smith, Pembroke, Radcliffe, and Simmons. At Amherst, as at all of the Ivy League colleges in the fifties, there usually were only two Negro students in each class, for a total of eight on each campus. We were far from the Little Rock Nine who had just integrated a hostile University of Arkansas. Nonetheless, we were culturally bereft. We compensated by reaching out to each other across campuses and state lines. More often than not, we knew or knew of each other through Negro social circles: the sororities and fraternities, Camp Atwater, the Girlfriends, Jack and Jill, the Links, summers at Oak Bluffs on the Vineyard, Sag Harbor in New York, or Highland Beach in Maryland.

As Negro isolates on white college campuses, we had developed a highly reliable word-of-mouth network about every brown face inside the loop. An important ritual every fall was to obtain a copy of the freshman class book from each of the colleges to check out the new Negro arrivals. The girls denied it but I'm sure they did the same thing.

While I enjoyed meeting and dating women during my undergraduate years, I remained fully committed to Pam. We weren't officially engaged, because I went directly from Amherst on scholarship to graduate school on scholarship and didn't have enough money to support myself, much less give her the kind of engagement ring I had planned. She was a senior at American University. So for years, we had gone steady as the couple who fell in love in the tenth grade and dated each other exclusively through high school. Later she wore my Amherst Phi Psi fraternity pin.

At Amherst and at Harvard, Pam was both my love and my conundrum. Twenty-one years old, lonely, and living with Dan and Vitz, who dated regularly, I burned up the telephone lines talking with her and rationalized any way I could my decision to seek "safe" dates without violating our trust.

For several weeks after our dinner party for Axel and his Wellesley Wonder, I kept hearing in the back of my head a replay of Harriet urging me to make a date with her friend Shirley. I had nothing planned for the upcoming weekend—except studying until I was exhausted—and I wondered whether this Shirley person was as great as Harriet had said. Nothing wrong with meeting and spending one evening with a beautiful woman, as far as I knew. So why not give her a call? I rationalized. Pam may be having a "safe" date as well, so why not? I needed to get out of the apartment, out of the library, and away from the books for a few hours.

I searched our collection of freshman class books in Vitz's room and found the Wellesley Wonder book from several years back. Under the "T"s, there she was: Shirlee Ann Morris Taylor. I noticed she spelled her first name with two "ee"s at the end, instead of the conventional "ey." "Interesting," I thought. She came from some place I'd never heard of. High school honor student. Cheerleader. Oratorical winner. Student government leader. Likes sports and music. Plans to become a medical doctor. Nice picture. Pretty girl. Bright smile. Harriet was right—at least in terms of the photo. Worth a shot. Maybe a study date, just to keep the lines clear and clean. Probably dating someone steadily. Definitely worth a shot.

"Hi. My name is Harold Haizlip, and I am a graduate student at Harvard. I met a classmate of yours—Harriet—a couple of weeks ago, and she spoke so highly of you that I thought I'd give you a call to say 'hello.'"

For some reason, I was nervous. I wanted to meet her, but I was sure she'd simply thank me for calling and hang up.

"Harriet told me a little about you," she said. "Tell me more."

I loved her voice, instantly. It was warm, almost lyrical.

"There's not much to tell," I said, lying through my teeth. "I'm from Washington, D.C. I graduated last June from Amherst College. I'm now living in Cambridge with two close friends and fraternity brothers from Amherst and studying Latin, Greek, and Classical

Philology at Harvard Grad School. I'm planning to complete my master's and probably get a doctorate in Classics or something else. My father died many years ago, and so I am supporting myself on a Woodrow Wilson Fellowship and other scholarships here at Harvard. I drive a great old car on weekends and bicycle everywhere during the week, to save money. I was wondering whether you might be free this coming Saturday evening. Perhaps we could have a study date. What do you think?"

I waited anxiously for her answer.

"Well," she said, "I was supposed to have a date this coming weekend, but I believe he's going to be tied up Sunday with some kind of function. Would Sunday early evening be okay?"

"Sunday's great. At seven?"

"I think so," she said. "Do you know where Freeman Hall is?"

"No, but I have a campus map. I'll find it."

For some reason, unlike all of the other "safe" dates I had had, this one seemed special. Maybe it was her voice. Maybe it was her spiritedness. Her openness. Whatever it was, I liked it.

I couldn't wait for Sunday evening to arrive. On Thursday or Friday, I told Vitz and Dan that I had called that Shirlee friend of Harriet's and was going to have a study date with her.

"Forget the studying! Get laid," Vitz said.

"Yeah, yeah. Not very likely. She didn't sound like that kind of girl. Besides, I'm just a Sunday-night filler while her steady is busy. So we really are going to have a study date. I'll probably never see her again."

"Get laid. That's my advice, Haizzy," F. Scott intoned. "You haven't been with Pam in so long you've earned it. Phone calls just don't cut it. Listen to your uncle Vitz."

I just looked at Vitz and grinned.

Dan fired at Vitz, "Why don't you just shut up, grow up, and get serious."

After showering on Saturday morning, I looked in the mirror and realized I needed a haircut, big time. I looked like a woolly sheepdog. What to do? Seminars and classes all morning, and after 12:00 on Saturdays, every Negro mother in town took her kid to the one black barbershop in Central Square. Where the barber is as slow as molasses. Shit! Maybe I can brush my hair down and slick it back, so she won't notice. Wrong. Got to get a haircut.

At my study carrel deep in the stacks of Widener Library, I awoke in a panic from my unplanned nap Sunday afternoon. Holy shit! It's 5:00 already. What to wear? Jesus Christ! Only two sport jackets in my closet—one nubby brown with black stripes, the other gray herring-bone tweed with subtle maroon stripes and leather patches on the elbows to disguise the worn holes. The brown one. Not too preten-tious, not too pushy. A black tie, my black pants, my white shirt, black loafers, black socks, and I'll be set. Pam's picture inside my breast pocket, to keep me honest. Just in case.

The imposing Gothic columns gracing the Wellesley campus entrance always reminded me of an earthbound Gateway to Heaven. Thirty or more feet high, weathered, sculpted, and majestic, when-ever I drove through them, I always thought about the vast number of girls I was either approaching or leaving behind.

It had been only about five minutes, but it seemed like five hours of shifting from foot to foot in the lobby of Freeman Hall, watching attractive white girls scurry excitedly about. I was trying my best to look cool and calm, but I was churning like crazy inside. What was my problem? My mind jabbered. "This is just a study date. We're going to walk to the library, find some chairs at one of the tables, pull out our books, and study until about 10:00, when I probably should ask her if she'd like to go somewhere on campus for coffee, ice cream, or a shake before heading back to her dorm. Then I'll drive home and never see her again. It's just a one-time study date."

A Mr. Personality, I tried to keep calm and pass the time by chat-ting with the Wellesley Wonder working at Freeman's Bell Desk. Mid-sentence, I glanced at the stairs and knew that was Shirlee coming down toward me. She was gorgeous! Wearing an open mixed-gray tweed coat, she had an ab-so-lute-ly perfect figure wrapped in a blue-striped dress. She walked toward me, moving with the elegance and grace of a professional model. Great legs! Small feet! She smiled brightly—"You're Harold?"—holding out her right hand.

I was dead. Speechless. That voice. That smile. That body. Her warmth was overwhelming. Jesus Christ! I'll never be able to study—or even pretend to study—with her near me.

"Uh, um, um, yes! I'm Harold." I tried to recover. "It's great to meet you," I said, extending my clammy right hand, fearing that I would drop the armload of books under my left arm and make a fool of myself at any moment.

"I have to sign myself out," she said. "How do you spell your last name and where does it come from?"

That voice. It's too much. It knocked me out. I came up with something inane, my heart in my throat. "You have a favorite place to study Sunday nights on campus?" Not waiting for her answer, I continued, "I don't know about you, but I've had a full day and didn't have time to have dinner. Would you mind if we had dinner rather than a study date tonight? I mean, if you're really pressed and have an exam or quiz to prepare for, we can find a quiet place where you can study while I grab a bite, and then we can both study. How about it?"

"That sounds okay," she said, demurely. "But let me show you Lake Waban first."

Yes! Yes! Yes! It sure as hell is okay, I yelled to myself as I reached for her hand and headed for the car.

I hoped she wouldn't notice that my shirt was already soaked across my chest and that because sweat was also pouring into my crotch, my underwear was knotting up and I was walking funny. And thank God I'd put on fresh deodorant: I could feel sweat running down my sides and arms inside my shirt. I was a mess. What the hell was happening? I didn't have a clue, but I felt like I was on fire. This had never happened to me before. I had to repeatedly tell myself to keep cool, stop perspiring, calm down, and see what happened.

As we approached the Chrysler, I opened the door for her and sur-reptitiously glanced at her again. "Jesus Christ!" My interior mono-logue rattled away: "This can't be our first and last date. I've got to see her again—tomorrow, if at all possible. The hell with Mr. Steady Date. One step at a time, old boy. Don't get ahead of yourself. Relax. Get a hold on yourself. And stop sweating so much."

I couldn't stop smiling, although I kept trying not to.

Bounding around the Chrysler, I saw a flash of Pam smiling at me from a large photo on my night table. For a second, I froze.

I didn't understand why—until much later, when I knew without any doubt whatsoever that on that Sunday evening, November 4, 1957, my life had changed profoundly. Forever.

The radio was playing softly. "Turn left at the next intersection. You like Nat King Cole, I see. Know any of his other songs?"

"Do I like him? Do I know his songs? You must be kidding. I know every song he ever recorded, line by line. As if demonstrating the point, I began singing along with Nat. She joined me. I couldn't believe what was happening. She even likes my kind of music. And knows the words. Was this a sign, or what? Unbelievable. Always have loved lakes on college campuses—especially with a beautiful girl at my side and The King on the radio.

"Because of my sister, Vira, I know a million songs, and I play quite a few of them on the piano—when I'm inspired."

"Frank Sinatra. Chris Connor. The Four Freshmen. The Weavers. You like any of them? Do you know their songs, too?"

"My mom has been singing in her church choir since I was born. I heard her singing before I was born. Vira has been singing since *she* was born. I listen to all kinds of music, including classical music, all the time. If I'm still studying around 2:00 A.M., on my broadband radio I always tune to WWVA in Wheeling, West Virginia. Bet you never heard of it. They play the greatest backwoods hillbilly and western music I've ever heard."

"If you park in the next pullout, there's a path to one of my favorite spots," Shirlee said.

Holding her hand in mine as we approached the lake seemed only natural, yet it was thrilling. It probably didn't mean anything special to her, but just touching her, just seeing with my mind's eye her beautiful soft hand with upturned fingertips curled around mine—MINE!—raised my temperature several degrees. The inner Harold was beside himself. "God forbid what would happen if I ever got my arms around her. Oh, Jeesus! The thought of it. And look at me. Getting excited already. Relax. She won't kiss on the first date, anyway. Besides, she's steadily dating that momma's boy from wherever."

Shirlee was joyous yet mellow. I hoped it was because of being there with me, but I couldn't be sure. She showed me her favorite study spot, a slight promontory midway around the lake, and I tried to imagine her on a fall afternoon, her books piled nearby.

> Moonlight in Vermont
> Falling leaves of sycamore . . .

She began singing, softly. Her voice was lovely. Sort of second soprano, with a natural but subtle tremolo that makes you pay attention. Smiling innocently, she said, "This is one of my favorite songs. When the Wellesley Widows perform, I sing the lead on this one. Did I tell you I sing with the Widows?"

"Widows? No. Let's hear some more of it."

When she started, I joined in, for a duet:

> Telegraph cables
> They sing down the highway
> And welcome each bend in the road

By the time we reached our starting point around Lake Waban, our hand-holding duets had exhausted a half-dozen repertoires. Anyone overhearing us most likely would have thought us Maniacal Music Majors. Each song that we shared seemed to heighten the intensity of our rapport. Or something like that.

"What kind of food are you in the mood for?" Regardless of whether she said Italian, French, American, Greek, or whatever, I didn't know a single restaurant in the area to call my favorite for that kind of food. And I had only about twenty dollars in my pocket, half of which I needed for my own survival next week.

But wait. There's another twenty-dollar bill in my wallet, folded in thirds, probably stuck together so tight that it will shred if I try to use it. Ma gave me that money nearly a year ago "for emergencies."

It seemed only seconds before we spotted an authentic-looking Italian diner, its red neon sign casting warm shadows over the cars in the graveled parking lot leading up to the canopied door. Not a loud greasy spoon filled with half-drunk college kids, I thought, and looks like they worry more about the food than a fancy exterior. Quiet and dimly lighted inside. I can handle this. No problem.

The green light circling the big silver speedometer was still fading to black as I opened the passenger door, extending my hand to help her out of the car. Her hand was warm and oh so soft as she lightly curled four fingers across my palm, her thumb seeming to caress the back of my hand. Instinctively, my thumb welcomed her with slow, long strokes down the length of her fingers. I had never been so excited by the touch of a woman.

Aromas of grilled peppers, provolone, roasted garlic, fresh-baked breads, pepperoni, wine, and simmering tomato sauce filled the room as the chefs nonchalantly banged the silver bell on the pass-through shelf from the kitchen announcing another masterpiece. Helping Shirlee with her coat, I couldn't avoid eyeing her fantastic figure again as I settled in the booth opposite her, took a sip of water, and glanced at the menu. My heart was pounding a thousand beats per minute. I wasn't at all hungry.

"See anything you really like on the menu? Shall I ask about tonight's specials? A glass of sherry or Chianti for starters? Want to share a salad? Oil and vinegar okay? I'm really glad you were free for a study date tonight. What's the name of that high school you went to? And where is Ansonia, Connecticut?"

I couldn't stop babbling. My mind kept up a parallel stream of thoughts. Had to find out more about this gorgeous woman while I had her undivided attention. "What a wonderful, warm smile. Does she like me as much as I already like her? Just calm down and be cool. Her steady is probably in New York City this weekend shopping for an engagement ring. Nah. She wouldn't pull a trick like that. Stop worrying. She's here now, so take advantage of it. Stay cool. There's still time. Forget the library after dinner. Anything but."

We ordered something—can't remember what—and kept on talking, no money worries weighing on my out-of-control pleasure. We ate. And kept on talking. I sipped Chianti while hanging on Shirlee's every word. She spoke animatedly about her father and mother, her sisters and brother. I listened intently to every detail, enthralled by them and—more important—by her lively eyes, her bright smile, and the promise of her curvaceous lips and beautiful hands becoming one with mine. But by the time she finished, I was in sheer panic because, while the two of us seemed to have so much in common even after only two hours together, I knew that our families were worlds apart.

It was my turn. Shirlee lifted her glass and settled catty-cornered in the booth, eagerly awaiting details. She immediately sensed my uneasiness about sharing my family story after hearing hers.

I didn't want the differences between us to interfere, but I couldn't lie about my own family. What to do? What if Shirlee was, at bottom, a snobbish, self-centered, rich, pampered little brat from a Negro middle-class cocoon in Ansonia with no firsthand knowledge of, empathy for, or appreciation of the daily struggles among the vast majority of Negroes simply to survive (not prosper) in legally segregated America? The majority I belonged to.

"You're from D.C.? I have a lot of family in Washington," she prompted. "Several of my relatives live just off Sixteenth Street in North West, near the Carter Baron Amphitheatre and the Maryland state line. You know that area? Where does your family live?"

Everybody in D.C. knows "The African Gold Coast," I thought to myself, where all the rich Negroes live in big houses and act like white folks. I knew it well because my childhood friends Bennie Ginyard and Claude Moten and I used to ride our bikes through its wide, manicured streets and choose the cars and houses we would buy when we got rich. Then we'd breeze down Sixteenth Street to Florida Avenue and race all the cars and buses east toward the Benning River and Deanwood, our home turf.

"Oh, sure," I said. "I know the Carter Baron area. I had a couple of friends who lived near there when I was at Dunbar." Loosening my armor a little more, I admitted that only my aunt and one or two cousins lived in North West, while the majority of my family had lived in North East D.C. for years and years.

"Is that the area where Minnesota Avenue connects with Sheriff Road?" she asked, tentatively. "I have a half sister who lives out there, on Eads Street, not far from the big Safeway."

"Yes!" I exclaimed, like a 440 distance runner crossing the finish line in first place, dripping with sweat, joy, and total exhaustion. "Yes! Yes! Yes! You know that part of D.C., too? You're talking about my neck of the woods now."

I told her about my mother and father not finishing high school in North Carolina because they had to work in the tobacco fields to help their large families survive. She seemed okay with this, so I tested her with my older sister, Vira, the self-styled International Singing Sensation, and my older brother, Allen, an Armstrong High School triathlete. She still seemed okay with what I was saying and obviously wanted to hear more.

I told her that my father died unexpectedly when I was ten and that shortly thereafter Ma took a job from 4:00 P.M. to midnight to support us. With Vira in places unknown and Allen at team practice after school every day, I soon learned how to prepare meals for myself, starting with cucumber and mayonnaise sandwiches after school, and graduating to hamburgers, fried chicken, and my aunt Dit's recipe for cherry drop dumplings made with canned cherries, cornstarch, sugar, and Bisquick.

Ma always raved about my food, strongly recommending it to Allen and Vira, even if she only "sampled" it herself when she got home from work. It wasn't until much later that I began to suspect that Ma's praise of my cooking was her way of being assured that I kept at it.

I didn't realize I was pouring out my life story in such a torrent until I heard Aunt Dit's recipe for cherry dumplings flying past my lips. I caught myself, glanced at Shirlee, and tried to regain my cool. As if we were a two-man team of relay racers, however, Shirlee grabbed the baton in the same stride and told me about growing up as a daughter of a much-respected Baptist minister whose flock had migrated to Connecticut mostly from the Carolinas. Many of its members lacked formal education, worked long hours in menial, low-paying factory jobs, and endured constant racism. She had known and cared about these people all her life. The more she shared, the more I realized that I'd known her "Ansonia" my entire life. It was Deanwood—with a different name.

So where did all the time go? What time was it, anyway? And no need to worry about money: we talked more than we ate or drank. Plus, no dessert. I was home free.

Shirlee seemed to sit a little closer as we headed back to campus, but I played it cool so she wouldn't think I was a grabber. Turning the radio dial, I came upon Nat King Cole singing "Love Is the Thing." My thoughts exactly.

At 12:50 A.M. the Chrysler rolled into the Freeman Hall parking lot, jammed with cars idling puffs of white steam far cooler than the frenetic last-minute kissing and hugging inside. This was the moment. I really wanted to kiss her good night but dared not.

She smiled brightly at me, extended her hand smartly, thanked me for a wonderful evening, and turned her head toward the door. I held on to her hand, put my left hand over hers and said something silly before dashing around to open her door.

Extending my hand to help her out, I asked, "Are you busy tomorrow? I don't think I can wait until next weekend to see you again."

"Call me," she said. "I have an exam to study for, but I might finish by early evening. I've got to be inside that door in less than a minute."

Just before vanishing she turned and kissed my cheek—ever so gently. She was gone.

I was weak-kneed. Delirious. Bereft. Happy.

As I stood there staring at the door, two Wonders dashed past me and began banging frantically, as if their lives would end if they didn't make curfew. I turned toward the parking lot and the Chrysler, hopped in, and headed out between the gates toward the lonely road home.

"Hello?"

My heart was leaping out of my chest. "Hi. It's Harold. Just wanted to tell you that I got home safely, that I really enjoyed our evening together, and that I hope, really hope, to see you tomorrow afternoon—anytime. Any possibility you've finished studying already?"

She laughed. "Tomorrow evening around six looks good for me."

"I'll be there."

"Good night for now."

I didn't sleep more than ten minutes all night. I relived our evening, minute by minute by minute, over and over and over. It was the best evening of my entire life. I loved her. No question about it. I loved her.

Pam was smiling at me from the night table. I whispered, "I'm sorry to do this to you. So very, very sorry. I didn't intend for this to happen, it just did. Please try to forgive me, someday. I'm really sorry."

CHAPTER 2

At Last

*S*HIRLEE: Of course, I never saw my Lexington beau again after my first date with Harold. I handled the situation badly, cruelly, in fact, although at the time I would not have thought so. Nineteen years old, I was still a teenager in some ways. Many of my real-life cues came from the movie melodramas I loved. When I needed the ultimate excuse to break off with my steady, I don't remember agonizing about it, if in fact I did. I told a lie.

At a time in my life when I had not yet experienced the deep pain of grief from death or dying, I told him by phone I had a brain tumor and needed to concentrate on my indefinite future. He should look for a healthier girl, I advised. From time to time I wonder if this lie will hold me up at heaven's gate. It's probably the worst thing, the most unethical thing I have ever done. Whenever I think of it, I feel embarrassed. And my daughters don't help. They were incredulous when I told them.

There is no doubt the news shocked him, hurt him. He came by the dormitory, sent notes, flowers, telegrams, Milky Ways. I remained incommunicado. I could not speak to him. Judy was flabbergasted at my behavior.

I wonder why I could not tell him the truth. I suppose I thought it would have invalidated for him all the experiences and feelings we had shared for two years. He was so earnest, so kind, so thoughtful, I could not bear to hurt him directly. And yet I did. How much he was hurt I'll never really know. I did hear rumors, though, through the Negro collegiate grapevine, that he was devastated for a while. Thank God twenty-one-year-old broken hearts tend to mend.

In any case, I was a coward. I was wrong. I was unkind. But I did not linger long in the land of guilt or cowardice. Love moves you forward.

Harold and I saw each other constantly that fall. I was always just meeting the curfew. I loved his extraordinary brightness, his wit, his sense of humor, and his charm. And I loved his gentlemanly ways. His manners were impeccable. He always opened doors for me, stood up when I came to the table, took my arm or held my hand, and walked on the outside. He could make anyone he met laugh. My dorm mates adored him. Some were fascinated. His particular brand of Negritude did not fit their stereotypes.

Nor did he fit mine. Northern Negroes had their own sense of superiority to southerners. Undeserved, but nonetheless there. I had imagined that a young colored man coming out of the segregated South would be passive, timid, unsure in his dealings with white people. I suppose I thought my father and uncles who were born in North Carolina and raised in Washington were "exceptions."

To my delight, Harold, too, believed his horizon was without limits.

His verbal skills were dazzling, honed by the poetic structures and harmonious cadences of the classics. In his words I heard the poetry of Catullus, the history of Herodotus, and the orations of Cicero. I thought he would give my erudite, word-loving father a run for his money.

He enchanted me with his encyclopedic knowledge of music. Then there was his talent on the piano. With his large hands moving furiously over the keys, he could go from Rachmaninoff to an imitation of Errol Garner, with a little Don Shirley thrown in. Switching to lounge lizard style, he could tinkle the songs he played as an earnest accompanist at weddings, "I Love You Truly," "Because," "Ave Maria." Best of all, for me, he could beat out a mean gospel.

Across the skating rink at the Boston Common, his whirling presence dominated the space; graceful, powerful, arms outstretched, scarf flying. Mastering all the latest dances the minute they came out, he had equal aplomb on the dance floor. Outdone, I felt my terpsichorean talents paled next to his. Perhaps I felt less colored, less authentic with this rhythm king. I began to wonder if there was anything he could not do well.

On a limited student budget he fed me comfort foods with his cooking, southern style with a continental flair. I had never had so many versions of tuna and noodles. And I was not a cook.

Harold had become my ideal. The iconic sweet-faced Winslow Homer brown boy I had dreamed about as an adolescent; the boy of the *Snow White* song "Some Day My Prince Will Come." The boy who was destined for great things, whose character and integrity were enviable. The boy who was too good to be true.

Now don't get me wrong, Harold was not perfect, by any means. His sense of time revolved around what he wanted to do and when. It was as if he had been born with his own personal clock somewhere in the center of his being, next to his soul and under his heart. His time had little to do with Greenwich Mean Time, Eastern Standard Time, or even Colored People's Time. It was Harold's Time. For most occasions he was late and quite comfortable in his lateness. We argued about that a lot. I probably spent too much time analyzing it. To no avail. I learned to strategize.

I loved and hated the fact that he was generous to a fault. He tried to please everyone, often not being able to keep promises he sincerely made in good faith because there was too much on his plate. He was supposed to drive a friend somewhere, go ice skating with another friend, read someone else's paper.

He was inconsistent on money issues, sometimes being frugal to the point of self-abnegation. He needed a new sport jacket but patched and repatched the old one. He smoked too much, drove too fast, and sometimes swore like a sailor, but only in private. I countenanced these blemishes as minor, human flaws that made him endearing—when they did not inconvenience me.

Boston held no overt menace for its darker citizens then. We walked everywhere, seeing the city anew. Leaving dappled Harvard Yard, pushing through the cacophonous crowds of Harvard Square, ambling along the Charles River, we crossed the bridge into a parallel world. We climbed the cobbled, winding streets of Beacon Hill, where we imagined living and loving in a tall, handsome house, with tall, handsome rooms and tall, handsome children.

Surprisingly, my class work did not suffer; it got better. I was more focused, and I was determined to be the intellectual equal of this bright nova. I also wanted to share with him all the new things I was learning, the tales of Langston Hughes's Simple, the music of Vivaldi, the literature of Gorky, and the wonders of comparative anatomy.

Signaling his intentions, Harold soon asked me to wear his fraternity pin, a serious display of true love in those days. Of course, I was curious about the circumstances of the pin's retrieval. Harold was sparing in his details. I chalked it up to gentlemanly discretion.

Most of Harold's dreams became mine, and many of mine, his. We wanted to achieve, to make our parents proud. We both wanted to have jobs we would love, travel abroad, raise a small family, spend summers in New England. We wanted to help other Negroes achieve. We assumed that material things like houses and cars would automatically come our way. We dreamed simple-minded dreams then. Together we would help create a country without racism and classism; a world without war and hunger.

That Thanksgiving weekend my father was just a bit more welcoming than Duchess, our dog. The two-legged master of the house folded his hands under his chin and with a fixed, unreadable gaze observed Harold from an Olympian distance across the dinner table. My mother smiled sweetly and passed the dressing. She asked Harold the requisite questions about his family and life in Washington.

In this unknown family terrain, Harold was a comfortable explorer. Unlike other beaus who visited, he was not at all intimidated by my father's imperial demeanor. As if he were conversing with an old friend, he told my father jokes, teased him, asked about the material for his sermons, and talked about their mutual alma mater, Dunbar High School in Washington. By Sunday afternoon, Harold could claim a new, if cautious, fan.

Before meeting Harold, I had not intended or wished to marry while I was in college. In fact, I did not think about it much at all. His arrival changed all that.

After spending a princely sum on a beautiful necklace for me, Harold had no money to come to Connecticut or to go home for the winter holidays of my junior year. I made a drastic decision. For the first time in my life, I left my parents on Christmas Day. It was not an easy thing do to.

Christmas for me had always been my parents and my sisters and brother. Often my uncle Percy from New York would join us, playing the piano and singing Christmas carols. Christmas Eve service at the church. Arranging the hundreds of Christmas cards my parents received. Time in the kitchen with my mother, watching her annual battle with the holiday turkey. Helping Pattee wrap her last-minute gifts, including some for herself. Telling Brother I really didn't want to know what was in the large box from Mother and Daddy. Ice-skating at a pond on Ansonia's East Side, or, later, at the Edgewood Rink in New Haven. That's how my Christmases had been.

My father was out on his annual all-day Christmas mission, visiting every family on the church's roll of members, when I left the house. More than likely each household would give him a Christmas treat, a cake, a pie, a pot of chitlins. But he was most interested in the little white Christmas envelopes trimmed with sprigs of holly. When he came home around four o'clock, the car would be full of sweet-smelling pastry, his pockets full of holiday envelopes.

The Greyhound bus pulled out of New Haven in a swirl of falling snow.

While I feasted on a baked chicken in the eternal springtime of Harold's apartment and in the light of one fat candle and Harold's adoring eyes, back in Connecticut, my father fumed, my mother placated. I had gone off without his knowledge or permission to see "some young man." Of course he knew who it was, but in his mind, *omen nomen* was an operating principle as far as the males in his daughters' lives were concerned.

And that Christmas Day he was obliged to welcome another young man from a "good family." I had met this particular suitor the previous summer while visiting his sister in St. Augustine. He had driven all the way from Florida, through the snowstorm, to see me, only to be told I was not at home. I suppose I had known he was coming.

On the bus I kept replaying the scene in my mind. An earnest, bookish-looking, gangly guy in dripping galoshes, dodging Duchess while asking where I was. My father, annoyed but gracious, inviting this friend of his daughter's but stranger to him to Christmas dinner; my mother making apologies and telling him that there must have been some kind of mix-up.

Long before Christmas I had tried to discourage the smitten swain from making the trip. He was determined. Blithe spirit that I was, caught up in my own romantic pursuits, I did not feel any guilt about not being there to welcome him. I had told him, hadn't I? Of course, later I would come to understand my no-show was a callow act. That kind of knowledge comes with a maturity I did not possess at the time.

Of more immediate concern was my father's reaction. I knew I would face more than the aftermath of a blizzard when I returned home that night. I also knew that my father had to realize how serious my feelings were about the new man in my life. Nervously, my mother awaited my arrival.

By the time I reached home, the Florida fellow had departed for warmer climes. My father was as frosty as the night air and gave me the look, a stern, uncompromising, unblinking glare over his glasses and down his aquiline nose, across his drawn lips. When he finally spoke of my decision to leave, his reference was to the "sanctity of family holidays and the maintenance of family traditions." He was quietly annoyed at me for days. I knew I was growing up, because ameliorating his anger was less important to me than enjoying my romantic buoyancy.

Instead of studying for my mid-year exams in January, the besotted girl I was then wrote:

Jan. 20, 1958

Dearest H.

Hope that you will find time to pore over these choice bits of knowledge, for I am sure they will reinforce your raison d'etre. After all, if one doesn't know that Achilles sacrificed twelve Trojans to appease the soul of Patroclus, how can one possibly exist (in erudite circles, of course)? . . .

I sincerely hope in your present search after that which is called knowledge, you are not impairing your well being.

Of course I realize that you usually perform in this schol-
arly manner, but may I remind you of what happened to
Milton (besides Paradise Lost, of course) . . .

Because of the intense and continued coldness of the
atmosphere, the lake has frozen from shore to shore. I
thought of you yesterday when I saw people skating and
falling in all directions. My thoughts of you were not just
confined to that particular time, but have been a subtle
influence upon my complacent frame of mind for many if
not most of my waking hours. . . . I shall leave you now to
your labours and your thoughts, hoping some of the latter
will concern me.

Shirlee

That same winter, on a bitterly cold night, Harold proposed. As he
held my hand, his mood was serious, almost solemn. He caught me
off guard. I had imagined I would receive my proposal dressed in chiffon and silk, with an unseen wind blowing my dress around my knees,
my stole fluttering around my shoulders, my face upturned at a
Jeanne Crain angle. Violins and harps would be playing in the background. Instead, Joan Baez was singing and playing her guitar. Harold
and I were both wearing blue jeans and heavy fishermen's-knit
sweaters. No flowing chiffon. My face was the face I saw every day in
the mirror. No dimples, no inch-long lashes, no upturned nose.

I accepted.

We wanted to get married in 1958, at the end of my junior year. I
wonder now if young people are more practical in their approach to
marriage than we were. Harold came up with a budget of eight dollars
a week that would fit within the financial parameters of his fellowship.

Jewelle and her husband, Jim, advised us to wait. They thought we
were too young.

A few weeks later, when he formally asked for my hand in a three-
hour, close-the-door-to-the-study session with my father, Harold
emerged chastened. We had to postpone our plans. Although I was
dying to know, I never learned the particulars of that heart-to-heart
from either of them back then.

As with most people in love, everything that happens to the inamorati was either sublime or horrendous. When my father put his two feet down on our college wedding plans, I was deeply disappointed.

March 4, 1958

Dearest H.

. . . in retrospect, I can honestly and happily say that from November to the present time has been the most exciting, happy and contented period of time in my life . . .

At present I am listening to Judy's copy of Nat Cole's "Love Is the Thing" and needless to say, my mind conjures up all sorts of exciting pictures. Now that winter is over (despite your own "winter slump") my mind is wishing spring out of existence, and anticipating a wonderful summer with you.

I hope you will both forgive and take lightly my sporadic moods of pessimism. This, I think, is part of my egocentric, childish orientation of wanting every desire fulfilled immediately, if not sooner. Slowly but surely I am learning that this, i.e. marriage, will come about in due time. The uncertainty of the date, however, I must admit, will continue to cast some small shadow of gloom, but said gloom will be immediately dispersed by your presence.

Perhaps you will be pleased to know that I'm not going home at all, before spring vacation. I would like to be with you as much as possible before the pressure of exams sets in, and after all, what does spring mean unless you're with the one you love.

Love always,
Shirlee

Now my letter seems stilted, unnatural. I laugh to think I wrote like that. I look at it and think I see some of my father's and grandfather's homiletic phrases. I guess I had not yet left their circle of formality. Or maybe I was showing off for my brilliant beau.

But I did go home, one time.

I fell in love for the first time in 1947, when I was ten. I played a lot of baseball and softball, the only girl in a group of neighborhood boys. Some of the boys were Polish, some Italian, some Irish, and some black. We played on a wide sandbank by an old trestle, where the docile Naugatuck River curved beyond our sight. I modeled my playing style on the pigeon-toed Dodger player who claimed my heart. The boys remained unimpressed.

My father called me one day at college and suggested I come home to meet a special guest, someone who would be spending part of his day with him at my old high school in Ansonia. When I found out who it was, my father did not have to ask twice.

I told Harold my father wanted me to come home for a special event he was hosting. I did not let my husband-to-be into the space I had reserved for my very first hero, the prince I had always hoped would come to my little town and sweep me into his life. Never mind that the prince had an adored wife and beloved children.

The reality did not diminish the dream. All I can remember about the day I met Jackie Robinson was his great smile and kind look when he shook my hand. I had planned to impress him with my knowledge of Dodger statistics and trivia related to his playing. The facts flew out of my head like a long, clean homer. In Robinson's presence I became the ten-year-old tomboy in braids. He was the giant I imagined him to be.

Harold was nervous about introducing me to his mother and the rest of his family. I think he was also apprehensive about what I would think of his home, even though he knew I had no illusions about his life or circumstances. They were less fortunate than mine. So what? My father had ingrained in me the understanding that modest circumstances were irrelevant to good character. I knew that to be true from the many good folk of my father's church. Besides, many of my high school beaus had come from such families.

The house was as small as he described, but more homey than he let on. It was nothing new to me. I had been in homes like that all my life. Somewhat tentative at first, Harold relaxed once he saw I made myself at home.

It was the thought of meeting Harold's mother that made me nervous. I imagined how proud she was of her youngest son's achievements and how she wanted to make sure he married "the right kind of girl." It was essential that she approve of me.

I knew that she and Harold had been particularly close. I knew that her life and mine had been vastly different. She had worked hard. Since she did not know me and I did not belong to her church, I expected she might be guarded. I dressed conservatively the day we met, wearing a dark madras plaid shirt dress and no makeup except for lipstick.

Much to my relief, that pretty, cheerful middle-aged woman sweetly welcomed me to her home with traditional southern hospitality. Her obvious sense of fun and charming sense of humor quickly endeared her to me. There was no gulf to overcome.

I studied Harold's mother as she busied herself in the kitchen. Her dark hair was curly with a few streaks of gray. She was tall, and her figure was firm. Her hands were large, like her son's. Her eyes looked as if she had seen one sorrow too many. Her color was one of the most pleasing I had ever seen, as if her skin had been washed with gold.

She insisted I eat mounds of her sumptuous chicken, beef, ham, yams, rice, collards, and sweet potato pie to "put some more meat on my bones." She was easygoing, open, and especially interested in my family life. I remember she said, "I guess I don't have to worry about your going to church." She seemed to hang on Harold' s every word. What was eminently clear to me was that she had utmost confidence in Harold's taste and judgment in all things. If I was all right with him, I was all right with her.

Harold's sister, Vira, was another story. Shapely, clothes-conscious, and world-weary—those were the words that came to mind when I saw her. I immediately noticed she had vee-shaped eyebrows like Harold's. They were perfect. Her jet-black hair was silky and carefully styled. I saw that her nails were long and well manicured. Mine were nubs and unpolished. Tall like her mother, her figure was sensuous, made more so because of a knock-kneed gait that caused her hips to roll like easy swells on a calm sea. There is no doubt she had been called sexy since she was a young girl.

She met me with cool detachment and dark, heavy-lidded eyes that did a good job of concealing what she was thinking. There was great drama in her languid movements. She took long, meaningful puffs on her cigarettes, starting a new one before the next was out. She offered only half-smiles and often raised one eyebrow, as if in bemused wonderment. She had a strange, unsettling effect on me.

Vira asked me a lot of questions about my dress, hairstyle, and makeup. I asked her about her career as a singer. She provided few details, keeping a polite distance. She said she would show me her clippings book sometime. I never saw it. She never fully took me to her bosom. I probably returned the feelings.

We went by Allen's house for a quick visit. The family resemblance was strong: lidded eyes, those eyebrows again, the same rich timbre to his voice as his brother. They both seemed to have inherited their mother's pleasantness. I thought Allen and I would get along just fine.

In a whirlwind of calls, I met all of Harold's uncles and aunts who lived in Washington and some cousins as well. The family seemed close. I liked that. An old, tattered scrapbook introduced me to the rest of the relatives, living and dead. I kept noticing photos of a stern, light-skinned man in the North Carolina contingent. A heavy mustache topped an unsmiling mouth. "That's my grandfather," Harold said. "The Scottish one."

We got engaged that junior year. To make it official, my parents gave us a formal party. I wore a tangerine silk halter dress with a narrow waist and full skirt. I had to wear at least three crinolines to keep the skirt as far out as I thought it should be. No one could sit close to me on the sofa. Harold was pleased about that.

The family rallied. My aunts from Washington became the Greek chorus for the night. All dressed up in their peau de soie and crepe, they gossiped behind the flickering candles on the dining room table. Somewhere within the stories of their own lives, they were gauging and measuring our chances for success. They all fell in love with Harold.

Oddly enough, what I remember most about the engagement party was Harold's cousin Ellis sitting like Socrates on the aubergine tufted love seat. At the time, Ellis, a theatrical producer, was studying at the Yale Drama School. His arm lightly encircled the shoulders of the dark-haired love of his life, the sculptress Eva Hesse, who later would achieve some degree of fame in her work and die an early death.

We all thought she was odd—retiring, in fact. There is no doubt she was unused to being in the home of Negroes where silver was on the table and Orientals were on the floor. Although there were other white people there, none were part of an interracial duo. I thought it daring that Ellis should bring his white girlfriend to the party and create a mild sensation, just by sitting sedately. It was a typical thing for him to do.

My wonderfully eccentric godmother, Gregoria, had given Harold a dainty heart-shaped emerald that had been her mother's engagement ring from the late 1880s. In the elegant old ring box was a thin piece of ecru-colored paper on which Gregoria had written, "Green is for everlasting love," in turn-of-the-century script. I wore it for the first time that night.

For wedding bands we ordered wide rings in which the Greek key had been deeply etched. We had been told that it, too, was a symbol of eternity. In both of the bands Harold had inscribed, "Forever and three days." We were not hedging our bets.

As my engagement photograph I selected the portrait taken by the yearbook photographer who made all Wellesley seniors look as if they had come from the same upper-class white family. His studio lighting made tan skins paler. A single strand of white pearls sat chastely in the hollow of my neck above a modestly positioned sweetheart neckline. I looked as if I were wearing a barely off-the-shoulder white evening gown. It was really the photographer's drape.

The New York Times, the New Haven Register, the Ansonia Sentinel, the Afro American, the Pittsburgh Courier, and Jet magazine carried news of our engagement and, in the custom of the day, my picture. In the engagement notice we wrote that Harold's people were from both North Carolina and Washington, a true statement but not intended to convey what the column implied: that they had substantial homes in both places. We laughed at the implication and the Times's use of it.

At that time, few Negro girls had their pictures in the Times. For weeks after the Sunday issue carrying my picture was published, numerous friends of my mother's called to ask how she had managed it, and could she do it for them. My mother took no credit for the feat. "Shirlee is a good girl who went to Wellesley. After all, she's marrying a smart, nice boy who went to Amherst and Harvard. The paper thought it was worth printing."

*H*AROLD: Harvard grad students either internalize the university's work ethic at the outset or fall by the wayside rather quickly. Everybody is extremely bright and energetic, extremely articulate and well read, and extremely motivated to maintain and demonstrate the extraordinary intellect that got them admitted in the first place.

As one of the dozen or so Negroes among the thousands of students in all of the grad schools combined—and the only Negro then enrolled in the Graduate Department of Latin, Greek, and Classical Philology—I saw myself endlessly auditioning for acceptance in roles or groups. But there was no doubt in my mind that I was as good as, and sometimes better than, the self-anointed gatekeepers.

Prior to the 1960s civil rights movement, Negroes in all-white schools were not assumed to be less-qualified, affirmative action admits. We were curiosities who had somehow gotten over their walls and into their sanctums. The unsubtle incredulity was everywhere evident: a professor asking in a private conference the name of the tutor who had helped me write my A paper; another professor asking whether I would mind reading aloud in Ancient Greek and then translating into English a difficult fragment he was allegedly working on for a professional monograph; a professor interrupting my response in class one day to ask if I was speaking from a hidden, prepared text; being called to a conference with a professor who wanted to know who had sat on my left and right—two rows away!—during final exams.

When curiosity or the competition got the best of them, students always wanted to know if I had graduated from the "real" Amherst College, the one in Amherst, Massachusetts, and with honors in what, specifically. And how had I paid for Amherst, what did my parents do, what high school had I attended, did I know anyone else who had gone to college, where/how had I learned to speak and write English the way they did, and how much scholarship money had Harvard given me, for how many years, exactly?

Sometimes out of arrogance, sometimes out of anger or reciprocal disdain, and always out of fear of not succeeding, I crafted my Harvard self by what I chose to share or keep private, depending on how I read the intent and integrity of my interrogators.

Most of all, I knew without doubt—but shared with no one— that, unlike most other students, including Dan and Vitz, I had no money, no powerful support group, and therefore no safety net. At the end of a good month at home, if the major bills were paid and Ma had $200 left over in the bank, we were rich, safe for another thirty days. And here I was at Harvard, paying more for my third of the rent than Ma's monthly mortgage on Sheriff Road, and paying Harvard, buying books, feeding and clothing myself, and keeping my car rolling on my scholarship, a bartending job, and any other nickel I could find. I was terrorized by the thought that if I did not succeed, the opportunity of my lifetime would vanish without notice, without concern, without a trace. The jig would be up.

I carefully organized my entire life around this fear. The "unthinkable alternative," coupled with my commitment to Pam, justified the necessity of studying rather than dating.

Until I met Shirlee. Without knowing it, she really messed up my carefully crafted study regimen, and I became her eager assistant. When I heard myself seeking that first Monday-night date with her, I knew that all of my rationalizations, the terror that had so motivated and focused me, and even my commitment to Pam were becoming scrambled. Only one thing was clear: I was going to spend time with Shirlee. She seemed to free me from the weight I'd been carrying for so long. She vaporized my screens, got through to the uncontrived, unprotected, real me, and seemed to like the person she found—on our first date, no less. I had to find out, had to KNOW, whether these connections were real for both of us, or whether I was totally out of control with a bad case of the hots.

I abandoned my pious self-denial so fast that I scared myself. It was as if I suddenly decided to take a free fall from my high wire, with full knowledge that there was no net below, no guarantees, no predictable outcomes.

Shirlee had a steady and so did I. She was beautiful; I was not handsome. She was used to having money; I didn't have a dime. She freely took time off from school; even as other students observed vacations and holidays I stayed on and studied, fearing the loss of my scholarship, my academic edge, my whole world.

Convincing Ma and Pam to accept, begrudgingly, my abandonment of loved ones and ignoring of holidays had taken a long time and caused a lot of pain. Occasionally, I even had insisted that Dan and Vitz entertain their weekend dates elsewhere so I could study undistracted in the Flower Garden.

I had never even remotely considered the possibility of a date on a Monday. When final exams were on the horizon, I routinely lost my appetite or "forgot" to eat, and spent days and nights in the Widener stacks. After meeting Shirlee, I turned a corner.

All day Monday I was at war with myself: I had more work than I could finish even if I studied straight through to class time Tuesday. If I raided my savings for extra gas and food, I couldn't also take her out next Saturday without still more time off from studying. And I would need to bartend my rent shortfall by the thirtieth.

Why was it so urgent, so important to see Shirlee again, so soon, when I hadn't seen Ma or Pam for nearly a year? I knew, secretly, that sometimes when I could have taken time off to go home, I hadn't done so because I really didn't want to. After catching up with Ma, Pam, Vira, Uncle Ellis, Uncle John, Aunt Bo, and a few others, I always wanted to leave, to return to my own world, which they admired from afar but knew and cared little about. Although I feigned concern, I certainly did not want to get bogged down again in their survival issues (which were essentially the ones I had grown up with) when my own were at the imminent catastrophe level with only myself—and not a single one of them—responsible for the outcome.

I even debated whether I should psych Shirlee out: cancel and see if she was really disappointed or just pretending interest in me. She, too, had an Hour Exam coming up. If she wasn't really interested, she'd graciously agree to cancel. If she was, she'd ask or leave the door open for me to reschedule.

"Right," I said sarcastically to myself, struggling to escape the shackles of my self-imposed workaholic lifestyle. My inner guide went on, "You're a class-A asshole if you think for one minute that after a single blind date, a gorgeous woman like Shirlee is going to kiss-off Mr. Lexington and all of the other horny bastards trying to get next to her until you can find time in your busy schedule to see her next Saturday. Especially if you cancel less than twenty-four hours after telephoning her in the middle of the night to confirm. Besides, you need to learn to study smarter, not longer. And just how much studying do you really think you'll get done with your mind constantly on whether Shirlee's seeing Mr. Lexington—precisely because you're too busy hitting the books? You can study two extra hours from Tuesday to Friday to make up Monday's time. Get your ass to Wellesley. You've earned it. She's waiting. You know you're going to do it. Why are you putting yourself through this agony routine?"

As the arch faded from the Chrysler's rearview mirror, we sang our way toward Boston on half a tank of gas, about eight dollars from last night's dinner, and Ma's twenty-dollar safety bill in my wallet. A few more bucks and I could have impressed her with drinks at the Harvard Club and dinner at Durgin Park, but we settled on sharing popcorn with the fearless pigeons on Boston Common, watching skaters pirouette around the ice rink, and decoding the cryptic plaques of Boston's historic leaders, talking incessantly to each other despite these distractions.

Beacon Hill's cozy, narrow streets and elegantly shuttered rowhouses triggered dreams and tastes I was surprised to discover we shared. Riding my bike in the Brattle Street residential area outside Harvard Square, I had greatly admired the large old houses, imposing and unchanged for decades. Fairly or not, they represented permanence, tradition, stability, and lifestyles of stress-free calmness, family activities, and memories—the good, important things I wanted for myself someday. Beacon Hill homes evoked similar yearnings in Shirlee, who, it turned out, saw in the longevity and permanence of those elegant structures the essence of the life she wanted for herself. Incredible.

Charles Street at the foot of Beacon Hill was replete with downscale smoke shops and coffeehouses frequented by students from Boston University, Simmons, Harvard, MIT, Wellesley, Lesley, Northeastern, and Boston College. At one of the candlelit basement coffee-houses we half-listened to a wailful guitar, probing each other's thoughts over multiple coffee and hot chocolate refills.

Later, Shirlee peered carefully at the sophisticated displays of understated women's fashions and accessories of specialty boutiques on Newbury Street, ignoring the price tags. If she really liked something she saw, its cost was irrelevant. She fantasized freely about wearing these kid gloves with her new black coat, or those suede and alligator pumps with a dress on layaway in Wellesley Centre. And the navy wool slacks and matching silk cardigan set would be "just perfect" for the Harvard-Yale game.

Having lived below or close to the poverty line all my life, my immediate reaction was to reject all of this stuff as overpriced playthings for people who don't know the value of money. Yet I admired her insouciance, her unwillingness to allow a lack of money to diminish her enthusiasm. She clearly believed that she could and should have the things she wanted, and that she would get them as soon as her financial situation improved. So it was perfectly fitting for her to move beyond the temporary inconvenience of having no money. She was freer than I was. Much freer. And more optimistic.

Without knowing it, she was cracking my deeply ingrained, automatic, and necessary response to being poor. Maybe I, too, could assume that someday I might have these things if I really wanted them. Imagine me thinking something as crazy as that.

"Lawd, have mercy!" my mother would say.

"I was just thinking I won't see you again for five days, if you're free Saturday night." We were in the Chrysler, driving back to Wellesley.

"I already have a date next Saturday evening . . ."

My heart sank.

". . . The Widows are doing a concert on campus with the Yale Whiffenpoofs . . ."

Jesus Christ! A Yalie?? I'm up against a Yalie? Shit! Shit! Shit! I should have known.

". . . Why don't you come? I can't eat before I sing, so I'll be starved. Maybe we could have a late dinner somewhere?"

"Sounds great," I boomed, masking my shitfaced fear.

The close harmony of the Four Freshmen's "It's a Blue World . . . Without You" softly spun from the Chrysler's radio while my mind skirted the idea of slamming on the brakes and wrapping myself around her. The fierceness of my feelings nearly overwhelmed me. Instead, we both joined the Freshmen for a sextet.

We were in front of her dorm again, this time standing very close to each other. Her back was to the door. She was beautiful. My heart was racing.

I slid both of my arms around her waist, pulled her close, and held her tightly, saying nothing. She put her right hand gently around my neck and kissed my cheek ever so slowly.

"Call me when you get to Cambridge. Good night, Sweet Prince." She vanished. Same as last night.

Sweet Prince? That's new. Was that Lady Macbeth's line? Was it Juliet's? Or did she make it up? Imagine me a prince. A Sweet Nothing? Or a message, for sure. Roll with it.

I wanted to roll down the windows and yell as loud as I could, "I found her! The beautiful, smart, lovely woman I will marry and live happily ever after with! The mother of my children! My best friend! I lucked out!"

At home, I slept fitfully as my mental screens replayed in gauzy, sexy slow relief every glance, every word, every titillating touch we had exchanged that evening. It was going to happen. Soon. I knew it. I drifted into sleep.

At first, I wasn't sure I saw us. I was wafting dreamily through the scenario of the mental postcard I had mailed to my subconscious at Amherst, on the day I heard Robert Frost read his poem "Stopping by Woods on a Snowy Evening." Although the forty-foot trees had shed all but a few leaves, their arms formed a lacy archway.

The couple were on a blanket in a circular clearing at the base of an old tree overlooking Lake Waban. I moved closer. They were making love. Her outstretched fingers gripped his bare waist and shoulder, pulling him deep into their synchronized rhythms. A closer look. It was Shirlee. It was me. Joy. Love.

"Harold, how could you?"

It was Pam. A voice I recognized anywhere.

I leaped out of bed in a flash, sweating and panicked as if she had fired at me with a shotgun. "Oh, my God. Where are you? How'd you get in? Where's Shirlee? Jeesus Christ."

When I finally found the light switch and realized I'd been dreaming, I let myself go and fell across the bed like a timber log. I was spent.

How do you tell your steady girlfriend of eight years—who's absolutely committed to a future with you and is waiting patiently for that future to begin—that you met another girl on a blind date and you're going to marry her? Whatever words you use, the meaning is the same. What do you tell her family? What do you tell your own family? What do you say to the friends you share? And, most important of all, what do you say to yourself? How do you live with yourself?

I couldn't help what happened between us, so there was no reason to feel guilty. But I did. And I couldn't shake it. I rehearsed again and again all of the scenarios, populated with formerly beloved people in my life—Pam weeping so uncontrollably that her mother angrily yelled from her bedroom, "What the hell's going on with you two out there?"; her sister, furious at news of the breakup, calling me a "no-good, selfish little shit!"; Bennie and Claude backing away from the friendship that had made us inseparable since childhood; and even my brother, Allen, who talked to me only when he couldn't avoid it, warning me to stick with people whose backgrounds were similar to my own.

I understood all of this and appreciated and respected their feelings and admonitions. But I was no longer the Harold these people once knew. I couldn't forgo the possibility of a fundamentally different life with Shirlee. My mind was made up.

Several times during the night I bolted upright from dreams of Shirlee and nightmares of Pam. By sunrise, I was an exhausted wreck, facing back-to-back classes all day, inadequately prepared. On my high wire, this was a real no-no.

I would have to tell Pam and everybody else soon.

Shirlee turned out to be the tonic I needed to get my act together. Being with her was so exciting, so enlivening, and so non-negotiable for me that I had to find a way to keep my studies under control according to my impossibly high standards, to let myself fully enjoy being with her, without guilt.

In the weeks following that second date I became more focused when working and seemed to accomplish twice as much in half the time at Widener. In class, on pop quizzes, in hour exams, term papers, and finals, I found myself expressing my opinions more openly and confidently, worrying less and less about how well I was representing the Negro race or whether I was winning over the bigots. I had one major hurdle facing me—weeks after meeting Shirlee, I decided the time was right to tell Pam.

Pam answered the telephone, half asleep.

"Hi," she said, brightening quickly. "I was hoping you'd call tonight. You've been so busy, and I've been so lonely. What's happened to your letters?"

"Pam, something important has happened." I was fishing for a way to begin, for an entrée to the bottom line of this horrible conversation. "I met someone on a blind study date and . . ."

"Harold," she said almost inaudibly, "I've had dates, too. But we decided long ago that we were meant for each other. That hasn't changed for me. So what are you saying . . . ?"

"I'm trying to say that the blind date was only the beginning, and that in a short period of time it has become a very serious relationship. I'm trying to say my future is with someone else."

She sobbed uncontrollably. I waited, feeling a mixture of guilt, pain, and regret. This was the moment I had avoided and dreaded most, ever since I first saw Shirlee walking down the steps in Freeman Hall. The price of that joy was the pain I inflicted on Pam and felt myself, here and now.

We agreed to talk again in a few days. Instead, the following day I wrote her a long, rambling letter about the love and memories we had shared and being best friends for so long. I wished her much happiness in the years ahead and promised to keep in touch, if she would let me. I also wrote a short note to her mother thanking her for being a surrogate mother to me. I told her that I deeply regretted the pain this news caused her and that I hoped our friendship would continue.

I admitted to myself that my letters were a cowardly act, more appropriate for a spineless soap opera weasel than me. They avoided a one-on-one confrontation and Pam's questions about my betrayal of our relationship—questions I couldn't answer without hurting her even more and making myself feel worse. I knew that for Pam and her mother, my canned phrases and schlock emotions were as hollow as those of the minister who urges grieving parents to rejoice that their innocent child, killed by a drunken driver, now sits safe and secure at the right hand of God.

"This Shirlee person must be the fucking Queen of England, the way you're carrying on!" Vitz shouted, after an afternoon listening to me bitch about the mess in their rooms. "If she thinks our place is too messy after we've vacuumed the wallpaper off the fucking walls, she can stay the hell out there in the Wellesley woods. Give us a break. No broad is worth all this aggravation, for Chrissakes!"

When Shirlee passed the "Vitz and Dan test," the news of my having a gorgeous, smart, and interesting steady traveled fast among our friends. Tom Herzog, my best friend for five years, my fraternity brother, and my former Amherst roommate, telephoned me and demanded to know who this Shirlee person was.

I'd met Herzog on my second day as an Amherst freshman in the lobby of our dorm. Looking directly at me, he exclaimed, "Oh, God! So there are two black sons-of-bitches in my class, also. My brother's class had only two. Wonder if they'll ever let ten of you people in. I'm Tom Herzog. Who the hell are you?"

For a moment, I was too shocked to respond. I didn't want to get thrown out of Amherst for putting my fist in the mouth of this funny-looking redheaded white boy with bushy black eyebrows. But I couldn't let it pass. Nobody can speak to me that way. To give myself time to think of an appropriate response, I said, "What did you say? Say that again. I want to be sure I heard you right."

"Well," he said, "if I were black I'd really be pissed off at a school that allows only two blacks to come in each year. Aren't you pissed? You should be. You sure as hell are black!"

"And you sure as hell are a funny-looking white boy with your red hair and black eyebrows. I don't run the place. Are you saying there are only eight blacks in the whole school?"

"Unless there're some real light ones that nobody's detected yet. What's your room number?"

When I couldn't afford a train ticket or hitch a ride home to D.C., we spent time together in all-white South Salem, New York, with Tom's family and their black maid, Leona. Incredulous that Herzog's best college friend was black, Leona kept her distance. Looking askance when serving me breakfast or dinner at the big dining room table, she conveyed the feeling that I should know by now that I really belonged out in the kitchen.

Ignoring Leona's standoffishness, Tom's parents and his older brother welcomed me warmly into the family, often as the resident expert on race relations.

I knew that Leona, ostensibly busy in the kitchen, listened quite intently to our feisty dinner-table discussions. At first, she never said a word to me. On my third trip to South Salem, however, she seemed delighted to see me. When the Herzogs were out of sight, she took me aside and in a stealthy whisper said she had prepared cornbread and a pot of blackeyes and neckbones for me, just in case I was feeling a little homesick for my mother's cooking. Just in case.

"So when are you two getting married? I know you will, because it's written all over your silly-ass face. I've been there," Tom expounded.

In our junior year, Herzog met Mary Andrews on a blind date at Smith and fell madly in love on the spot. I met her the following weekend and fully understood why. Tall, blond, and pretty, Mary was as iconoclastic, bright, and fun-loving as Tom. They became inseparable, and despite her parents' strenuous objection to Tom's being Jewish and his best friend's being black, they married at the end of that year at Mary's family home in Pound Ridge, New York.

"Slow down, Tom. We haven't gotten that far yet. But I'm sure we will—soon. Shirlee invited me to Thanksgiving dinner with her family. Her father is a Baptist preacher. I'll have to watch my mouth."

A few weeks before Thanksgiving, Shirlee telephoned me late one evening and said that the Widows had a crisis and needed help. They were to perform in Canada at McGill University's Winter Carnival. If they paid for my meals, gas, and tolls, could I possibly drive her and four other Widows to McGill?

The Chrysler was in only fair mechanical condition because I couldn't afford the needed maintenance. It was uninsured for the same reason. My spare was far from new. Not the best vehicle for a seven-hour nighttime drive along winding country roads.

After listening to my anxieties, Vitz and Dan volunteered to lend me fifty dollars each in case of a catastrophe.

For the five Chrysler Widows who seemed to forget I was in the car, the drive was a grown-up girls-only sleepover. They chattered and chattered, sang and soloed, laughed and shrieked until, mercifully, one after the other they began napping.

Alone in the crowded Chrysler's silent darkness, I gave full rein to my fantasies and fears as my inner voice took over. "I put the two most worn tires on the rear, so if I have a flat I shouldn't have a problem bringing the Chrysler to a safe stop, but I'll stay in the far-right lane just in case . . . A highway patrolman will probably stop me after sunrise on some kind of ruse. He really wants to arrest this Negro pimp on federal interstate solicitation charges . . . for taking five young white women across the border into Canada to make money. If I am arrested, I'll call Herzog because he has no fear of the police and will get his parents to help me if I need it. The law says they MUST allow me to make one telephone call . . . I don't have a bartending gig lined up and won't be able to repay all of the emergency money Vitz and Dan loaned me next week, as I promised . . ." If the women hadn't been sleeping, I'd have turned on the radio so I could stop thinking so much.

We turned around directly after the concert for the trip home. Once again, the Widows soon fell fast asleep.

On the way home, on a deserted stretch of the highway, the Chrysler's engine suddenly began misfiring. The engine coughed and shut down altogether. We rolled to the side of the road and stopped. Silence. It was pitch black outside.

"Where are we? Why are we stopping here?" The girls were now wide awake.

"I'm having a car problem. The engine shut down. I don't know why, but I'm sure it's nothing serious. Keep the doors and windows closed. I'll check under the hood to see if my distributor cap came loose. We'll be on our way in a jiffy."

The distributor cap was just fine. And there were no loose hoses, no disconnected wires, nothing obviously out of order. Now what? If I start walking down this dark highway with four white women, I'll be arrested in minutes. And nobody, nobody driving by will stop to help us.

I climbed back into the Chrysler, offered no explanations, turned the ignition switch, and tried to restart the engine. It turned over several times but would not start. I tried the ignition a second time. Again, nothing.

With gloved hands shoved into our pockets, scarves wrapped tightly around our heads and ears, and collars turned, we trundled along the side of the road puffing steam like five miniature Lionel locomotives following a single dim beam in the freezing cold night air. After about a mile, we came upon an unpaved driveway leading toward a small, dimly lighted farmhouse nestled in a stand of trees. I thought I saw a vague outline of a car or truck near the back of the house.

Despite my ostensible bravado, I was scared shitless. If anyone is at home, and I sure hope to hell someone is, they're no doubt white. When they see my black face at the door, they'll think it's the Gingerbread Man run amok. If it's a man and he has a shotgun, he'll grab it and start shooting in self-defense, no questions asked.

As we approached, I told the girls to take their hands out of their pockets, their scarves off their heads, turn their collars down, and stand near me so that all of us could be seen right away. I rang the doorbell.

We waited.

Nothing happened. I began to think no one was at home. Finally, the light on the the porch came on and an elderly gentleman slowly opened the curtains covering the small vertical windows in the door. A gray-haired woman in flowered bathrobe and slippers was standing behind him.

"Our car broke down about a mile down the road," I enunciated loudly through the double doors. "May we use your telephone?"

The curtains closed abruptly. The inner door swung open. They stared at us, obviously quite uncertain what to do.

"Sir, we're on our way to Massachusetts. We need to find a mechanic so we can get back to school."

Unlocking the storm door, the man said, "Come on in. We'll get you some hot tea, won't we, honey? Take off your coats. Have a seat. We'll see what can be done."

"Yes! Yes! Of course!" his wife said.

The girls huddled together on the edge of the sofa. I sat in the oversized armchair, returning the husband's quizzical gaze.

"Did you say you're from Massachusetts?" he asked.

"Yessir! My name is Harold, and I'm a student at Harvard. These young ladies belong to a singing group called the Wellesley Widows, from Wellesley College, which is also in Massachusetts. They sang at McGill in Canada, and I'm driving them back to school."

As the girls sipped their tea, the farmer said we were free to use the telephone, but there were no mechanics within twelve miles or more and they were closed at that time of night. He said he knew enough to fix his own car but not the new, fancy ones they're selling now.

"My car is a 1953 Chrysler New Yorker, with fluid drive."

"Those were great machines," he said. "They'll run forever, if you take care of 'em. What happened to yours?"

After I described the Chrysler's coughing, he asked, "When's the last time you put dry gas in your fuel tank?"

"What kind of gas are you speaking of?"

"All gasoline has a small amount of water in it, and during the winter in this part of the country, if you don't add dry gas to your fuel tank, crystals will form in your fuel line and, if it's cold enough, shut your engine down."

"I'll be damned!" I exclaimed, quickly apologizing for my language.

"I keep a couple of cans in my truck for emergencies. We'll see whether that's the problem."

The dry gas did its job. The Chrysler roared back to life.

I offered the farmer my famous twenty-dollar bill. He declined the money, saying he had done nothing to deserve it.

The traffic was a bitch. Everybody and his mother seemed to be driving from Boston to New York for Thanksgiving, and only the mothers were at the wheels. Slow as hell. Jesus! What a mess out here. Bumper to bumper.

In no time at all, there were signs announcing a tunnel ahead, followed by the Whalley Avenue Exit, my exit, according to Shirlee's directions. Within minutes I was on West Park Avenue and saw the tall three-story white house with shutters, facing a park. A long, smoky-gray fishtail Cadillac took up the entire front section of the driveway. The blue Connecticut license plate identified "REV T" as the owner. I parked the Chrysler at the curb so REV T would be sure to see it when he greeted me. It was older but spotless, and to me it looked just as great as his Caddie.

I decided to leave my suitcase in the trunk of the car. I didn't want their first image of me to be some awkward jerk trying to hold a suit-case and shake hands with twenty people at the same time. Besides, I never once saw Gatsby making an entrance while grappling with a suitcase. Elegance can be natural. And sometimes it's contrivance and hard work.

The house was quiet from outside. I was a little nervous. I rang the doorbell and waited.

Suddenly, I heard a dog barking furiously, gargantuan paws and nails grabbing at the floor sliding out from under him as he ran pell-mell toward the door. Unable to stop, he skidded and banged his weight against the glass panes. Still barking ferociously, he stood up on his hind legs and stretched his front paws above the top windowpanes.

"All right, Duchess! Get down, girl. Come with Momma!" A woman with a gentle, high-pitched voice beseeched the Monster to back off. To no avail. Duchess roared angrily, bouncing front legs up and down in sync with each bark, her long molars clearly visible through the curtains.

"Hold on a moment until we get Duchess in the kitchen," Shirlee shouted.

Duchess must have been wearing a choke chain, because her bark-ing became garbled and intermittent as Shirlee and the soft-spoken lady pulled her backward. I heard the talons scrape the floor. Then she resumed barking at a much lower volume, as if she were trapped in a distant echo chamber.

Shirlee opened the door looking somewhat frazzled.

"Sorry that took so long. Duchess thinks she's the Lady of the House. Please come in and say hello to my mother. Duchess is locked in the kitchen."

I took in my surroundings urgently, perhaps out of fear that the Duchess would suddenly reemerge to chase me out again. Ahead, an elegant stairway led to the second floor. On the left was a large, open sitting room with a long green sofa with a boy doll and a girl doll sitting close together at one end, as if watching television. On the leather-scrolled coffee table was a copious supply of magazines and books, including the largest Holy Bible I'd ever seen. Opposite the tan-brick fireplace was an oversized leather lounge chair with a large tapestried and fringed throw folded into a triangle over one arm. A door led to a room with a piano, the music room. Beyond that was a small study.

On the right, French doors opened into a spacious pale pink living room with a fireplace flanked by more French doors. Pale pink wall-to-wall carpeting and custom-made heavy pink draperies suggested an endless flow of luxurious space. A triangular glass-topped coffee table separated two wine-colored antique velvet sofas. Richly upholstered antique chairs and lamps were ornamentally positioned throughout.

An arch led to the dining room, where a banquet-size table, surrounded by a dozen chairs, had already been set with gold-rimmed plates and stemmed glasses, lots of nut bowls, a floral centerpiece, and candles. On the buffet were silver platters, bowls, carving utensils, and trivets. The mirror over the buffet reached up to the ceiling, reflecting a chandelier with gleaming crystals. The door to the kitchen was closed, but I heard Duchess parading back and forth, waiting to check me out again.

Holy Jesus! I said to myself. The foyer, sitting room, and living room are bigger than my whole house on Sheriff Road, and there are two more floors plus an attic upstairs and a basement downstairs. This is some HOUSE.

"Where are your things? I'll show you to your room and then we can relax until it's time to get ready for dinner," Shirlee purred.

I wondered if my room was near hers and whether, after everyone was asleep, I could tiptoe over there for a long goodnight kiss. Probably not. An idea, though. But where did the dog sleep?

An attractive white woman emerged from the door at the far end of the foyer, struggled to close it tightly, and walked toward us, smiling brightly.

"Mother, this is Harold Haizlip."

"Nice to meet you, Mrs. Taylor. Thank you for inviting me to spend Thanksgiving with you and your family. You have a very nice place here."

"We're so pleased you could come. Just ignore my Duchess. She's a lovely, friendly dog, once you get to know her.

"I'll have to join you in a few moments. I've got to get back to my kitchen, or there won't be any Thanksgiving dinner. It's nice to have you with us, Harold."

Now, Shirlee was very fair and had an interesting mix of what looked like Greek, East Indian, and Italian features. But her mother was definitely white, without question. Maybe Irish, Italian, or Jewish, with curly, dark hair around her oval face. In some ways she also reminded me of Merle Oberon, one of my movie idols. First Duchess, this mansion, then a white mother who looked like a movie star. I wondered what other surprises Shirlee had for me.

I retrieved my bag from the car and followed Shirlee up to the guest room. Shirlee's room, dammit, was directly opposite her parents' suite. Pattee's room was just down the hall. Christ! When I heard Shirlee's footsteps on the stairs leading down to the foyer, I closed my door and locked it. Although I wasn't afraid of dogs, I felt my formal introduction to Duchess should be with Mrs. Taylor holding her choke chain—tightly.

Before emerging again, I listened intently for sounds of a dog breathing. Hearing none, I decided to risk getting downstairs as quickly as possible and without appearing to be concerned about the dog. I tiptoed toward the stairs through swirling aromas of roasting turkey, sweet potatoes, green beans, gravy, and rolls and walked nonchalantly into the sitting room, where Shirlee and a row of dolls were watching TV. I sat as close as possible, sliding my arm around her shoulder.

"Are the dolls yours?" I asked.

"No, but don't disturb them. They're Pattee's. She's fifteen years old but will still have a hissy fit if anyone touches them. This is *their* sofa; you are *their* guest. They're her children. Do not touch. Those are the rules for everyone. Can you imagine?"

She clasped my hand and raised it over her head, and brought it down beside her. "My father is very formal and would not approve. You'll understand when you meet him. He'll be in here any second to watch his news program from his favorite chair."

"Glad you told me. I wouldn't want to start my relationship with him by sitting on his chair."

"The lounge chair is his. We sit in it when he's not here, but when he is, nobody goes near it."

The front door slammed, and a beautiful girl resembling Shirlee appeared before me.

"You must be Harold with the funny last name. I'm Pattee, Shirlee's baby sister. Shirlee must like you a lot to invite you for Thanksgiving."

"Hi, Pattee. I met your children already. They're quite nice."

"They told me they like you, too. And they said you had your arm around Shirlee before I came in, but I won't tell anyone."

Pattee was clearly a live wire. Bright, self-confident, outspoken, with sharp aquiline features and a great body, she was a force of constant energy and movement, mostly centered on herself and her rapidly changing whims. Her every sentence began, "I . . ."

More footsteps, then . . .

"Might this be the young man who's having Thanksgiving dinner with us, Shirlee?"

Nattily dressed in a three-piece, navy blue suit, with a blue and white pocket square and a matching necktie held in place by a sizable diamond tie tack, Reverend Taylor walked deliberately toward the lounge chair, dropped in with a huge sigh, and raised both feet so Pattee could slide the ottoman under. His elbow resting on the arm of the chair, he raised his right hand toward me, outstretched. "Welcome, son, to the Taylor home. We're pleased to have you. Your name is?"

"Harold! I'm Harold Haizlip!" I had jumped to my feet, stood over him, shaking his hand firmly (but awkwardly, since he was sitting and I was standing). "So nice to meet you, sir, and to have Thanksgiving with you and your family."

Shirlee and Pattee fell silent, glancing alternately at their dad and at me, waiting for the chemistry. I took him in.

A rich cocoa color, Reverend Taylor was a relatively small, thinly built man, about five feet nine, with keen, Indian-like features: a sharp nose, high cheekbones, deeply set and piercing eyes behind round gold-rimmed eyeglasses, a pencil-thin mustache over thin lips, his hair waved back from his forehead and cut close to his small head. The feet resting on the ottoman were incredibly small—half the size of mine—probably size six and a half or seven. His shoes gleamed like mirrors.

Later I noticed that he walked upright and purposefully, as if measuring his stride and counting the steps toward his goal. And even when speaking about the simplest things with family or friends, his phrases were measured, his cadence rhythmical, his elocution perfect, as if he were addressing a crowd of thousands.

"Shirlee has told me a lot about Macedonia. I'm looking forward to hearing your message Sunday morning."

"Is your family Baptist?" he asked coolly, glancing at his newspaper headlines with seeming disinterest in my response.

"My mother's family is and has been for many, many years. My grandmother was a founding deaconess of Oak Spring Baptist Church in Stokesdale, North Carolina. Many of my aunts, uncles, cousins, nephews, and nieces are members today. After moving to Washington, my mother joined the Church of God. I grew up in that church."

"Is that the holiness church?"

"No, sir. It's a fundamentalist church. Are you the founder of Macedonia in Ansonia?"

Pattee became bored with this talk rather quickly and went to the kitchen. I heard a strangled sound from Duchess, but the door closed on her. Shirlee pretended invisibility but listened attentively as Reverend Taylor and I began discovering each other.

He spoke authoritatively and with self-confidence, offering pronouncements on every topic. When I disagreed with him, saying, "My understanding was somewhat different . . . ," he was challenged to amplify his position and diagnose for me the errors of my misunderstanding, thereby enabling me to agree with him, of course. If I persisted in my different points of view, he adopted a fatherly tone and reminded me of my youth, adding that when I grew up and had more experience, I would ultimately agree.

I liked and admired Reverend Taylor from the first. After my father's death, his brothers, Ellis and John, became my surrogate fathers in my early years, but they never completely filled the void of my adolescence and young adulthood. This chasm grew after I left Washington for Amherst, a world totally unfamiliar to my mother, sister, brother, and fatherly uncles. Reverend Taylor had traveled comfortably in both the Negro and white worlds far longer than I. He had been able to control and rise above the inherent anxieties of Negro second-class citizenship in America. Except for many of my Dunbar teachers, until meeting Reverend Taylor I had considered my entry onto this stage my private battle, the major, lonely challenge of my life.

By 5:00 P.M., many people were chatting amiably over lemonade and punch in the living and sitting rooms when I ventured in. In a blur of new faces and names, I met Uncle Percy, Reverend Taylor's wildly cheerful, piano-playing brother from New York City; a half sister, Margaret, a half sister, Althea, and her husband, Darryl; another half sister, Margie, Shirlee's only brother, Julian, Jr., whom everyone called "Brother," and Reverend Knight, an aspiring Baptist minister being tutored by Reverend Taylor. Missing were Shirlee's older sister, Jewelle, and her husband, Jim, spending part of their honeymoon year in Africa.

Once everyone was seated around the dining room table, Reverend Taylor told us to bow our heads while he asked the Lord's blessing, an extended sermonette with references to his wonderful wife and chef of the day, the wonderful children who had blessed their lives, the family members who had passed on to their just rewards, the hungry and the poor, the members of Macedonia Baptist Church, and the new members joining the family circle on this wondrous Thanksgiving Day.

Immediately, as if released from a long, sworn silence, everyone began talking loudly at once, in a cacophony of unending noise. Pattee complained about the food she hated and would not eat. Margaret offered uncanny imitations of her Yale boss, who had a heavy Russian accent. Margie engaged Althea in a conversation about her sons. Brother wanted to know what happened to the last guy Shirlee brought home to meet the family. Mrs. Taylor gave him a stern look meaning "Hush."

The conversation percolated as the food whizzed by in all directions. It was a dinner melee unlike any I had ever experienced before.

And, despite the simultaneous conversations, everyone seemed nevertheless to know what each individual was saying and to whom. Sometimes in the middle of a sentence to one person, somebody would abruptly answer a question raised by another—at the opposite end of the table. I felt as if I were watching a high-speed, high-decibel verbal tennis match.

By the end of the main course, I had begun to appreciate the spiritedness of this family and to learn about what brought them together.

Most important to me was discovering that the "half sisters," Margaret, Althea, and Margie, were not children of a previous marriage by Reverend or Mrs. Taylor, though I would later learn he had, in fact, been married before. Still, because of the girls' family situations, Reverend and Mrs. Taylor had arranged to become their surrogate parents. Somehow, I wasn't surprised by these revelations; I was impressed that this family not only talked compassion but lived it.

There was one more revelation. Shirlee's mother wasn't quite white after all. Her immediate ancestors included blacks, Indians, and whites. Shirlee told me she would tell me her mother's story later.

By the end of the evening, I had bantered with everyone so openly and freely, often with exchanges of uproarious humor, that I felt I had known Shirlee's family for many years.

After most of the guests had left, Shirlee and I offered to help Mrs. Taylor clean up.

I opened the kitchen door slowly, trying not to give off the scent of fear that people say dogs readily detect. I probably failed. Duchess squinted her eyes, backed away toward Mrs. Taylor, flashed her molars, and began barking as best she could in defiance of the choke chain.

I sat in a chair at the breakfast bar in the middle of the kitchen. Petrified.

Mrs. Taylor brought Duchess closer. She growled, looking at me sideways.

"You see," Mrs. Taylor exclaimed. "She likes you, Harold."

I pretended I believed this. For the rest of the weekend, whenever Duchess and I were in the same room and out of Mrs. Taylor's sight, Duchess would quietly approach me from behind, sniff the seat of my pants, open her mouth as wide as possible, and practice taking a huge bite. It was as if she were behind a plate-glass door. She performed this one silent maneuver for years thereafter. She never bit me.

That evening on a walk in the park, Shirlee told me that she knew her father had taken a special "liking" to me, much more so than to any of her previous dates, but that he was trying not to be too interested too soon. I told her that he had been quite pleasant toward me, but nothing more. Out of the range of his patrician glare, I was more interested, frankly, in holding and kissing her.

As we were leaving, Reverend Taylor said, "Young man, drive carefully. You've got precious cargo on board." I knew that he was indirectly warning me to take Shirlee directly to her dorm—without a stopover in my apartment. Men understand each other.

After that Thanksgiving, I spent as much time as possible with Shirlee, much of it walking around Boston and Cambridge. As far as I knew, we were dating each other exclusively, although I sometimes wondered what she had told Mr. Lexington.

Seeing Shirlee so frequently had increased my weekly expenses to the point where I absolutely had to get a bartending gig every week. To have additional money for the Christmas holidays, I would have to bartend even more. This was out of the question, because I needed the time to prepare for my semester exams. I had only one choice: to remain in Cambridge and study.

Throughout my childhood, Christmas was my favorite time of year. Although we were always on the edge of disaster because of serious money problems—and perhaps precisely because we were—I found joy and freedom in the temporary relief of celebrating and shopping for that one special gift for Ma, Vira, Allen, and Pam. As a teenager, I worked part-time in a dry cleaning plant and every year began saving "Christmas money" immediately after Halloween. Until this year, I had always found a way to celebrate Christmas.

I told Shirlee that I could not visit with her during the holidays. Not believing it, she pleaded with me to go over the possibilities again. I tried to find a way but couldn't.

Ma said she understood and would try to send me twenty-five dollars to cheer me up. Both Vitz and Dan offered to lend me a few dollars, but I declined. I didn't want any more debt. I finally decided to get one additional bartending job so that I could buy a gift for Shirlee.

On the evening before she left for the holidays, Shirlee and I had a pizza dinner date in Boston, exchanged gifts, and admired the city's Christmas windows. Back on campus we sat in the the Chrysler listening to Christmas carols, holding hands, hugging and kissing. I was nearly delirious with self-pity.

Cambridge became a ghost town. There were no more than six or seven students in all of Widener Library. Our apartment seemed desolate. Most nights, after a tuna salad, potato chips, and a beer, I studied until midnight. I was deeply depressed most of each day until my nightly telephone call to Shirlee, after which I would feel better for an hour or so, only to fall into a slump again. Christmas Eve was unbearable.

It was early Christmas morning and I was sound asleep when the phone jarred me awake. "Hello? Hello? Who's calling?"

"It's me, Sweet Prince!" Shirlee shouted. "I'm at the bus station in New Haven about to leave for Boston. I'm coming to spend Christmas Day with you. Can you meet me? Got to go or I'll miss my bus. See you at 12:45. Love you." She was gone.

In my pajamas, I sat at the kitchen table over a cup of instant coffee, unable to contain myself. She *is* coming. She wasn't kidding me. She wouldn't kid me about something so important. What should I do first? Get some food? Pick up a small Christmas tree? Get some red candles? Clean the apartment? Wash the Chrysler? Make a dinner reservation somewhere? Find the old Christmas records in our LP collection? "Your best bet, Harold," I said to myself, "is to stop drinking coffee and get your ass in gear. You've got the best date ever in just a few hours."

I arrived about 12:20, parked the Chrysler, found her arrival area on the bulletin board, and sprinted outside to a cold bench. To honor the season and the occasion, I wore my big, heavy fishermen's-knit red turtleneck sweater under my black topcoat and wrapped my six-foot crimson Harvard scarf loosely around it so that its tasseled ends fell to my knees, front and rear.

Heavy snow slowed down buses arriving from the south. I knew that but nevertheless swore incessantly as 1:00 came and went without a bus in sight. Finally, around 1:15 a bus appeared in the distance, lumbering toward the depot. Despite the cold, I began to feel quite warm.

As soon as the doors opened, hordes of people clutching luggage, children, boxes, and shopping bags bulging with brightly wrapped gifts rushed down the stairs. I looked frantically in one direction and then the other on tiptoes, trying to catch a glimpse of Shirlee. No luck. My heart sank. No Shirlee. Had she been kidding me, after all? Maybe something happened and she missed the bus. She probably telephoned to let me know while I was out shopping. She'll be on the next bus. I kept looking in both directions. No luck.

And then, there she was, smiling and waving, her red scarf and red beret warming up the white snow. I ran toward her as fast as I could, clutched her in my arms, and kissed her over and over again, twirling both of us around and around.

"Merry Christmas, Sweet Prince!" she whispered.

Except for the usual mess behind the closed doors to Vitz's and Dan's rooms, the apartment was spotless, with subtle suggestions of Christmas here and there: two tall red candles on the kitchen table, bright red apples in a Pyrex dish; a big, round blue "snowball" candle flecked with red and green glitter, an arrangement of fir twigs salvaged from a nearby Christmas tree stand; and, in the living room window, a small green ceramic Christmas tree covered with multicolored dots that glowed brightly when the bulb underneath was turned on. Thank God for Woolworth's.

I lit a blue snowball candle, put Nat King Cole's Christmas LP on, turned the volume down low, asked Shirlee to dance, and held her close.

"If he kills you, he'll have to kill me, too!" I said, half jokingly.

"He'll be very upset, but I know he'll get over it after a while. He already asked me if I was serious about you, and when I told him I was, he said you seemed to be a nice young man from a nice, religious family." We both knew why he emphasized the "religious family" part.

As the last bus back to New Haven pulled away, I heard myself saying softly, "I love you and want to spend the rest of my life with you. Will you marry me? I'll be as good to you as humanly possible, because I love you dearly and cannot and will not live without you. Marry me and I'll marry you!"

Three weeks into the second semester, we had a long, casual dinner in Boston and stopped by our favorite coffeehouse on Charles Street. We held hands over coffee and hot chocolate. Shirlee was radiant and cheerful, wistful, in love. So was I. The time was now.

"Shirlee," I began slowly, "there's no question in my mind that you are the woman I must spend the rest of my life with. I love being with you and hate being without you. I want to to be with you forever, to love you, to have children with you, and most of all, to be the love of your life. Will you marry me?"

"Are you sure?" she asked.

"Never been surer of anything in my life. Will you marry me? Will you let me marry you? Will you marry me? I know your answer will be 'Yes.' I know it."

"Yes," she said. "Yes! Yes! Yes!"

"When?" I asked.

"You'll have to talk with my father. Let's drive to New Haven for a weekend soon. You can ask him then."

A few weeks later, we arrived at the Taylors' home late on a Friday evening. I had agreed to drive Reverend Taylor to Ansonia early Saturday "on business." A good time to talk, I thought. When the family came upstairs to bed, I heard Duchess's I.D. tag tingling lightly outside my closed door.

The next morning, a quick cup of coffee sent Reverend Taylor and me on our way. A small leather-bound notebook stuffed with opened envelopes, folded pages of notes, official-looking documents, and other papers seemed to be our guide. Reverend pulled out various pieces randomly and, as if suddenly remembering where he had to go, told me to turn here or there until we reached his destination. Whereupon he instructed me to park and wait until he returned.

By noon, we had stopped at one business in New Haven and two in Ansonia, four or five homes in different areas of Ansonia, a Chrysler/Plymouth car dealership, Macedonia Baptist Church, the offices of the *Ansonia Sentinel*, the Ansonia Elks Club, an Esso station, where he gassed his car for free, a dry cleaning store, and a car wash. Before and after each stop, he concentrated on the papers bulging in his notebook, reading different pieces, writing notes on various ones, and returning them to the pile. He spoke infrequently, except to give directions to the next stop.

When we returned to New Haven, Shirlee was disappointed to learn that "the subject" had not been discussed. I promised to find a time later in the day.

After dinner, Reverend Taylor retired to his chair. Scared as hell, I joined him and began chatting about nothing to get a conversation started. He pretended preoccupation with the TV, grunting approval at intermittent points during my chatter at him. Frustrated, I finally said, "Reverend Taylor, I want to ask you a very serious question." He continued watching TV and waved his hand offhandedly for me to continue, as if he were the starter waving the checkered flag from the sidelines of an auto racetrack.

"I would like your permission and blessings to marry Shirlee."

He remained expressionless and still for a few minutes, as if he had not heard me. I waited because I knew he wasn't hard of hearing. The next move was his. He invited me into his study.

Finally, without looking at me, he said, "Do you have a particular date in mind?"

"As soon as possible, sir. But no date yet. That's why I wanted to talk with you."

"And as a full-time student, just how do you plan to take care of my daughter in the manner to which she is accustomed?"

"Right now, I make good money bartending parties for a group of women pilots in Belmont. After I get my degree, I plan to get a good job to support us."

"And will these lady pilots pay you enough to cover your tuition at Harvard and Shirlee's at Wellesley, plus your other expenses?"

"I don't think so. But I can find another part-time job."

"Do you need time to study at Harvard? Or are you a genius who knows as much as your professors?"

"I'm no slacker in the brains department, but I study quite a lot."

He changed the subject. "Tell me more about your parents and family."

Interrupting me at various points for clarification of a detail, he listened quite closely to the Haizlip family story. I crescendoed to my conclusion and exclaimed, "All of which brings me to your doorstep asking to marry your beautiful daughter."

"That was pretty good," he said. He paused for what seemed to be a full hour and finally said, softly, "I'll give you my blessings to marry Shirlee, and we'll be proud to have a young man like you join our family. But there are two conditions."

My joy was a shout in my throat. But I couldn't breathe until I heard the conditions.

"Shirlee will complete her junior year at Wellesley in a few months and graduate in June of next year. I plan to pay her tuition and other expenses until she graduates, and when she does, she will be a Taylor only. Shirlee Anne Morris Taylor. You two can get married the day after graduation, if you like, but not one day before. That's the first condition."

He waited for my response. I remained absolutely silent.

"The second is there will be no Taylor-Haizlip babies at the graduation, and she will not be pregnant. Do I make myself absolutely clear?"

"Yes, sir. Very clear. Absolutely clear." I was wiping perspiration from my face so rapidly with both hands that Reverend Taylor pulled a handkerchief from his pocket and casually waved it in my direction.

"Reverend Taylor, I want you to know that I love Shirlee more than life itself, and that I will honor and protect her for the rest of my life in the same manner as you have done to this point. I consider myself fortunate and honored to have her as my wife and the Taylors as my new family. I will always do my best to live up to the trust you are extending to me with your permission to marry her. I will thank you for the rest of my life."

"Welcome to the family, son. But remember that my two conditions are non-negotiable. I'll talk with Mrs. Taylor tomorrow about the best time for a wedding."

I shook his hand for a long time. Then he hugged me. My eyes began to fill. I said good night and went to find Shirlee to share the good news.

CHAPTER 3

~❧~

Not Far from the Tree

*S*HIRLEE: I was the third of four children, and the second daughter of three girls and one boy, born to a couple whose own marriage of forty-nine years would be interrupted only by death. Two older half sisters from my father's brief first marriage, which ended in divorce, completed my family. They lived in Washington, D.C., my father's hometown, and, until each married, they spent their summers with us. Also included in our family circle at various times were five young girls, foster daughters, who would become women in our home and whom my siblings and I regarded as our sisters.

I lived most of my childhood and all of my adolescent years in a church parsonage in Ansonia, a small mill town in southern Connecticut, eight miles from New Haven. If anything, Ansonia was known for its steep hills, its factories, the Naugatuck River, which bisected it, and its championship high school football team.

Directly across the river, passenger and freight trains chugged and whistled by every few hours. At that time, you could catch a train in Ansonia directly to New York City. I remember my father in a space reserved for dignitaries, holding me up to help greet President Roosevelt when he made a campaign whistle-stop in our town on a train from New York to Waterbury. A few years later, when I was eight, my mother interrupted my cartwheels in front of the parsonage, calling me to come inside. My father sat slumped in his chair, his shoulders heaving as he wept. I was startled to see my father cry. "Go upstairs and change your clothes. President Roosevelt is dead," my mother whispered.

Our street, Clifton Avenue, was generally quiet. Mail came twice a day, and the milkman left bottled milk at our side porch door. I insisted on having the cream at the top for my oatmeal.

Few people had two cars. We walked everywhere. It was a town of ones: one theater, one library, one newspaper, one high school, one department store, one opera house.

A few doors away from the church, on the opposite side of the street, the nondescript parsonage was built by factory owners in the 1850s, originally to house a mill manager and his family. Five bedrooms upstairs and four rooms down made it adequate for our family of six. It was unpretentious, sitting two stories above the Naugatuck, whose waters were iridescent miasmas, brewed from polluted factory waste. Nothing lived in the stretch that flowed by our house. We understood without being told that we could not fish or swim in the river.

Although it was home, the parsonage was a busy place, used for committee and club meetings, pastoral counseling and tutoring, and sometimes weddings. I never knew who would be there with my father when I came home from school. It might be a factory worker needing a letter of recommendation, a couple receiving marriage counseling, or a visiting politician. If any famous Negro came to town, he would end up at our house. And so I always had to be mindful of my behavior.

When my older sister, Jewelle, was a teenager and held her first party with records and dancing at the house, word got back to some of Macedonia's deacons and members. The conservative ones in the group felt it was inappropriate for the minister's family to have dancing parties. Both my parents quickly squelched that concern, making it plain that their children would lead normal lives in their home— "normal" including parties and dancing. No more was ever said, and the parsonage became the scene of many a lively teenage party.

We inhabited a place rich with differences. Most of my schoolmates seemed proud to be first-generation immigrants. I wondered a lot about the "Old Country" they frequently mentioned. Their parents spoke a lively mixture of pidgin English and Polish, Russian, Czechoslovakian, Italian, Hungarian, Armenian, Greek, and Yiddish. Of the town's 25,000 citizens, 2,500 were Negroes. Their number never exceeded 10 percent of the overall population, so they were never viewed as a threatening group.

And so all of us believed we were free. We could pat ourselves on the back and say that our town was not like those horrid places below the Mason-Dixon line.

Much of Ansonia's Negro population had arrived there after enduring the long physical and emotional journey from the rural South, mostly North and South Carolina. In family groups they poured in for the "good-paying" factory jobs that blossomed in Ansonia's mills during the Second World War. They cherished new dreams of freedom and success, yet they brought with them their ground-in sense of subordinated place and, often, powerlessness. Theirs was a state of mind acquired in fear and maintained by uncertainty.

Although on the face of it Ansonia posed as an integrated town and racial tensions rarely surfaced, residential segregation was the unquestioned standard practice. The parsonage where we played out our lives sat in a mixed neighborhood. The bank helped my father finance the purchase of a large, multistory apartment building on our street. At the time, all of its tenants were white; some were my schoolmates.

Yet for years my father could not buy a home for his family in a white neighborhood in Ansonia, although he had the down payment, excellent credit, and an unimpeachable reputation. (When he finally did purchase a lovely, large colonial house, it sat in the middle of a desirable white neighborhood in New Haven. Our family's integration of the block was quietly opposed by some but loudly endorsed by the majority of the neighbors.) Now a street in one of Ansonia's newest, most exclusive subdivisions, way up in the hills near Woodbridge, has been named Reverend Taylor Drive, after my father.

All of the teachers in Ansonia's schools were white, as were the police force, the city government, the business establishments, and the other members of the controlling group that exists in every hamlet, every town, every city. Those who, by virtue of birth, skin color, fortune, or elective office, decide who can do what, where they can do it, and under what circumstances.

Nonetheless, in that strange quilting of American ways, there were genuine friendships among Negroes and whites in the town. There did exist some opportunities to move back and forth across the color line. My parents included a number of whites in their inner circle. My mother was the only Negro member of the women's college club.

Within the town's seductive mosaic, the citizens began their friendships in school, mixed in bars, attended each other's weddings, christenings, and funerals in the Polish Hall, the Catholic rectory, the Italian restaurant, and the Negro Elks Hall. Their children joined Scouts together. Fathers toiled side by side in backbreaking, greasy jobs in the factories, although no blacks were in management positions. Some mothers, Negro and white, worked in the rubber factories in nearby Naugatuck. Colored and white played together on local sports teams. But interracial dating was rare and frowned upon.

We were all thrown together in some of the town's elementary schools and the one academic high school. No black faces could be seen in a few of the elementary schools because of residential patterns. On a gentle hill, not far from a beautiful Russian Orthodox church, there was a vocational training high school for boys, the Pine School, to which the counselors assigned most of the Negro boys and the poorer white boys. I didn't think too much about those patterns then, although I often heard my father discussing such matters at home or in church.

My first place of learning was Willis School, a tan wooden elementary school high on a hill, Grove Street, about half a mile from my home. On Howard Avenue, at the top of another nearby hill, the "Crooked S," was the high school I would attend and love.

Not until I was in college did I realize how fortunate I was to have had as best friends from the first grade on children from two groups of people: those whose parents were my father's church members and those whose parents had so recently chosen America to live out their dreams.

Every day, Georgie Spader, my handsome blond Polish neighbor and classmate, stood in front of my house after school and called for me to come out to play softball with him and his brothers. Breathlessly, we ran to the sandbank. The Negro boys from nearby Wooster Street joined us to fill out the rosters of each team. In the winter, all of us would brave the light traffic of Wooster Street to sled down its long, sloping hill, the soft whoosh of the runners in the snow heightening our excitement. Yelling and calling, our voices parted the lovely silences of purple twilight on gleaming winter nights.

My classmates of the citywide eighth grade elected me class president. That year I joined the band and played first the French horn and then the slide trombone. My circle of friends grew to include students who had mastered their ABCs in parochial and other primarily white schools.

High school was a golden time for me. I did not have to strain to be an honor student since I loved to read, write, and study. I was an overachiever, a cheerleader, class vice-president, school newspaper reporter, and yearbook editor. I thought then I wanted to be a doctor. It was not a burning desire but something I believed to be honorable and important, something that would make my family proud, make my race proud, and help people live better lives.

This idea of achievement came not only from my parents but also from the other professional role models, mostly male, in my family. I knew I had two cousins, one a woman, with Ph.D.s who taught at Howard University Medical School. There had been several teachers on my mother's side. My father had grown up with four brothers, all of whom were college graduates, in some cases with graduate degrees, who did important things, including editing a newspaper, chairing a college art department, practicing dentistry, and playing the piano professionally. And I adored those uncles of mine, none of whom lived in Connecticut. Their wives were the beautiful, glamorous women who materialized in our lives in the summertime, as if out of afternoon dreams, chattering, sweet-smelling, and mysterious, wafting about in wavy hair, sheer dresses, and white gloves.

I still made time for dating; local boys, boys from New Haven, Waterbury, Bridgeport, and Hartford. I even had a swain in Alaska, sort of a cousin from Washington, who invited me to attend his senior prom. I didn't go.

My most handsome date, a boy with curly hair, smiling eyes, and a profile that could have graced a Roman coin, lost his looks in the Korean War. Somewhere near the Yalu River, a flamethrower melted his face and fused his fingers. I thought a lot about him while he was recuperating. His return to the States caused me to write my first political essay for an English class. A righteous piece, it was not about war but, rather, the racism faced by those returning Negro soldiers who served their country wisely and well. I remember reading it aloud in class to a strangely quiet group.

It was difficult to see my veteran friend at first. While he was away I had lost romantic interest in him. But after a while, his jolly manner triumphed over his disfigurement. We remained friends until I went to college and lost track of him. I heard he eventually became a social worker.

My father's tenure at Macedonia Baptist Church began the year I was born, 1937, and would end in 1980, the year before he died. He arrived in Ansonia a highly literate Howard University man. During most of that time, he also pastored a small Baptist church in the northeastern part of the state, to which he drove seventy miles every Sunday evening for a ninety-minute service.

Although he was determined to have his way, his was not a confrontational style. Above all things, he believed in and relied on reason and goodwill. He pushed quietly for civil rights beginning in the early forties, when he founded the local chapter of the NAACP. Later he led the fight to integrate the local YMCA. Among his dreams was better housing for Ansonia's Negroes. Most lived in poorly maintained tenements in the low-lying areas just off Main Street on the east side. When in 1957 hurricane floods tore through the center of the town, washing away many of its housing sins, my father began to realize some of his dreams.

He ran for alderman (and lost), served on the town's planning commission and the state parole board. He became an aide to the popular Democratic governor Abraham Ribicoff, and was named Connecticut's first black delegate-at-large for the Democratic party. Like his father before him, he was a powerhouse in black Baptist circles. For years he served as the president of the New England

Black Baptists and as a vice-president of the national group.

His high visibility, acknowledged leadership, and home training created a family atmosphere in which achievement had no limits, as long as we behaved in ways that would reflect well on the Taylor family and, in those days, on the entire Negro race. Early on, I believed that all doors would be open to me; all people would be kind to me; everyone would have my interests at heart.

An extremely private public figure, my father could be as ebullient as he was thoughtful. In church he transformed into a dynamo, full of charm for the ladies and wisdom for the men. Sometimes his sermons featured high drama and low sarcasm. At other times he would recite essays or the poems of Longfellow he had committed to memory.

In his messages, he always started out softly and calmly and ended in crescendo. A favorite passage began, *sotto voce,* "It's Friday," then loudly, "but Sunday's comin'." By the end of the sermon, the whole church would be exclaiming in response, "but Sunday's comin'." Heads would be bobbing, toes would be tapping, sweat would be running, and fans would be waving.

Often he sang solos with the senior choir. When he sang "I've Done My Work," "Jerusalem," or "Something Within Me" in his dulcet tones, the sisters would move their shoulders from side to side and wave their handkerchiefs up and down as tears rolled down their cheeks. The church women were especially attracted to the charismatic, polished man smiling down on them from the pulpit. Fortunately for his wife and family, he did not succumb to the wiles of those who needed "special prayers" or "private consultations."

At home his was a quiet but powerful presence. He rarely raised his voice. Instead, he reigned by a series of looks that we came to know only too well. The rueful smile, the unblinking stare, the clasped fingers over his lips, touching the tip of his nose.

Before dinner, he plinked at the piano and either whistled or softly sang along. He possessed a high tenor voice with a distinct vibrato. Sometimes we giggled at his trills, which seemed to go on forever. Among his favorite selections were the songs he had once sung in concert with his four brothers. Pieces he called "the light classics." I grew up hearing in his sweet, pure voice German lieder, French chansons, Negro spirituals, Irish airs, American classics, and popular operatic arias. No one could sing "Danny Boy" or "Motherless Child" more beautifully than my father.

From my father I inherited—osmosed, in fact—my love of music, reading, and words. Commanding exquisite enunciation, he expected ours to be the same. "You cannot reach people if they don't know what you are saying," he'd pronounce without looking up from his newspaper. If I told him something that had happened during my day and mispronounced or misused a word, he politely interrupted, gently corrected me, gave me the Latin derivation of the word, then invited me to continue on.

He was delighted when I began to make my mark as a public speaker. The first time my picture appeared in the *Sentinel* was on the occasion of my winning the citywide eighth-grade oratorical contest. The photo was two columns wide and the headline began, "Minister's Daughter Wins . . ." Every year after that, I entered and won the school's public speaking events. My father said he was not surprised. He expected it.

Often he worried crossword puzzles, played solitaire, or read a mystery. It was clear that his mind was seldom idle. Listening to the news and commentary on the radio and reading the paper were part of his routine. At least once a week he would say to me, "Read the paper so you can learn about the world beyond Ansonia."

Most agree he was a handsome man. His color was that of freshly ground nutmeg. His bearing commanded instant attention, suggesting royal origins. And my father understood well the importance of image. His manners were flawless. He spared little expense on a wardrobe for himself and the rest of the family. He knew how to dress well, understanding the fall of a drape, the precision of a crease, the drama of monochromatics. His feet were small, and he shod them handsomely. He never owned a pair of sneakers.

And he never left the house without some type of hat, usually a handsome fedora. Hats defined him, were as much a part of him as his shirts and ties. Sometimes he drove up to a hat factory in Danbury to explore the full range of possibilities. On those occasions, he returned home with a backseat filled with hatboxes of all shapes and sizes.

He had a delicate, courtly way of tipping his hat to the ladies, nodding his head as he just barely touched the brim with two slender fingers and a thumb.

In addition to hats, my father loved cars, big cars. When I was very young he favored Buicks; then he switched to Cadillacs. Every two years, a new shiny sedan appeared before the front door. For the first few days after its arrival, we children would sit in it with the windows open, waving and calling to all those passing by. For many years, his was one of only two Cadillacs in town, so everyone could tell us where he was on any given day.

My father's car became his finite kingdom. Permitting no one else to drive it, he kept it in sparkling condition. Sometimes he sat out front of the house in the car, reading his mail or looking to see whether the grass needed mowing. He reminded me then of the country squire on his horse, inspecting his fiefdom.

I never saw my father kowtow to anyone. Even the time when, on vacation and driving through West Virginia, he was pulled out of a long line of cars by two state troopers. Glancing at my mother and the four children in the car, they checked my father's license and registration and ordered him to follow them to the courthouse. Polite yet nondeferential, he complied. I watched in the hot noonday sun as the tall troopers towered over my father, escorting him inside a lovely red brick building graced by gleaming columns. I don't remember how long we waiting, swatting at buzzing insects and wishing for some cold water. After a while, he came out alone, walking determinedly, as usual. "Big fine for speeding," he said to my mother as we drove away. My mother's face flushed.

My earliest memories of my "place" in the scheme of things was my father saying, "Remember you are a Taylor." At first I thought the name had some mystical meaning. When I was old enough to use the dictionary, I looked to see what "Taylor"s were. I didn't get much help there. At the same time that he was extolling the Taylor universe, he taught his children another lesson. We were the same as everyone else, just a bit more fortunate. Everyone's role in life deserved respect. Somehow we got the nuances of this mixed message.

Despite all he had seen and experienced, my father lived most of his life without bitterness. In conversations, exchanges, transactions, he was always an equal. At times there was just the hint of superiority about him. He tried not to let it show.

There were some white people, he thought, who had goodwill in their hearts. He was optimistic and even hopeful that life for Negroes would get better and better. We had to work at it, though, he said. That is what he taught me. For a long time, I believed it.

Three things I wanted in my childhood but didn't get were a pony and grandparents. My grandfather, William Taylor, died the year I was born. My only living grandparent, Will Morris, existed beyond a barrier I could not cross: my mother's father, he experienced life as a white man, "somewhere in Maryland, on the Eastern Shore."

Everyone said that Grandfather Taylor was quite a man. Educated at Shaw University in Raleigh before the turn of the century, a time when most people in America, black or white, could not even dream of going to college, he seemed determined to be part of the burgeoning expansion of America. Opportunity beckoned in the form of Newport News, Virginia, where my grandfather pastored a city landmark, the First Baptist Church, then the tallest structure in the town. Some say God, others say greater glory, summoned him to Washington, D.C., where he founded his own landmark, creating an historic institution, the Florida Avenue Baptist Church. (When I was young, I imagined Florida Avenue to be inhabited by swaying palm trees and daintily stepping pink flamingoes whose thin legs tested the waters of the baptismal pool behind the altar.) It was in this church and in the Shaw neighborhood of Washington that my father and his brothers grew up.

Along the way Grandfather Taylor became a history teacher, a headmaster, a divinity school professor, and a man of property, including a grocery store. He also became a ladies' man. Twice widowed, he married a beautiful woman decades younger. He died a few months after the wedding. Newspaper accounts tell us that thousands thronged to the funeral service, witnessing the young widow swooning on the steps in my father's arms.

On my father's side, our lineage included Africans, Indians, and whites. My grandfather married the daughter of an Indian woman and a black man. My father never let me forget that he was proud of all of his background. Long before "multiculturalism" and "mixed" race became buzzwords, I knew that my family's personal history reflected the creolization of America. It was no big deal. It was a heritage most other Negro families could also claim.

Over the years, I would come to realize my father believed that the family was expected to behave in a certain way, to carry on a tradition, to pass on certain values. Not just because we were the minister's brood but because the Taylors had made a secure and special place for themselves in a country that did not have their interests at heart.

The way I grew up, which at the time I thought was ordinary, might be characterized by some as privileged and insular. By no means were we rich, but we were comfortably upper middle class. Our parents indulged us, showered us with lavish Christmases, bought wardrobes of clothes for winter and summer, gave us music lessons, packed us off to camp, kept us free of housework and chores, and sent the three girls to the best of colleges. My brother, too, was enrolled in a residential school for boys. My father took him on trips alone and gave him a car.

Jewelle was four years older than I, Pattee five years younger. Brother was between Jewelle and me by two years. Just as Jewelle or Brother walked me to school when I was first starting, I took Pattee by the hand and led her up the hill.

We had the usual fights over clothes, bikes, toys. But as children we realized early on that we were "the minister's family," perceived by the townspeople as a monolithic unit that ought to be perfect. That awareness molded our interactions with each other, where at home we were determined to be distinctly different. We fell into roles. Jewelle was the boss, the leader; Brother was the iconoclast; I was the quiet one, the peacemaker; and Pattee was the baby. For my sisters, at least, the spacing was far enough apart that we were never consciously competing with each other. Jewelle achieved an exemplary scholastic record and was the first girl from the town to attend Radcliffe. Brother went his own way and Pattee and I carved out singular niches. But not without our parents drumming into us the importance of close family ties and support.

We were proud of each other's achievements and, like our parents, expected them. We appreciated each one's special attribute: Jewelle's articulateness, Brother's ingenuity, my intellectual curiosity, and Pattee's charm. As sisters we enjoyed being the "Taylor girls," and each of us had her turn as "Daddy's girl." Brother's status as the only son was a double-edged sword, which he figured out how to use just before he died.

We celebrated our milestones at every opportunity. For my six-teenth birthday, I had a formal party for one hundred guests at the luxurious home of a family friend in New Haven. When all three girls graduated in the same year from college, high school, and eighth grade, respectively, our parents hosted a reception in an elegant con-servatory in a leafy Stratford park.

When I was twenty, my father gave me a trip to Florida for a birth-day present. It was my first airplane flight. I headed south for a friend's formal coming-out party, held at her home. On arrival, the ugly reality of segregated facilities enervated me far worse than the blasts of Florida's heat and humidity. Once we arrived at the debu-tante's home, we were in a protected enclave of Negroes who lived well. As her mother, in regal silk, and her father, distinguished in tails, presided, a string orchestra played for these daughters and sons of privilege to dance their way into adulthood.

Living in Ansonia in no way circumscribed our lives. With our par-ents we traveled throughout the state and other parts of New Eng-land. Each summer my father drove us to North and South Carolina, stopping in each state in between. We also refreshed ourselves at Highland and Arundel Beaches in Maryland, exclusive resort play-grounds for well-to-do Negroes. A number of our relatives had homey beach houses there. August vacations took us to Canada, upstate New York, Chicago, St. Louis, Iowa. Sometimes we joined our father in his trips to the National Baptist Conventions.

I had mixed feelings about traveling south. There was always a tenseness about the journey, which I wouldn't understand until later. On the way down, I loved passing the docks on the West Side of New York in the early-morning hours, spotting with excitement the *Queen Mary,* the *Isle de France,* or some other great liner resting quietly in its berth. My father said one day I would sail on those.

After New York, we were not easy again until we reached the homes of pastors who were my father's friends. Their houses were our overground railroad. Their homes became ours, because no public places would have us. It was that and the fact that I would have to sit in the "crow's nest" at the movies that made me indignant. No matter how attractive the offering, a Roy Rogers or Gene Autry number, I would not go.

Of my mother's family, the Morrises, I knew little. Her origins were said to be black, Irish, and Italian. What I did know was that my mother had been abandoned as a young child and grew up in a series of foster homes in Washington, D.C., while the rest of her family passed for white. Beautiful, soft-spoken, and somewhat melancholic, she married my father when she was twenty years old, and his large family became hers.

My mother had dark curly hair, large dark eyes, and a heart-shaped face. Her skin was the color of French vanilla ice cream. High cheekbones gave her a permanent pleasant expression, which was accentuated by a soft, girlish voice. Her most distinctive feature was her prominent nose, which some said made her look Jewish or Italian.

My parents married during the Depression and, despite a small inheritance that had been settled on my mother, experienced some hard times. In a nine-year period, my mother bore four children. For a while the family eked out a living on the tiny salary of a small-town pastor.

They moved several times before they settled into a comfortable life in Ansonia. Eventually they would purchase rental property and two homes and establish a reputation as a solid, attractive, productive twosome.

My mother grew comfortably into her role as a minister's wife, supporting my father in his church activities and assuming many of the leadership roles expected of a pastor's spouse. The parishioners were said to admire her gentle, ladylike manners, which could accommodate a high tea and a chitlin dinner equally well.

Rarely did they experience her flashes of temper, the lusty swearwords, and the steely determination. Those gargoyles made their appearance if anyone said or did anything even vaguely hostile to her husband, her children, or her pets. Once she snatched a deacon's tie on the front steps of the church when he voted against giving my father a raise. The time she kicked the shins of a giant school nurse after the nurse tried to push her down some steps made the local tabloid. Many called her "Lady Margaret," a title she enjoyed.

Like my father, and perhaps even more so, my mother indulged her children without apology. She wanted to give them the family life, the emotional undergirding, and the material things she had not had.

Once married, she never held a job outside the home. Not because they didn't need the money. Not because she did not want to work, but because my father insisted she stay at home with the children. I didn't know what a babysitter was.

How does one measure a good mother? By the food she cooks? The values she instills? The achievements of her children?

Psychologists tell us that good mothering begins in the womb. Yet the jury is still out on the precise ingredients that produce the mother the football player salutes, the mother the daughter calls daily from anywhere in the world, or the mother who the son believes is a saint.

My mother had no one to teach her to be a mother. Her own mother died when she was four. A series of guardians, one mad, one busy, and one cold, raised her. Somehow, from the deep spaces of her heart, she patched together her own formula for mothering.

I don't think she sang or read to me while I was in her womb. She probably was too busy taking care of my older siblings. I'm sure I heard those transactions, though.

Generally sweet tempered, my mother became a Fury if her children were threatened. Once she spanked the legs of a neighborhood bully who had knocked me off my new tricycle. Another time she ran down the street coatless in the middle of winter, holding my baby sister in her arms, to reach for my older sister, lying still under a car that had just knocked her down.

I cannot remember my mother sitting down during the day, and she was rarely ill. She was constantly involved in some household task, washing clothes by hand, ironing, cooking, or cleaning. When we were small, she made pretty little pinafores for my sisters and me.

Each morning she would get up, wash up, make up lightly, and put on a light red lipstick. She always looked pretty when she was working, wearing a freshly starched, well-fitted "housedress," which, on her, looked like a going-to-lunch outfit. I especially loved her in sleeveless summer dresses that showed off her beautifully formed arms and swished softly around her calves. From my mother I got my first sense of glamour, the upswept hair, the red lips, the white dress with fuchsia flowers.

Frequently she reminded us she wasn't "raising my daughters to be maids," so we did no regular household chores. When we got to high

school, we helped out a bit, but not in any significant way. The only
thing my mother's attitude about our working around the house
might have done for me was to endow me with a decidedly casual attitude about housework and no burning desire to have floors upon
which I could eat.

In the evenings Mother divided her time between helping us with
our homework and sitting with my father as he listened to the radio
or, later, watched television. More often than not, she would come
into the bedroom I shared with my younger sister and listen to the
mystery program *The Inner Sanctum* just before we fell off to sleep.

She extended her maternal wings. With the profound sorrow of
her childhood as a subtext, she gathered and nurtured other motherless, wounded children. Although they were not the children of her
womb, they were the children of her heart. Our family blossomed as
she sheltered, loved, and spoiled five other girls.

I know that until we left her nest, she and my father protected us,
actually hid us, from America's foulest wind, racism. She made me
know that I was a special person in this world, no matter what anyone
else thought or said. I believed her implicitly.

When my mother was eighty years old, I found and reunited
her with her only sister and the rest of her missing Morris family. But
that is another story. Our family is still feeling the ripples of the
reunification. I often wonder what my father would say about this
closing of my mother's family circle, especially when I tell people
now that I am "a Taylor *and* a Morris."

And so I came to marriage with a good, perhaps even exaggerated,
sense of my self, and of self-worth. I expected that the man I married
would provide for me in the same way that my father had. That he
would be a well-dressed, dignified man and an excellent communica-
tor. That he would be proud of me, dote on me, and encourage me to
do whatever in life would bring me satisfaction. Was I, in fact, thinking I was marrying a man just like my father? Not at the time.

In turn, I planned to do whatever my husband needed to help him
succeed. I would be faithful, helpful, and look good all the time. I
knew I was in no way a homemaker, but I saw little challenge in learning how to cook and keep house. Such things would be a snap, I

thought. They would be secondary to my pursuit of a career.

Along with my bouquet of yellow roses, those were the old fairy tales and the newly minted dreams that I carried down the aisle of Dwight Chapel on a sun-bright day in June.

*H*AROLD: Recently, in an envelope holding a faded snapshot, I found a small, heart-shaped locket my dad gave Ma when they were teenagers. As I held the keepsake in my hand, I imagined my father fastening the locket at the nape of my mother's neck, her hand holding her hair to one side.

The locket, on a long, golden chain, came from a time when my parents were young and hopeful. Inside, there was a picture of Ma when she was about seventeen, wavy, long, black tresses cascading around her shoulders and a sunny smile radiating from her oval face. In the faded snapshot accompanying the locket, Ma and Dad were about ten years older. She smiled only slightly in her fur-collared storm coat. Dad, slender in a neat overcoat and wide-banded fedora, smiled not at all.

Around the turn of the century my dad, Allen, and his twelve brothers and sisters were born one right after the other in Belews Creek, near Winston-Salem, North Carolina, to Isaac and Laura Starbuck Haizlip. Isaac, son of Sam, a breeder slave forced to travel across the South to increase the slave population, was a strict, no-nonsense disciplinarian who ruled his home with his fist, his belt, and tree switches. He required his sons to work on the large family farm long hours before and after school, and all day on Saturdays. Along with his farm, he purchased one of the first automobiles in Kernersville but rarely allowed his sons to drive it.

It is not surprising that Isaac's children married early and fled the family home. Ellis, the eldest, moved to Deanwood, in Washington, D.C. Shortly thereafter, his brothers John, Allen, and Clarence, and his sister, Levolia, followed. As they moved north, they lived with one another until they could find work and get started. Within a few years, there was a Haizlip compound in Deanwood.

Uncle Ellis had found a job as a redcap at Union Station. All of his D.C. brothers, including my dad, worked as redcaps or Pullman car porters for years. Their pay was customers' tips. To supplement unpredictable "salaries," they drove taxicabs, catered lunch for Union Station employees, and did handyman jobs. Aunt Bo (Levolia) worked in-service until she saved enough money to open a beauty salon. Years later, she became a practical nurse.

Deanwood was the Negro community I knew as home from the 1930s, when Ma and Dad bought the two-bedroom bungalow on Sheriff Road, until I left for college in 1953. Most Deanwood houses were small, without central heat, on minuscule lots. No two homes were alike. Many had been upgraded and winterized with asbestos siding that pretended to be slate. Our gray/brown/red sandlike siding had a fake brick pattern, and we were proud of it.

In many ways, Deanwood was like a large, poor Negro family burdened by limited education, inadequate health care, menial jobs, borderline poverty, unremitting racism, legal segregation—and World War II. I never knew we were poor. We were Negroes—with very little money. Like us, most of our neighbors had migrated from far worse living conditions in the South. The indoor plumbing; the living room coal stoves; the kitchen gas water heaters; the window screens, storm windows, and weatherproof siding vindicated the move up north.

On Sunday mornings, a parade of adults and children wound through Deanwood toward Sunday school and 11:00 worship services in stately-to-storefront Baptist, Methodist, Holiness, Episcopal, and Catholic churches. Uncle Ellis and Aunt Sarah joined a storefront Church of God in North West, pastored by Brother Benjamin, a well-educated West Indian.

Dignified, kind, and elegant, Uncle Ellis became a faithful pillar of the Church of God: a deacon; an usher; a handyman for church repairs; a chef for church events; and a major fund-raiser. He urged his brothers to join. But Brother Benjamin forbade women and girls to wear lipstick or makeup, pants, jewelry, or "revealing" clothes. Movies, dancing, and popular music were sins, as were consuming beer or liquor and smoking cigarettes. Absolutely no "intercourse" before marriage and certainly no divorce.

After being warmly welcomed by Church of God members, Ma

got "saved" and joined the congregation. Why she chose that church and not the Baptist faith in which she was raised is a mystery. I suppose that for a country girl from a speck of a town in North Carolina, the Church of God provided rootedness, a family, and a support network otherwise difficult to tap into in the anonymity of Washington. For years, she prayed that Dad would find salvation. When he steadily refused, she then fixed her eyes on her own salvation—and mine.

She attended prayer meetings on Wednesdays like clockwork, choir rehearsals on Thursdays, sang with the choir Sundays, went to ushers' meetings twice monthly, Pennsylvania prayer camps every summer, and, whenever she could, she bussed all over the city to pray for sick members at home. Every Sunday, she put exactly ten percent of her week's earnings in the collection plate. I spent nearly all day each Sunday at the Church of God for years and dared not complain. Vira and Allen, Jr., escaped, along with Dad.

Over six feet tall and lanky, Dad was a serious, hardworking, and often humorless man who lived by the ethics and self-discipline of his father. Because he always worked two jobs, I remember him in jigsaw pieces.

Memory fragments slip into place, like his unsuccessful attempts to set curfews and limits for Vira, and his quiet rage at her rebelliousness, flirtatiousness, and independence. Their clashes always ended with Vira talking back to him, threatening to run away, and slamming the door to her room as she prepared to pack her clothes and leave. In the silence that followed, I overheard Ma reminding him of Vira's age and pleading with him to be less strict and more affectionate. Ma seemed to understand that Dad loved Vira dearly. He died in the year we celebrated the end of World War II.

The war was the darkest cloud in my sky. I never understood what it was about. I only knew that everyone said that for Negroes, the draft was a thankless, one-way ticket to death in a foreign country.

Food was rationed, so once a month Ma returned from downtown with stamps for sugar, butter, cereal, milk, and other staples. She must have had good credit at Chasen's Market, two doors from our house, because as the end of every month approached she got food without stamps or money. She settled her charge slips later.

Several times a week, earsplitting sirens signaled Emergency Air

Raid Drills at my school, George Washington Carver Elementary. Our teacher led us in timed seconds to Safety Zones in stairwells or the basement. Other times, she directed us to crawl quickly under our desks and cover our eyes with our hands. We waited in terrified silence, listening for the whining sound of Japanese bombs that would blow up our school and kill us. When the all-clear bell finally rang, we were allowed a short recess before returning to class, where our teacher assured us that the Air Raid Drills would one day save our lives. We said, "Yes, ma'm" in unison, but I had difficulty believing her.

The war denied everybody something important. When the silk stockings Ma proudly wore to church vanished from neighborhood stores, she ignored the new nylons until the nail polish she repaired her silk stockings with made her legs look like she had chicken pox or measles.

Dad died without insurance. Although Uncle Ellis, Uncle John, and many neighbors helped us with the funeral and later gave us money, food, school clothes, and coal, in May, Ma took her first paid job as a housekeeper at the Pentagon. That summer, the seasonal rhythm of my life changed dramatically.

On the day after school closed for the summer, Ma packed my clothes. She, Vira, and Allen, Jr., drove me to Union Station, where Uncle Ellis introduced me to porters he and Dad knew on *The Senator,* a huge silver train heading south. Wiping away tears, the women in my family told me to be a good boy and not to get off the train until a porter or conductor called out "Greensboro." There, Aunt Minnie would be waiting. Mom handed me a shoebox stuffed with fried chicken, biscuits, and cookies. They rushed off the train as it clanged toward my first summer vacation with Ma's family, far from the "bad Deanwood influences" she couldn't protect me from while working.

Ma was the fifth child among seven boys and two girls born to Robert and Kitty Hill, my grandparents, who married in 1893. Grandpa was white, with piercing blue eyes and long, sandy-brown hair, and died in 1926. Grandma was very dark, with sharp features, high cheekbones, shoulder-length hair, and perfect bright-white teeth. Her mother, Kizzie, a former slave, lived vigorously until age 104.

How Grandma and Grandpa survived as a married couple in seg-regated North Carolina, where miscegenation was illegal, is a story I never heard. Ma and her siblings arrived tan-skinned, with sharp features and wavy, "good" hair. Grandpa was often asked who were the parents of the nigger children with him. Grandma told stories about going to the rear "Colored Only" window of the local variety store to buy an ice cream cone while her children were invited through the "White Only" front entrance.

By the time Grandpa died, he and Grandma owned, free and clear, 114 acres of arable farmland in the woods of Kernersville. Their land was reachable only on foot, over miles of unmarked trails and paths off the road to Greensboro.

After clearing the crest of a hill, they built a large cabin of hand-hewn logs sealed with mud-mixed hay, and topped it with a corrugated tin roof. Heat for the house came from the woodstove on which they cooked in the kitchen. Water hauled from a well or spring nearby was used for cooking, drinking, and bathing in a large tin tub in the kitchen. At night, kerosene lamps cast long shadows against walls papered with old newspapers. About thirty feet from the cabin was the outhouse, stocked with old newspapers.

When I first went to Kernersville, all of Grandma's children had married and moved away and left her alone in the cabin. She had given Ma's younger sister, Aunt Minnie, a few acres of land near the new road as a wedding gift. Uncle Howard had built enough of their new two-story house so that he, Aunt Minnie, and their three children could live on the first floor in winter and expand to the unfinished attic in summer. Far more modern than Grandma's cabin, Aunt Minnie's house had real windows with glass panes, front and rear porches, store-bought wallpaper, and a rug in the living room. They dreamed of indoor plumbing, running water, and electricity.

As a city kid, I found Kernersville a wondrous place. I was one year younger than Leonard, Aunt Minnie's oldest son, almost the same age as Bobbie, her younger son, and two years older than Dot, her baby daughter. I suddenly was living with two "brothers" nearly my own age and a younger "sister," none of whom had ever been to a big city like Washington.

Knocked off my special perch as the precocious fatherless baby in a grown-up family, I had much adjusting to do, including fights to establish myself with Leonard and Bobbie. Aunt Minnie was a fun-loving, warm, and kind surrogate mother, but Uncle Howard's moods went from joviality to rage on one shot of corn likker.

In D.C. I rode my bike, learned to cook, and kept keen eyes on Vira. In Kernersville, we kids had real work to do, every day, before sunrise: feeding table scraps to pigs squealing and sloshing around in smelly, muddy pens; dragging stubborn cows out to pasture; feeding dried corn to countless chickens decorating the yard with droppings; hauling buckets of water from the well to the kitchen; splitting firewood and stacking it near the kitchen stove; and picking corn, apples, tomatoes, berries, beans, peas, watermelons, and greens from the garden.

By midsummer, as far as we could see in every direction, thousands of tobacco plants stood as tall as Leonard, Bobbie, and I. Most of the crop belonged to Aunt Minnie; the rest was farmed by cousins and neighbors who leased plots from her. Added to our daily chores was the job I hated most: picking worms off tobacco plants to prevent them from devouring the crop that would become the family's major income for the winter.

The worms were horrible. They looked like bright, lime-green translucent rolls of clay, with hundreds of tiny black-tipped legs curling out. Inching slowly up the stalks to the underside of the leaves, they ate big, asymmetric holes before moving on. Ugh.

Toward the end of summer, after Aunt Minnie's sunrise breakfast, Leonard, Bobbie, and I hooked the family mule, Daisy, to a homemade tobacco sled and went to the fields. Dripping sweat, we laid tender-ripe tobacco leaves one by one in the sled and dragged it to one of our lopsided barns, where Aunt Minnie and others tied them into bunches for curing. When one barn was filled, we moved to another. Midday, we had a break—and supper, our largest meal of the day.

Late at night, under Uncle Howard's watchful eyes, Leonard, Bobbie, and I made slow-burning log fires in the rock-enclosed openings of the barns. Steady heat over several days "cured" the green tobacco into dried brown leaves ready for auction. I spent many nights huddled on old blankets in the glow of those fires, amber-red against midnight skies flickering with fireflies and distant stars, listening to Uncle Howard's endless stories.

Leonard, Bobbie, and I became an inseparable trio, but I always knew I was on their turf. Sometimes we "escaped" and walked three miles into town to Mabe's Variety Store. Although we went barefoot all summer and wore shoes only to church on Sundays, their feet were much tougher than mine. They glided along the gravel road as if walking on velvet carpet while I lagged far behind looking for bare spots between each pebble to avoid shredding the soles of my feet.

They weren't bothered, either, by Mrs. Mabe, the wizened, craggy old white woman who, with her even older husband, owned the store and a gas station. The Mabes had known Aunt Minnie since she was a baby, and I think Grandma had done housework and laundry for them years before. Nevertheless, whenever the three of us went into her musty store, which reeked of kerosene and sour pickles, Mrs. Mabe warned us not to touch anything, to point to what we wanted and show her how much money we had, implying that we couldn't count. If she decided we had enough, she handed us what we wanted.

Leonard and Bobbie dismissed Mrs. Mabe and her husband as "poor, old white crackers" living off Negroes. But I hated her because she was uppity, so we invented a scheme to get even: we entered her store and scattered in different directions, looking at different things as she tried to follow first one of us and then the other. When she wasn't looking, we stuffed gumballs or a Baby Ruth in our underwear. Then we called Mrs. Mabe, pointed to what we wanted, and showed her our money. On the road home, out of her sight, we celebrated our winnings. If Uncle Howard had ever found this out, we would have been buried the following week in the family cemetery plot across from the Oak Spring Baptist Church, which Grandma founded.

There always seemed to be a "Do what I say, or else" threat—unspoken but real—that all Negroes knew well, more so in Kernersville than in Washington, D.C. As we talked ourselves to sleep in Aunt Minnie's attic, Leonard and Bobbie told me stories about carloads of white men forcing Negroes off deserted highways into ditches late at night; about older boys being tailgated by drunken white farmers; and about young Negro girls dragged into cars and raped by white men.

I learned about white farmers who shotgunned Negro sharecroppers accused of stealing a bushel of peaches. My cousins explained why I shouldn't speak to a white girl even if she spoke to me first; how, when shopping for new shoes, we had to place the soles against the bottom of our feet rather than try them on; and why Aunt Minnie made her own clothes rather than buy them in town, where she couldn't try them on. What I learned from Leonard and Bobbie made me confused and angry. I knew my life in Washington was constricted, but I didn't know all the details. My mother never really spoke of those things at home, maybe because her father was white.

A few days before Labor Day, I arrived at Union Station laden with boxes. In one were fresh country hams. In another, fresh-picked green beans, limas, spice apples, cabbage, collards, carrots, and potatoes. In another, two or three watermelons. In still another, jars of Aunt Minnie's or Grandma's homemade "chowchow relish," spiced pears, and pickled okra.

I returned to Kernersville for emotional and physical nourishment every summer until I was fifteen.

The year my father died, Mrs. Nora Gregory, sister of Dr. Charles Drew, the eminent scientist who developed blood plasma, was my fifth-grade teacher at Carver Elementary. After that she regularly stopped by our house or telephoned Ma to tell her how proud she should be of my schoolwork. In sixth grade, she scheduled weekly meetings to talk about how she expected me to get outstanding grades in every subject because I had the brains to do it. I tried because I believed her and didn't want to disappoint her.

Bennie, Claude, and I became best friends in school and out. Both of them were the only children in their families, and with my father dead, with Ma working full-time, and with Vira and Allen, Jr., in their own worlds, I also felt like an only child. Bicycles were our freedom trains. With Vira's help, I got an after-school job at Chillum Cleaners in Brookland and saved enough to buy my first bike, a brand-new maroon and gold three-speed Schwinn with whitewall tires and an electric generator for the headlamps and taillights.

On weekends, even in winter, Bennie, Claude, and I packed a sandwich and soda in our saddlebags and liberated ourselves. Friends for life, exploring and free. We rode as far as Baltimore and back, or to Rock Creek Park, or through downtown D.C. I never told Ma where we went. After several "Lawd, have mercy"s she would have grounded me, for sure.

A year or so after Dad's death, Uncle Ellis's wife also died, leaving him to raise four children—including Ellis, Jr., whom we called "Ellis B."

Ellis B. became a fixture at our house, showing up several times a week to chat with Vira and Ma. Ellis B. was different in a way I couldn't put my finger on. With his sharp wit and funny stories, he kept Ma and Vira holding their sides with laughter. Allen, Jr., often said in private that Ellis B. was a sissy and left the house whenever he came.

One of the things I admired about Ellis B. was that he seemed to have escaped Deanwood and survived. A drama major at Howard University, he frequently went to New York to see plays or for parties with friends we heard about but never met.

Sometimes I'd come home from school and find him wrapped in Ma's bathrobe in our kitchen (he had a key to our house), cooking crab cakes to go with the fruitcake he said he'd brought Ma from Italy. He insisted on serving her on her best china. Then he vanished. Uncle Ellis later told us that Ellis B. had moved to New York and that he hoped "the boy would find a good woman, get married, and settle down soon."

After a long hiatus, Ellis appeared—dressed to the nines and carrying a tan double-breasted car coat with leather buttons. I couldn't take my eyes off the coat. I finally asked him if I could try it on.

"Baby, it looks better on you than me," Ellis B. said. "It's yours. Wear it for both of us."

Again, we didn't see him for a long while. Uncle Ellis said he was producing shows in someplace called Greenwich Village and still hadn't settled down or married.

By eighth grade I was still leading the pack with As in every subject, running the 440 on the track team, and directing the student government of Browne Junior High School along the narrow path prescribed by The Tyrant, Principal William Stinson. When Negro students were invited to participate for the first time with white students in a city-wide science fair, Mr. Stinson wanted to know what my first-place project would be. I settled on providing the definitive answer to the question "Which came first? The chicken or the egg?"

I designed an elaborate display of eggs being incubated from fertilization to birth, followed by chicks, live midsized chickens, and a rooster I named Henry.

On the night before the fair, I set up my display in the lobby of the Department of Education and went home. Around midnight, a security officer telephoned to say I had to remove Henry immediately because, in violation of building regulations, he would not stop crowing. In a box in my room, he continued to cluck and crow all night.

I won second place.

Henry was such a hit that I decided to keep him and built a wire cage in our backyard. One Sunday I returned home from church and found a huge roast chicken in the center of a feast already on the table. After Ma said the grace, Allen told me to let him know whether Henry was tough or not. Food sprayed from my mouth. I ran from the table to Henry's cage in the backyard. No Henry—anywhere.

From the backyard I yelled to Ma, "Where's Henry?"

"On the table." Allen chuckled. "Let's eat. He's getting cold."

I couldn't. I got my bicycle and rode around the neighborhood for several hours, tears nearly blinding me. In my valedictory speech at Browne Junior High School's graduation, I memorialized Henry for all time.

Eventually, Allen made himself even more scarce in my life. He went away to Hampton College in Virginia. At the end of his sophomore year, he married Elnora Monago, his high-school sweetheart, who had also been our neighbor. In quick succession, they had two daughters. Allen worked two full-time jobs to support his family.

Vira went to Cardozo High School for the commercial course of study, Allen went to Armstrong High School for the football team and mechanical arts course, and I went to Paul Laurence Dunbar High, the high school for college-bound Negro students. Mrs. Gregory, the teacher who had encouraged me through grade school, told me not to worry about how to pay for college, just to keep up my straight-A average and college would be taken care of. I believed her.

But I worried anyway. I had often heard at Browne and at church that only white-looking Negroes with thin lips, good hair, and parents who were teachers, doctors, or high-level government workers were placed in the advanced college courses at Dunbar, while brown people like Claude, Bennie, and me were assigned to the "general" courses.

When I asked Mrs. Gregory about this, she told me that a majority of the kids in the advanced classes would come from Brookland and North West Washington. I knew that meant they came from money and nice houses. She said it also meant they were competitive and accustomed to succeeding. Many years later I learned that Mrs. Gregory also lived in the land of rich Negroes in upper North West D.C. I never noticed how white she looked.

All summer, I didn't tell even Bennie and Claude how concerned I was about going to Dunbar. I told Ma, Vira, and everybody else that I couldn't wait for school to open in the fall, but deep down, I was scared shitless.

In homeroom on opening day, I found a note telling me to report to the office of the principal, Charles Lofton, attached to my schedule. At lunchtime, I checked with Bennie and Claude. No notes to come to the principal's office. I sweated the rest of the day.

"So you're Harold Haizlip," Mr. Lofton said, directing me to sit down opposite him.

"Yes, sir."

"Last week, I had lunch with Mr. Stinson, Mrs. Gregory, and some of your Deanwood teachers. They told me that you are a very promising young man, sure to become one of our best students. That's a tall order here at Dunbar. Do you know that?"

"Yes, sir."

"Well," he said, looking at a large chart he pulled from an envelope, "you've gotten all As since third grade. Let me know if you have any problems."

"Yes, sir."

The light-skinned Gold Coast Negroes must have stopped having children, sent them to private schools, or moved to Virginia or Maryland, because in my class there were many students who looked like me. Although many kids lived in nicer neighborhoods, in bigger houses, not everybody was rich.

I did wish my family could be more like some of those kids' families, talking more softly and being nicer and more helpful to each other. We always seemed so edgy at my house, as if we feared our lives would fall apart at any instant: the electricity would be shut off because we couldn't pay the bill, or we'd run out of coal on the coldest day, and we couldn't do anything about it except pray.

Most of the teachers at Dunbar were graduates of Ivy League colleges, state colleges, and universities, Negro colleges and universities. Most had master's degrees, many had Ph.D.s. The Ivy League graduates had been pioneers who, often as the only Negroes in their college or university, had graduated with honors.

Segregated by law in D.C., the teaching profession gave teachers an opportunity not only to pursue their intellectual interests but to vindicate and replicate themselves by preparing other Negro students to follow in their footsteps. This personal dedication went far beyond any standards set by the school department. Every teacher had a packed agenda in class and piled homework on without mercy. They reinforced every day their belief that we were the brightest students, capable of doing outstanding work, and they accepted nothing less. I responded without restraint, basking in the attention and rewards that being a good student generated. More important, I established a place for myself among so many other able students who had the money, privilege, security, and educated parents that I didn't. Despite a full academic and extracurricular plate, I continued working at Chillum Cleaners.

In my senior year, with Mrs. Gregory's advice and help from Mr. Lofton and Dunbar counselors and teachers, I was offered full tuition and expenses by Harvard, Dartmouth, Amherst, Williams, Yale, Columbia, Oberlin, and Stanford. Mrs. Gregory, whose brother was an Amherst alumnus, arranged for the Amherst Dean of Admissions to meet with me at Dunbar. A friendly, fatherly man, I liked him immediately and decided on the Amherst offer. Dean Wilson assured Ma that he would personally take good care of me. He didn't mention the fact that among the 250 men in the freshman class, I would be one of two Negro students.

At Dunbar's 1953 commencement exercises, five valedictorians, each with identical perfect grades, set a new record. As the only male, I made the last speech. Ma wept with pride, wishing Dad could have been there. Vira made sure everyone knew that I was her baby brother.

And Pam, whom I had been dating exclusively for four years, and I became unofficially engaged.

CHAPTER 4

⚛

Promises to Keep

*S*HIRLEE: In our living room, a bride and groom stand expectantly beside the fireplace. It is the moment just after the minister has pronounced them married, after they have kissed and turned to face the assembled witnesses of family and friends. They are slender and well formed: he elegantly turned out in white tie and tails, she in embroidered lace with a sweetheart neckline. The bride clutches her groom's elbow in formal fashion. In her other arm she carries a bouquet of white English roses, tightly packed together.

If one did not see the bridal finery, one would say the couple looked like brother and sister. The shade of their dark brown hair is identical; their patrician noses and thin lips rest on their faces in exactly the same way; they have dark eyes, deeply lidded, with thinly shaped eyebrows, one arched, one not. Like everything else, their skin tones match: pale with a hint of pink. Two-thirds of the bride's lace skirt are mocha-colored, stained from the sugared icing of the top tier of our wedding cake, where the pair first stood.

In 1959 in New England, wedding cake figurines were not designed to resemble people of color. Nor did we have a conscious second thought about ordering the standard—that is, the "white" couple for the cake. Our acceptance of this *mos* was a sort of cognitive dissonance, rampant in the 1950s, relentlessly exposed in the 1960s. We saw the couple, internalized them, and they became us. We did not become them. They were all those people who had penthouses, pools, convertibles, and condos; those Barbie and Ken people who knew nothing about hard times and difficult places.

The day before our wedding, we ended up in jail over a traffic incident. It began on the way to pick up our wedding bands, en route to the wedding rehearsal. The rings had arrived late at a New Haven jeweler whose store sat opposite the New Haven Green. Anxious to get to the store before it closed, we went through a yellow traffic light on Chapel Street, one of the city's main thoroughfares.

Although I did not yet have a driver's license, I quoted the Connecticut driver's manual, chapter and verse, to the policemen who stopped us, in a "you idiots" tone of voice. I knew my rights. They did not know what they were doing, and I let them know in no uncertain terms.

Whether because of Harold's politeness in the face of unfair treatment or my own mounting nervousness at being late for the rehearsal, I raged at them. "Fascists, Nazis, Communists, idiots, bureaucratic incompetents." With each insult they gripped Harold tighter. With as much disdain as I could muster, I told them we would not follow them to the station. "We have a wedding rehearsal to attend."

At the police station, I could only imagine what was going on in the holding cell to which they had hustled Harold. Frantic with Harold now out of sight, I called my father and blurted out our plight. Dad and the family lawyer arrived within ten minutes. Because of his civic activities, my father was well known to everyone in the police department. They welcomed him cordially. I interrupted their pleasantries.

After quiet requests from my father to me failed, he ordered me outside so that he could hear the officers' version of what had happened. I continued my less than ladylike rants from the front steps. Nevertheless, I heard my father ask in his most calm, precise voice, "Now, officers, just what is the problem you think these young people created?"

Within a few minutes, the police released Harold on twenty-five' dollars' bond with an order to return for a hearing, right in the middle of the honeymoon. (My father got the charges dropped while we were away so we didn't have to go to court.) The jeweler was about to lock his doors for the night when we finally arrived to retrieve our rings.

For a while, I seethed about the incident, but the good humor and joshing of the wedding party and guests restored my focus. I did not understand that I had put my groom in grave danger. I believed then, somehow, that policemen were fair and impartial, at least in New Haven. I was wrong, of course. It did not occur to me until later that the arresting policemen were offended at seeing me with Harold. In their eyes I looked white. They became enraged because I was not only riding but siding with a black man.

The rest of the wedding weekend passed with its own momentum. Short of making the bridal and bridesmaids' gowns, my mother had planned all aspects of the wedding like a quiet, determined general. She already had a model, having orchestrated Jewelle's rites two years before. My father had insisted on addressing five hundred invitations in his precise, beautiful, calligraphic style, a lovely, backhanded slant. Other than selecting the engraving type, performing the ceremony, and paying the bills, his role before the wedding was secondary to my mother's. He was not used to second billing.

There was one major bill he did not have to foot. Abel Prince, a small West Indian man who had passed my house every day for twelve years, paid for my gown as a wedding gift. Each day of those twelve years I had greeted him as I went to school, and he to work. Each day of those twelve years the man with the skeletal black face wore the same stained white panama hat and dark gray, ill-fitting jacket. Each day of those twelve years he asked, "How you do in school?" My answer was always the same: "Getting all As."

The straight-A record impressed him. He was "proud of al' your schoolin' and al' your As an tings." I had attained what he always wanted, a college education. On grease-stained, yellow-lined paper that served as a wrapper for five crisp one-hundred-dollar bills, he wrote a spare note. "This is for al' dem As an' makin' me proud. This is for your wedon dress. Love, Abel Prince."

His gesture took my breath away. I was deeply moved by the precious sentiment and the generous gift from a man who lived some of his dreams through me. At that moment, he became the grandfather I never had. I hoped I would continue to do him honor.

During the rehearsal, my dad, who was always punctual, proclaimed that the wedding, like all the ceremonies he performed, would start on time, not CPT (Colored People's Time).

With all the seriousness I could muster, I advised Harold, "If you are late for our wedding, I won't be at the altar when you get there." I meant it.

I did not know it then, but on our wedding day, my parents were in their high prime. Everyone said my father was handsome, dignified; my mother, beautiful, serene. She had chosen a pale green, tiered, Dior-inspired gown and looked as fragile as an after-dinner creme mint. A wide, high crown hat, a style made popular by Audrey Hepburn, added mystery to the chiseled planes of her face. Her white gloves came well above her elbows. "A page out of *Vogue*," someone whispered.

Wearing a single strand of pearls and turning every head, she stepped lightly down the aisle on her son-in-law Jim's arm. Her own head turned graciously from side to side as she nodded or smiled at every guest as if she were the queen of England.

When the university carillon struck the twelve o'clock notes, Harold, his hair cut boyishly short, handsome and slender in his morning coat and gray striped pants, stepped into the chancel of Dwight Chapel. As I followed the bridesmaids up the steps, I heard Uncle Percy's rendition of Purcell's "Trumpet Voluntary" soar up, out and beyond the stained glass windows, the notes dropping on the old campus like tender cherry blossoms.

The bridesmaids seemed to waft down the aisle in their hoop-skirted dresses. Their pastel bustles fluttered like butterflies hovering over slender poppy stems. The sun shone through the layered organza of their wide-brimmed hats, and they looked like delicate escapees from a southern belle's garden party. They were a mélange of sisters, foster sisters, college friends, and roommates, with a tot from my father's church serving as the flower girl.

Sister Jewelle selected her favorite peach shade to show off her tan skin and dark eyes. Sister Pattee wore lavender and looked like the beautiful woman she would become. Brother Julian, dashing and tall in his morning coat, was on his best behavior. My roommate, Judy, wore blue to match her eyes.

In the fashion of those who had gone to New England colleges, the wedding party was integrated beyond tokenism. The measure of our liberalness, our commitment to an integrated lifestyle, was on view. Black-haired ringlets were followed by blond waves, red-haired bobs, and auburn pageboys.

Images of our wedding day fuse, open, and recombine. Memory shifts, retreats, bursts forth again. Governor Abraham Ribicoff, Mayor Richard Lee from New Haven, and my father's bosom buddy, Mayor Frank Fitzpatrick of Ansonia, State Democratic Chairman John Bailey, and other politicians in dark striped suits serve as exclamation points and parentheses for the rows of brightly dressed ladies of Macedonia. Prints, stripes, polka dots, florals sit side by side. Elaborate hats block many a view. Handkerchiefs daintily wipe foreheads. Funeral parlor fans prissily cool faces.

On the arm of my oldest uncle, I enter that Church of England–style place of worship. A blinding midday sun lights up the ceilings and makes gray columns white. Golden dust motes glint, suspended in the slanted light. I pause to take in the scene. Uncle Bill squeezes my arm. I draw in my breath. It is not yet time for tears.

I am so proud my mother has created all of this for me, and my father has made it possible. Before me I see the people from the church that I have known all of my life. The people who patted my bottom and called me "Pumpkin" when I was an infant. The people who pinched my cheeks when I was a toddler. The people who cheered with me at the football games, and clapped for me when I came marching down Main Street as a majorette. The people who hugged me when I was a teenager, and palmed dollars into my hand when I got accepted to college.

Toward the front I see my relatives from Washington—on my father's side, that is. My mother's are missing, living another life in another world.

I see Harold waiting at the end of the long aisle. How handsome he looks; how young and vulnerable, and yet so strong. He smiles at me. I catch my breath. My chest feels crowded. My heart swelling?

I knew then what it felt like to be a princess. This is my kingdom. I am a member of a royal family going to meet my prince, my betrothed. I move slowly, gracefully, with a bride's gait. Down the aisle past the flower-laden pews that the Macedonia ladies had decorated that morning. Down the aisle past a proud Abel Prince, toothless, waving, gleaming in a new white linen sport coat, stained crumpled panama in his lap. Down the aisle past the friends, the relatives, the schoolmates, the politicians. I move toward him. He takes my hand. My uncle releases me.

Only one week after my college graduation, I believe I have fulfilled the first part of my life's dream. A dream covered in the filmy wrapping of endless love, eternal romance. I have visions of dancing like Fred and Ginger, living like Bogie and Baby.

My father loves the centrality of his role at this moment. He stands erect and resplendent in the light. Sunbeams dance off the prisms of the tiny diamond on his small finger. His voice is at its finest, clearest pitch. He speaks effortlessly yet with emotion.

It is his duty to issue the admonition that no man dare tear asunder his daughter's union. It is his duty to pronounce me the wife of the new son in his family. His words bring rivers of tears to our eyes. We kiss through falling streams.

Sometimes I wonder if daughters who are married by their fathers feel a special obligation to keep their marriages intact, for to do otherwise would be not only to break a sacred commandment but to dishonor thy father.

At the edge of a mirror-calm Housatonic River, we held our wedding reception in a stately inn in Stratford, the town where I was born. To the chagrin of some of our guests, my father provided no alcoholic beverages, which would have been a political problem for him. Nonetheless, a good band and a sort of universal joy created a lively atmosphere. Herzog passed out on the lawn.

Looking back, I'm glad we had the kind of wedding we did. The wedding's formality and its adherence to traditional rituals were important to me, giving me a deep sense of continuity. But if I were to plan it now, I would add a little more playfulness and a little less pomp. I would have Champagne for everyone, even my father.

Late in the afternoon we returned to my parents' house to change and start on our wedding trip. Scores of relatives and friends gathered on the lawn to see us off. Harold had just acquired a mini-car. Not much luggage would fit into its tiny trunk. Wanting to wear the extensive trousseau I had purchased or been given, I solved the problem by bringing my wardrobe loose.

While waiting for us to emerge for last kisses and handfuls of rice, various guests passed groups of my clothes hand over head from the house to be loaded into the back of the car. That was the beginning of a major, lifelong, marital problem—closet space.

As we embraced our parents and sibs, there were tears and bowed heads. My mother and father looked sad, something I could not fathom until I, too, became the parent of young adults. There is a picture of my father sitting in the family room after we had departed and most of the guests had left. His head rests on his upright arm as if he had just accomplished a major task.

That day, I left my father and mother behind. That day, wrapped up in a white dress of tulle and bombazine silk, I left my girlhood behind.

Thirsty from hours of talking and smiling, we made our first stop a roadside stand at the edge of town to get root beer floats. They arrived complimentary because of our "Just Married" sign. We took that to be a harbinger that the rest of the world would also be kind.

After driving for several hours, we reached the "secret" place Harold had chosen. The resort's glossy brochure, which he now carried dejectedly in his hand, was far better than its reality. In the end, though, the place where we spent out first night as a married couple became blissfully irrelevant.

When one of our grown daughters learned that we would be writing a book about our marriage, she said, "Mom, please don't talk about your sex life. I can't deal with that. What about my friends?"

There is no way that I would discuss intimacy with anyone but my husband. In my case it may be due to nothing more than old-fashioned prudishness. I like to think it is a respect for privacy and the honored belief that what happens between Harold and me is ours to own and claim; to guard and cherish; to relish and remember. I *will* say that Harold has been my grand passion and that we have loved both wisely and well.

We rambled around for a week in green places and established a lifelong love of Vermont. My wardrobe was holding out quite well. There is no doubt I had more clothes than honeymoon days to wear them. I was still setting my hair in curlers after Harold went to sleep, and taking them out before he woke up, so that he would not see his beloved in pink and green plastic. And Harold was as kind and courtly to me as he had been while we were dating. He was funny and thoughtful and constantly looked for new ways to surprise and please me. To make my rainy days beautiful, he gave me a white umbrella decorated with one long-stemmed pink silk rose. "I'm going to love this," I thought.

At twenty-one, I believed I was a full-fledged adult who would simply grow older and more mature. It would take another twenty-odd years before I fully realized that the bride in the Yale chapel was an overgrown, spoiled, highly romantic teenager whose vision of life grew out of a happy, protected, nurtured childhood and adolescence.

And so we married in the quiet of the Eisenhower years. A time when most of America was still confident and growing. Alaska and Hawaii became states that year, and the federal advisory council on Social Security reported that the U.S. Social Security System was in sound condition. The very first seven astronauts had been selected that spring, but two monkeys beat them into space. And we had a new hero. General Benjamin O. Davis, Jr., became the first black major-general in the armed services. Some illusions were shattered, though. One of America's iconic couples, Eddie Fisher and Debbie Reynolds, divorced. It was 1959.

Now my wedding cake figurines are flanked by a collection of sterling silver dinner bells. All around them, on a small oval surface I call "the wedding table," are pictures of the brides in my family, including me. There is Jewelle, in point d'alençon lace, and I in bombazine silk, in a full-skirted, small-waisted gown of the fifties. There is Pattee, in her slender sheath gown and square train from the sixties. In a gilded frame is Pattee, a bride again, this time in the seventies, her face accented by ringlets and an off-white Mexican wedding dress. Outlined by a silver-blue frame, our mother-bride of the eighties poses in living color with her daughters and granddaughters after her second wedding, which was held in my garden. Looking serenely at the camera, in tiers of lilac chiffon and a large hat swathed in gauzy tulle, our mother is closest in skin tone and looks to my wedding cake topper.

The rest of the family's brides had tan, olive, and yellow casts to their skin. Our grooms were the warm color of young Brazil nuts.

*H*AROLD: By the time I reached West Park Avenue Thursday afternoon two days before the wedding, cars lined the driveway from the street to the garage in the rear; others were parked bumper to bumper along both sides as far as I could see, and still others were slowly circling the block for parking spaces. Streams of Macedonia church members; New Haven, Ansonia, and Hartford politicians; ministers from around the state; Shirlee's high school teachers and classmates; Reverend Taylor's Ansonia tenants and business associates; Mrs. Taylor's club members; Jewelle's old cronies and Pattee's school buddies; and a host of folks I had never seen before were exiting their cars and walking across Rev. T.'s freshly mowed lawn, laden with bulging shopping bags and white boxes elaborately decorated with silver and white ribbons, bows, and forget-me-nots. Others were leaving for home with napkins full of pound cake, mints, and peanuts, exhorting reluctant children toward cars somewhere in the neighborhood.

As I walked into the jammed foyer, a chorus broke out: "Here's the lucky guy. The groom's here. Congratulations, Harold."

Smiling, hugging, and handshaking my way through the shoulder-to-shoulder crowd, in the music room I saw Shirlee beaming in a sea of wrapping paper and ribbons, oohing and aahing amid a gaggle of ladies as she opened gift after gift and handed them to Mrs. Taylor for a number, while Althea recorded the name of the giver and description of the gift in a lace-covered book dripping with long ribbons. I was lamely gesturing to Shirlee over the chattering heads when a hand firmly grasped my shoulder.

"How's my son?" Reverend Taylor asked as I turned toward him. We briskly shook hands, then, acknowledging without words that we weren't expressing how we really felt, we wrapped each other in a mutual bear hug for what seemed a full minute, oblivious of the crowd. His eyes became teary, as did mine. Folks nearby applauded. He recovered quickly, patted me on the back, and resumed welcoming his minions. I gave up trying to reach Shirlee and began handshaking my way through the room.

Around 7:30 P.M., Shirlee and I were saying goodbye to several departing well-wishers when the Haizlip caravan of eight or more cars arrived. Weary from the six-hour drive from Washington but delighted to be in New Haven for the occasion, Ma, Vira, Allen, Elnora, Uncle Ellis, Uncle John and his wife, Aunt Bo, Cousin Zella, Ellis B.'s older sister, Doris, and her husband, Wallace, Ellis B.'s younger sister, Janet, and numerous other relatives poured from their cars, clutching armloads of gift-wrapped boxes and shopping bags.

As I hugged and kissed Ma, she began sobbing, and seconds there-after everyone was fighting back tears in the middle of the street with all of the car doors open, hugging and kissing Shirlee and me. Hearing all the commotion, Reverend and Mrs. Taylor, Jewelle and Jim, Brother, Pattee, Althea, Margie, and Margaret all rushed from the house for first-time introductions of the new families. Pattee introduced herself to everyone first, emphasizing the correct spelling of her first name.

The Taylors' house was ablaze with lights. I was deeply relieved that from the moment they met the Taylors, my family stepped imme-diately into the role of proud relatives eager to welcome the union of bride and groom. Their decision to participate actively in the wedding and the warmth they exuded were important to me. I suspected that until they got to know Shirlee and her family, some of them—possi-bly including Ma, and definitely including Vira, Allen, Jr., and Uncle Ellis—felt (but would never utter publicly) that I was marrying Shirlee more for upward mobility than for love.

Within hours of the first introductions, Shirlee, her family, the Macedonia congregation, and all of the friends who had gathered shattered any such unspoken suspicions. Despite Reverend Taylor's obvious prominence and success, my family quickly came to under-stand that he was still one of us, still identified with us, and that Mrs. Taylor and Shirlee regarded them and me warmly and lovingly. That was the real "wedding": the exchange of signals that brought the lovely comfort of understanding, acceptance, and oneness of two families, despite all differences.

My groomsmen—best friends from Amherst, Harvard, and Wash-ington, D.C.—arrived from Canada, New York City, New Jersey, Tennessee, Washington, D.C., and elsewhere, ratcheting my excite-ment skyward and sending Pattee into a state of delirium at being surrounded by so many handsome young men. Bennie and Claude were not among them. I think their decision to boycott the wedding had something to do with who they thought Shirlee was, who I wasn't, and who they wanted to be. It wouldn't be the truth if I said that their absence did not matter. It mattered a lot and hurt even more. Right then I made up my mind that some of my old allegiances should be stored away, along with the fur tails from my bicycle, in my trunk of neighborhood memories, far back in my closet of boyhood dreams.

While the ushers tried on their suits for last-minute fittings, Shirlee and I ventured downtown for our rings in the new, royal blue, subcompact Renault Dauphine I had purchased after the Chrysler died and refused resuscitation. Talking animatedly to her in our few moments away from the crowd, I suddenly heard sirens, and saw a police car's flashing lights in my rearview mirror and a hand above the driver's window motioning me to pull over to the curb. As I did so, my pulse quickened instinctively. I knew from my own experience and years of hearsay that Negroes had no rights and police officers had daily quotas.

The officer walked to my window and demanded to see my license and registration. While reaching for my wallet, I asked as deferentially as possible, "What's the problem, Officer?"

"Driver's license and registration," he replied, ignoring my question.

"Here they are, sir. What's the problem, Officer?" I repeated.

Holding on to my license and registration, he commanded, "Follow me to the station house."

"I'll be glad to, but why? What for? I know my license and registration are in order. So what's the problem, Officer?"

"Moving violation," he finally offered. "You drove through the caution light at the intersection back there."

I was being as solicitous and demurring as possible to avoid a pissing contest with this officer or becoming caught up in a booking at the station house. I knew that any Negro who challenged the authority of a white police officer would also be charged with resisting arrest and any other phony offense the officer could think of—with assistance and support from fellow officers at the station. At the station, they could have lunch or whatever and I could be locked up for hours before any charges were filed and before I could call an attorney.

Because the jewelry store was closing in less than an hour, I took a calculated risk—not to challenge the officer, but to agree with him and at the same time explain that I was aware of the law and suggest, nondefiantly, that I had adhered to it.

"Officer, I was in the middle of the intersection when the caution light came on. I believe the rule is to proceed with caution through the intersection in such a circumstance, not stop in the middle and block oncoming traffic." I was as solicitous as possible and kept my voice as evenly conversational as I could.

"Oh yeah?" he snarled. "Follow me to the station, mister."

I knew my gamble had backfired when he called me "mister" with all the sarcasm he could muster, signaling that he knew very well how to deal with a smart-ass like me. In New Haven, as elsewhere, Negroes "talked back" to white police officers at their own peril—even if the officers were dead wrong or lying. On the streets, we had no rights.

At that point, Shirlee, whose sense of injustice and personal insult I knew was rising as rapidly as my own, became a Fury, and a haughty one. She yelled angrily and defiantly at the officer that he knew he was wrong, that he was doing this because I was a Negro, and that if he insisted on taking us to the station house, her father would see that his badge was removed immediately.

"If you keep it up, lady, I'll cite you, too. Follow me."

"Hon, hon," I whispered desperately, "calm down. You're making everything worse."

With her hands on her hip, she challenged him, "You just try it. Just try it."

I held my breath.

The officer, determined and angry, said nothing. He whirled around and jumped into the police car, quickly pulled alongside us, turned on his flashers and siren, and beckoned me to follow.

At the station house, Shirlee ignored my pleas to stop making matters worse by shouting threats at every officer in the station. When one of the officers handcuffed me and was leading me toward the lockup, I heard Shirlee demanding a telephone so that she could get her father to come and have everyone fired.

Within half an hour or less, my handcuffs were removed and I was escorted to the station entrance, where Reverend Taylor was waiting. The arresting officer was nowhere to be seen. Reverend Taylor said he had sent Shirlee outside to the car and had taken care of this "unfortunate misunderstanding." Shirlee and I should continue on our errand. I asked no questions and left immediately.

In the car, Shirlee was so outraged and insulted that she began to cry, upsetting me more than anything else that had happened. I masked deep anger at my own powerlessness and the insult to my manhood in front of my bride-to-be, saying "Forget it. The important thing is to get our rings before the store closes."

When we returned home later with our wedding bands, I was raging silently at my humiliation. Everyone in the house, however, was doubled over with side-splitting laughter as Reverend Taylor regaled them with a fully embellished description of his future son-in-law locked up in jail and the berserk bride-to-be raving like a maniac at every police officer in sight. I went along with his humor and laughed halfheartedly with everyone else. In fact, I was furious and still smarting for the revenge I would never get—on my own. I appreciated Reverend Taylor's help, but the score, from my point of view, was never settled. Now I understand that part of my reaction was generationally based; I had not had Reverend Taylor's breadth of experience along the lengthy fissure of race. I had not yet had to negotiate in the most serious of circumstances. I know now that I got off easily, for which I am grateful, because black class differences mean nothing to white policemen. To them, unknown black men become one and the same faceless perpetrator, dangerous felons close to or at the center of impenetrable darkness.

My edginess subsided considerably at our rehearsal at Dwight Chapel—with Reverend Taylor announcing ponderously how the ceremony was supposed to be and demonstrating, by turning out his feet dancer style, the proper "step-step-hold" gait for groomsmen and bridesmaids walking up the aisle.

As the rehearsal ended, Ma pulled me aside in the rear of Dwight Chapel, saying she wanted to tell me some good news. She reminded me how long Dad had been dead and how hard it had been for her working full-time and raising her children alone. Now that her baby was getting married, she said, she had decided to live some of her life for herself. She added slowly that she had married Glenn Sutton, a co-worker at the Pentagon whom she had been seeing for some time, and that she had sold our old house on Sheriff Road and put the money in a savings and retirement account for herself. She added that she and Glenn had purchased and moved into a larger, brand-new house in D.C. She wanted me and Shirlee to see the new house and meet Glenn as soon as possible.

"Is this Glenn person a member of the Church of God? How old is he? Has he been married before? Does he have children? Do Vira and

Allen, Jr., know him? Like him? Why has this been kept secret from me? When was the house sold? Who bought it? How much did you sell it for? Why didn't this Glenn come to my wedding with you?" I asked a tumble of arrogant questions without thinking until I saw Ma's eyes filling up. I caught myself.

"I'm really happy for you, Ma. You deserve the best. Shirlee and I will come to meet Glenn and see the new house as soon as we return from our honeymoon. I promise. Congratulations."

I was angry at her for keeping secrets until she was ready to share them. I found Shirlee and told her the news. She said I should be very happy for my mother, regardless of any other feelings I had.

The bridesmaids, Shirlee, Mrs. Taylor, and all the other women returned to West Park Avenue. The groomsmen, my uncles, male cousins, friends, and I drove to a friend's cottage on Milford Beach for my stag party.

Tom Herzog bartended, pouring two glasses of every highball requested and drinking one himself. He soon passed out. Allen, Jr., told the story of Henry, mimicking my screwed-up face and shrieking voice as I yelled from Henry's cage in the backyard, demanding to know where he was. Dan regaled everyone with the story of my shit-eating face after my first blind date with Shirlee. Brother told everyone exactly how he made women scream with pleasure during lovemaking. Patrick, from Tennessee, added stories about my Amherst dates, particularly all of the "uglies" I seemed to bring to the frat house. With each new round of drinks, the stories got more graphic, more detailed, the laughter more loud, more boisterous.

We partied until early morning and would have continued on, but I announced that I wanted to be sober for my wedding and ready for the first night. All of us got back to New Haven and into bed without incident.

It seemed only ten minutes later that Allen was shaking my bed, saying we had to be dressed and ready to leave in an hour for my BIG DAY. He had shaved and showered and was almost dressed. I needed to get going, pronto. I felt as if I had two heads. Allen gave me two aspirin, which didn't help at all.

When he and I arrived at Dwight Chapel about half an hour before the ceremony, I was astonished that so many people were milling around the common, and that the chapel itself was nearly full. Reverend Taylor's brother, Uncle Percy, was showing off his virtuosity at the pipe organ. The seated guests waved, applauded, and began taking photographs as Allen and I strode toward a room in the apse where Reverend Taylor and two other pastors were waiting. I began mopping perspiration from last night's booze from my face and smiled feebly at the guests and cameras.

"It's time," Reverend Taylor said authoritatively, opening the door to lead the way. Once the clergy were in place, Allen and I followed and took our places below the altar.

The chapel was jammed to capacity as first Ma and then Mrs. Taylor were escorted to their seats on opposite sides in the front pews. Bouquets of white flowers filled the altar and broad white ribbons decorated the ends of each pew all the way to the rear. Dan and Brother, handsome in their morning coats and gray gloves, walked to the front and expectantly unfolded the white carpet down the length of the chapel, out the front door, and down the stairs.

With another of Uncle Percy's elaborate flourishes on the pipe organ, the first bridesmaid appeared at the chapel entrance, framed by the massive oak doors, and began Reverend Taylor's "step-step-hold" march down the aisle. Shirlee had told me about the dresses, but I never imagined them to be as romantic as they appeared. When one bridesmaid was halfway down the aisle, another materialized and began making her way toward Allen and me. Then the groomsmen stepped up and repeated the process, until bridesmaids and groomsmen stretched from end to end across the altar, behind Allen and me, facing Reverend Taylor and his two assistant pastors. A little girl holding a basket trailing ribbons and filled with rose petals then shyly made her way down the aisle, daintily casting petals with each step.

Uncle Percy's next and most elaborate flourish brought the audience to its feet. Amid oohs, aahs, and flashing cameras, Shirlee was suddenly outlined by the huge doors on the arm of Uncle Bill. Unbelievably beautiful with her wispy veil, a bouquet of flowers, and a majestic gown that swept the pews on both sides of the aisle, she moved slowly forward, her train trailing. Allen nudged me with a handkerchief because tears were pouring down my face as I watched Shirlee coming down the aisle to marry me.

As Shirlee and I reversed our overloaded Dauphine out of the West Park Avenue driveway, waving to our teary-eyed families and friends showering us with rice, I finally understood the true significance of baptisms. Although never baptized myself, as a preteenager I had accompanied Ma to Church of God baptisms. During summers in Kernersville, after the 11:00 o'clock service every fourth Sunday, Aunt Minnie required Leonard, Bobbie, Dot, and me to join her, the pastor, the deacons, and the congregation of Oak Spring Baptist Church in a somber, hymn-singing procession through dense stands of tall pine trees to a small, muddy-red pond deep in the woods behind the church. There, as at the Church of God, the pastor and two deacons waded waist-deep into the water, their white robes circling on the calm surface around them, and beckoned one by one to the sheet-clad candidates ready to begin new lives as faithful Christians. The entire congregation shouted and thanked God as the pastor and deacons immersed each penitent and quickly raised each Christian.

Invariably, they seemed transformed. Sometimes coughing (possibly because they couldn't swim), often trembling, and always crying, the newly baptized men and women invariably stretched their hands toward the sky, praising God.

I always wondered what had happened to them, what had changed them so fundamentally, what made them feel renewed, reborn. At dusk on my wedding day, I knew.

Watching our families and friends fade from our rearview mirror, I felt a joy that I had never known before. I had loved Shirlee since the moment I saw her sensuously gliding down the stairs of Freeman Hall for our blind date. She was it for me. I didn't care whom I had known before or might meet in the future. Shirlee was my dream—a dream I never imagined I could actually live. And that we had so much in common—so many values, so many hopes for a way of life that I secretly wanted but doubted I had a right to because I was poor and Negro in the 1950s—confirmed the connection between us.

For the first time in my life, I had a soul mate who understood my innermost aspirations, my hurts, my fears, and my foibles—who encouraged me to free myself from the shackles and mind-set of the second-class citizenship that had defined me, my family, and friends since Deanwood.

I, too, was born again—baptized, perhaps—on June 27, 1959.

For months I had explored options for our honeymoon, which I wanted to be romantic, memorable, and spectacular, sending for brochures on resorts all over New York State and New England. Somewhere along the way, I decided that for the first night we should stay at a beautiful, Negro-owned resort so there would be no ugly incidents or race-related problems awaiting us on our night of nights. After numerous telephone calls, letters, brochures, and photographs, I settled on the renowned Peg Leg Bates Hotel, where I reserved the bridal suite for our late check-in on June 27. I prepaid for it to be stocked with champagne, stemmed glasses, Cokes, and ice, orange juice, fresh cheese, fruit, and finger food, and, most important, dozens of fresh red roses and a king-size bed.

I kept these arrangements secret until Shirlee and I were en route, so that I could surprise and please her. We stopped for floats and coffee, got lost, refound our way, and finally arrived around 10:00 P.M., exhausted and exhilarated.

To my absolute horror, the resort was a dump. The bridal suite was a small, ordinary room, neither well furnished nor clean. Saltine crackers, a Coke, and two plastic glasses were on one of the dressers. Three plastic flowers were in an old wine bottle on the night table next to the bed. The bed was small and lumpy.

Before we unpacked the car, I went to the registration desk a second time to be sure there hadn't been an awful mistake. That was the room I had reserved, according to their records. No one knew about any special arrangements or champagne or roses I had paid for. They were the weekend staff. The regular staff would return Monday morning and I could settle with them then.

It was too late to try to find another hotel. Greatly disappointed, we decided to spend the night and leave the following day. Besides, we needed and wanted only each other.

We didn't get to sleep until after sunrise. We were deliriously fulfilled. Once out of our room, we were unable to stop holding hands, hugging, kissing. I had never known such bliss.

We left by noon the next day and headed for Vermont and New Hampshire. We found old country inns overlooking lakes and during the day explored the vast open hillsides and off-road antique shops. We stopped at a Rockefeller resort, made a dinner reservation, dressed in our finest, and spent a delightful, romantic evening dining in the warm glow of a huge open fireplace, basking in the surrounds of old money. When we happened upon country fairs, we bought mulled cider, delicious cheeses, and maple syrup. Our days were great and our evenings even better.

Back in Boston, Shirlee's wedding pearls and gifts for my groomsmen had seriously dented my cash flow. With our honeymoon expenses added in, the outflow went more quickly than I anticipated. The discrepancy almost caused our new landlord to change his mind about leasing to us. Good soul that he was, he relented and let us move in with more silverware, silver bowls, ice buckets, fancy vases, cheese boards—and clothes—than could be found in any upscale home furnishings store in Boston. With only a new bed and our wedding gifts in the apartment, we didn't need furniture. We felt we had everything.

Embarking on Homer's "wine-dark sea" of marriage, I held tightly to one very important piece of history from my past. My paternal grandparents, Isaac and Laura Haizlip, my maternal grandparents, Robert and Kettie Hill, and twenty-one of their twenty-two children (including my parents) established, during the most adverse times and circumstances for Negroes in America, a record of solid, long-term, monogamous marriages. On my wedding day, I made another vow, a private one. I promised myself that throughout the future, I would work toward upholding my family's tradition as best I could by being loving to, respectful and supportive of, and honest with Shirlee at all times. I believed that if I continuously tried to hear the feelings behind her words and learned to share my feelings with equal openness, trust, and honesty, we would continue a positive family custom. Instinctively I knew she would find a good job and be a good mother, but of more immediate concern to me was her role as housewife. I had my fingers crossed that she would grow into that. But for the moment, thinking about clean houses and good meals was not my top concern.

CHAPTER 5

Sipping the Wine of Cana

*S*HIRLEE: There is a yearning, a need to feel at home in one's life. The French have an expression for it, *bien dans sa peau*—"well within one's skin." The feeling that you should be just where you are, doing what you are doing, and at ease with yourself about the whole thing.

Children who are greatly loved have this feeling. But then for many, something happens, slippage occurs, the fit gets wrinkled. Maybe it's because one isn't popular, pretty, smart, or thin enough. Maybe it's because one doesn't dance well, compete well, make enough money. Whatever, the feeling of at homeness slips away, like a shadow in the fog.

Most of the time I knew what it felt like to be at home with myself. Sometimes a hairline crack appeared in my wall of comfort. A voice slipped through. In my ear I heard the story that someday, I would live a life far different from the one I knew. Something would happen, someone would come who would change my life forever. Little did I suspect that it would be me. But that would take a while.

We came home to closed doors—our apartment, that is. The fact that we had gotten the place on Gloucester Street in Back Bay was a small miracle in the first place. The homes in that neighborhood were uniformly closed to people with dark skin. Harold had happened upon a landlord who, for whatever reason, had escaped or lived beyond the customs of his time. As long as we had green money and paid it on time, he said, we could live in his house.

But now the Irishman, a no-nonsense retired military man, wanted no part of us. The check Harold had written for the deposit and first month's rent had bounced. The funds were in the bank but had not cleared. In the hot July sun I waited outside in the Dauphine with all my clothes, wondering if we would be sleeping back in my father's house that night. After a few hours, Harold and the bank resolved the matter, the owner gave up the keys, and we transferred the clothes from the car to the closet.

The ground floor-through apartment was sunny, facing south. The two main rooms were spacious, with tall ceilings. A small alcove, just off the entryway and big enough to eat in, opened onto a tiny kitchen, large enough for one cook. Next to the kitchen was a closet-size room we grandly called a study. We squeezed a desk and a chair in there. A charmingly antiquated bathroom was one of the largest spaces in the place, bigger than the kitchen, the dining alcove, and the study combined. I had grandiose plans for it. It would be my special place, my spa, my study, my space for dreaming.

Turning away from the dark, heavy traditional furniture of our parents, we homed in on avocado and hunter green, teak and rattan. Harold made green striped drapes for the living room, pink swags for the bedroom.

I convinced him that a marigold-colored sofa would bring sun into our living room all year. He cajoled me into believing that a tall-backed chair in alternating stripes of green, yellow, and orange was just the place he needed to rest his head at the end of the day.

We congratulated ourselves in making a cinder-block bookcase elegant by covering its shelves with dark green velvet to display the silver trays and other silver "stuff" that came in our wedding boxes.

That first Christmas, we had a silver foil Christmas tree filled with bulbs of green and gold. We had become sleek; we had become moderne.

The only thing neat about the bright yellow room I shared with my sister at home had been the bed. Clothes, books, papers, dolls, and other sundries were the artifacts of my daily dig. We had transformed my grandfather's dignified rocker, sitting in a corner near the room's one closet, into a capacious trunk that held our out-of-season clothes.

When I got to college, things were easier. Wellesley did not assign me a roommate in my freshman year. I had a homey room in Homestead, an old colonial house that had been converted to a freshman dormitory. I felt lucky. Little did I know it was the college's unwritten policy not to room black and white freshmen together. The woman who would become a friend and the secretary of state, Madeleine Albright, lived on one side of me with her Catholic roommate. On the other side were two Jewish girls. Blissfully segregated, I kept my room spotless.

Sophomore and junior years, a quiet blonde from Chatham, Massachusetts, who was politely interviewed by a college dean "to see if she really wanted to room with a Negro" shared a double room with me in one of Wellesley's new modern dormitories, Freeman Hall. Although clutter and I were easy companions, for the most part my neatness matched my roommate's.

For Harold, neatness was a beatitude. Orderliness was an idol. Fastidiousness was a word created for him.

Whenever anything is not in the place for which it has been designated, Harold moves it. Partially filled glasses, ballpoint pens, magazines may end up in the Bermuda Triangle.

He says I leave a trail wherever I have been in the house. He erases the trail. He has become known as Harold's Moving Service.

I found that his housekeeping admonitions might have come from my mother's rule book. "When you dust, lift things, move things. Don't practice the art of kamikaze dusting. Clean the kitchen every night so bugs will not look for food on plates or water in the sink. The living room is not the place for discarded clothes or old newspapers. A good housewife makes the bed every day."

I began to post quotes about women's lives, freedom, and creativity on the refrigerator.

For the longest time, his insistence on neatness bothered me. I made myself feel better by attributing his attitude to childhood and cultural issues. He made me feel as if I were among the world's ten worst housekeepers. I felt as if I could publish *Bad Housekeeping*, the Magazine for Women Who Couldn't Care Less. I would commission articles on "How to Ignore a 17-Inch Dustball" or "Defrosting with Dynamite."

We agreed, in principle, on maintenance and upkeep. I did what made me feel the most comfortable—dusting, washing, ironing—as needed. Early on Harold told me he'd rather iron his shirts. I knew I fell far short of his view of housewifely perfection.

I had majored in sociology at Wellesley and thought I wanted to be a doctor, so I'd taken pre-med courses as well. After meeting Harold, I decided I did not want to commit all that time to a rigorous post-graduate training, so in the fall of my senior year I applied to law school instead, on the East Coast and West Coast, since we didn't know where we would settle. Boston University and Stanford accepted me.

When I returned from our honeymoon, I knew my heart was not into going to law school in the fall. I was tired of the intense kind of studying that I had been doing for so long and wanted to concentrate on making my marriage solid. I wanted real life for a while. I was convinced that whatever I was meant to do, I would do it at the appropriate time. I took so much for granted. Now I shudder to think how easily I made the decision not to go to law school.

My parents never pressured me about any of my decisions. What they wanted for me was a good marriage and a satisfying career. My dad and mother never said, "You ought to be a doctor, a lawyer, a social worker, or a teacher." What they did say was, "Get a degree so you can take care of yourself and be a credit to your race." So when I told them I was not going to law school, they were not disappointed. They were eager to hear about my new job.

Two months after our wedding, my mother wrote. It was my first letter as a married woman. Yet from her tone, I knew I was still her little girl. I didn't mind.

August 1, 1959

Dear Shirlee

We're happy to hear from you and to know that you are enjoying your little job.

Pattee was ill last week with an acute attack of indigestion. I thought it was polio because New Haven has so many cases. She went to the Emergency Room where they gave her capsules. She also has a cyst in the ear but she is better today. We attended a lovely garden wedding today, canapes and everything in style in West Haven. Julian married them.

We were pleased over your decision about going to Law School. I think it was very wise to wait until next year. Things will work out fine for you.

Please write and tell Jay Storm what size pictures you want in the (wedding) album.

It is hot here and I am just tired out.

Please write soon and come down.

With love,
Mother

On good days, I walked to work on Commonwealth Avenue. When the weather was bad, I hopped on the bus or subway for the fifteen-minute ride.

My day life was a world of words, jargon, and esoteric medical terminology for which my pre-med courses had prepared me. My boss, Dr. Ethan Allen Brown, became another in the series of men in my life whose love of language defined them. Dr. Brown was British, a former member of the Royal College of Surgeons. In some ways this chunky white man reminded me of my father. His joy in finding just the right word; his interest in etymology. His absolute certainty about the rightness of what he was saying.

A world-renowned allergy and asthma specialist who edited numerous medical journals, Dr. Brown had pioneered a one-shot allergy treatment that brought him patients in droves. A brilliant, mercurial tyrant, he ran his practice and his editorial offices like a Napoleonic campaign.

He allowed as how he had never employed a black editorial assistant before. How did I get so comfortable with the language? he wondered. Ultimately, I became his chief editor.

My days at the allergy center were a genteel introduction to the world of work. Some days, Brown would call me into his office to discuss the poetry of Robert Frost or the work of William Faulkner. On certain afternoons, as the Charles River flowed beyond the great bay windows of the place and the sun set on the red-stained leaves, I felt as if I were at a college colloquium, listening to a particularly chatty, avuncular professor.

At home, *Joy of Cooking* had become my best friend and intimate companion. I vowed to try each recipe in the book. That oath did not last long. Once I sent Harold to find truffles. I had never tasted them; nor did I know what they looked like. But I had to have them. Harold went everywhere to find them. Adding them to scrambled eggs, I expected an epiphany. Nothing happened. Their taste was vague, almost nonexistent. Harold laughed for weeks.

My cooking was serviceable and, once in a while, inspired. I tried to extend our taste range beyond the mix of New England and southern fare we both knew. Harold had only disdain for frozen food and deli offerings. He would cook wonderfully tasty meals on weekends and holidays. His southern fried chicken became legendary among friends and colleagues.

Good food and eating together were essential to Harold's contentment. Since my family had had dinner together every evening, this was an extension of my own home training. Harold went further, though. Candlelight was also requisite. Great for romance and your complexion, he'd say. He preferred late dinners, nine o'clock or so. Sometimes I wondered if there was a cultural influence from Spain hidden in his background. A taste for midnight dining was something I had to acquire. My stomach and I adjusted.

Negotiating differences was something I had to relearn. Growing up in a family of four children, you learn one set of skills. They're not always transferrable. My parents had no physical fights, not even loud screaming ones. From time to time I saw my father petulant and scowling, usually over something "the devilish children" had done. My mother's temper flashes were as ephemeral as a feather floating down from a passing bird. It was easy to tell when she was angry: her face flushed a deep red. My symptoms were less subtle.

When Harold and I had a difference of opinion I liked to argue to the end and win. I tried to convince him he was not just wrong but totally wrong. I was stubborn and determined. It seemed as if Harold did not enjoy the battle, did not enjoy confrontation. His body stiffened; his eyes grew more lidded. He got quiet. Sometimes I wanted to shake him into action. I got nowhere. Then I sulked. He withdrew. Silence and politeness conspired against closeness. Days would pass with few words.

We disagreed mostly about money, what to do with it, where it should go and whether I *really* needed all the new clothes I liked to buy. Every major purchase for the household called for a summit meeting. Not wanting to negotiate *all* the time, sometimes I just went out and bought what I thought we needed, like eight crystal sherry glasses that we had to have. (Sherry was our favorite drink then.) Harold's good nature and his desire to please me usually prevented an outbreak of hostilities.

Once during our first year of marriage Harold loaned his barber four hundred dollars for some business scheme. He had known the man just a few months. "Shirlee, this man has not had our opportunities, but he is really sharp. Don't worry, it's a great investment. We'll get our money back."

Four hundred dollars. That was a big part of his paycheck. Never mind that we had no savings. I was not feeling particularly socially responsible to a man I did not know. We never saw the four hundred dollars again. I was mad for weeks.

After experiencing my trousseau, Harold was certain I would not need new clothes for another twenty-five years. For me they represented a summer's wardrobe for my new life. I had been brought up to expect dozens of new outfits for winter and summer. My father enjoyed refurbishing our wardrobes each September and May.

In spite of Harold's belief that I "had everything in the way of clothes" and his fussing and grumbling if I brought something new home, that first Christmas he lifted a huge, exquisitely wrapped box from under the gold and green tree. A designer coat. I didn't analyze it, I just wore it.

I saved a memento from our most serious fight. One evening during our first year we had a couple to dinner. They had both been in our wedding. Harold thought I was flirting. I thought I was behaving normally—besides, the guy was not even my type.

The couple left. Harold was livid. Anger puffed his face like a blowfish. I protested my innocence. Indignation took one hand and self-righteousness held the other. We went for a walk by the Charles River. Cool air and quiet water did little to break the tension. I pulled off my wedding band and threw it to the ground. For the rest of the night, we did not speak. We averted our eyes. Back to back, we huddled at each side of the ice floe that had been our bed. He got up early and left the house before I awoke.

When I went into the bathroom, I found my wedding band, newly polished, in a black velvet box sitting on top of my toothbrush.

During the middle of the day, a messenger delivered a telegram to me at work. The message: "Forever and three days is a long way off. Let's talk tonight. Always, Harold."

Many who write about the sixties write from class-, gender-, or race-based perspectives. The privileged saw it as a terrible time, when people lost respect, when cherished values were trashed, when an "unsuitable element" took control. Those were the views of people who had been in control, people who had power, money, education. Some women, blacks, and working-class people use a different prism. For them, the sixties was a time when previously powerless groups came into their own. Their messages were heard; their existence was validated. I fall into the latter category. The sixties were some of the best times of my life.

In his State of the Union Message, President Eisenhower proclaimed that 1960 would be the best year in United States history. Someone misread the entrails. A month later, black students from North Carolina's Agriculture and Technical College staged a sit-in at Woolworth's in Greensboro. Physically, I remained hundreds of miles away, in Boston. Spiritually, I had flown to North Carolina.

A & T, as the college was known, was no exotic location for me. It was part of my life. My uncle, H. Clinton Taylor, had founded its art department. As a little girl I had walked its campus, visited its classrooms, drawn in its studios. I knew I did not have the freedom in downtown Greensboro that I had on the campus. Even as a child that bothered me greatly.

Pattee, a college freshman at Fisk, called to tell me she was joining her fellow students at sit-ins in Nashville. Her happy and exited voice had a chilling effect. Nasty visions of the danger she might face made the sit-ins real rather than romantic. She called with daily bulletins. There were encounters with racists who spat on her, spouted epithets. Some mistook her for a white woman and labeled her a "nigger lover."

Once two Fisk football players physically carried her out of a local store because she was about to bean a bigot. How I wished I had been there with her, protecting her *and* egging her on. With my mother's temper and my great sense of outrage, I wouldn't have been scared. I would have been ready and spoiling for a good fight, never mind the turning the other cheek business. After all, it was because of *them* that I couldn't go to the movies or get an ice cream cone in the South when I was a little girl. I was tremendously proud of the fact that Pattee was a foot soldier in the front lines of this new war. She would carry the Taylor banner into the fray. And she would meet her first husband during a skirmish.

At home, the growing civil rights movement was all we could talk about. In our lifetime, Harold and I had not seen or heard anything like this new vocabulary, this new set of postures and expectations. We could feel ourselves growing and changing. Harold, who had lived in the tightly controlled world of segregation, was reserved about storming the barricades that had been so dangerous and deadly for black men. He examined the issues with restrained passion. Was this because of years of being cautious with white people?

As for me, I was indignant. I was ready to jump in anyone's face. I had known the ostensible freedoms of the North. Every summer I was thrown up against the irrational restrictions of the South.

I was feeling a deepening oneness with my colored brethren, one that I had especially experienced at the National Baptist Conventions where there were tens of thousands of ordinary black folks. Nowhere else had I seen and been with so many people who were colored like me. Nowhere else did I see masses of brown folk in frills and finery, enjoying the days and rejoicing in the nights. Nowhere else did I see the ministers, the leaders, like a flock of elegant black herons, resplendent in white linen or sharkskin summer suits.

My father journeyed to Los Angeles as Connecticut's first black Democratic party delegate-at-large. We saw his face in close-up on the network news jumping for joy as the Democratic party named John F. Kennedy for president on the first ballot. At Kennedy's request, my father went on to play a key role in getting out the black vote in West Virginia. The candidate wrote an appreciative letter:

> May 19, 1960
>
> Dear Dr. Taylor:
> Sarge Shriver and other members of my organization in West Virginia have told me of your very effective work on my behalf in the West Virginia campaign. This is just a note to express my appreciation of your efforts in making the two trips to West Virginia. I am hopeful that you have fully recovered from the illness you experienced upon returning to Connecticut.
>
> Many, many thanks
> Sincerely, John F. Kennedy

Shortly after President Kennedy announced the formation of the Peace Corps, I wrote away for two applications. I filled my head with notions of wearing a natty safari suit and handsome leather boots while doing good deeds. Perhaps I was influenced by Jewelle's living with her anthropologist husband in the African bush for a year, although she had assured me it was no picnic.

Harold was not enthusiastic about our possible Peace Corps participation. He was not buoyed by the thought of his education being delayed by an uncertain new venture. He wanted to go back to graduate school for a Ph.D. I tried to convince him that there would still be time for getting his degree after we emerged from the hinterlands. For a while I lobbied heavily, dredging up every humanitarian argument of importance I had read, seen, or heard. Harold did not budge. We would not save the world in matching outfits from Abercrombie and Fitch after all. I regret not having done it and often wonder how Peace Corps service might have affected our lives.

We celebrated our first anniversary with a trip back to our honeymoon territory, minus the black resort. The Sunday we returned home, I ran from the car to the apartment, doubling over from excruciating cramps. I lay on the bathroom floor. Suddenly, I felt soaked. Blood all around. I screamed for Harold.

In pain and hemorrhaging, I met a doctor at the emergency room of Beth Israel Hospital. My first pregnancy ended in miscarriage after two months. There is no doubt I was in denial about being pregnant. I was not ready. It was not part of our plan. Overwhelmed by the suddenness of the incident and surprised at the conscious level, we did not feel too badly about the loss. We knew there would be other chances. But you always wonder who that embryo would have become.

It did not bother me that my life, like the fetus, had not yet taken shape. I thrived in a world of possibilities. I had a bag of dreams, all of which I knew could be pursued, *if I wanted to*. I knew I was still becoming, that there were marvelous things ahead.

After two years, I left the editorial job. Getting to work involved using the subway. My new job, at the Boys' Clubs of Boston, was just down the hill from the Bunker Hill Monument to the American Revolution, in Charlestown, in a tight-knit blue-collar Irish neighborhood.

The executive director of the club, a cheerful, blustery Irishman with piercing blue eyes, was my new boss. A cigar never left his hand. His other hand was constantly at his temple, smoothing back a heavy headful of thick, graying hair. With regular features and a dazzling smile, he was quite handsome.

During our initial meeting, totally without context, he asked me why my skin was so light. "It's in the genes," I answered. "Some of my relatives are Irish. Who knows, I might be related to you." This usually shut Irish people up.

"Someday you should write the story of how that came to be," he said. I told him I planned to do just that.

There were no other black employees in the Boston Boys' Clubs then and no black boys in the Charlestown club. My job was administrative, far removed from the daily programs involving the boys. I was confident that what I did, publicity and fund-raising, ensured that there would be recognition and money for programs, for materials for staff. I believed my work was one of the keys to keeping the institution alive.

I had to pass the Bunker Hill Monument every day. The only way I could relate to it was by thinking of Crispus Attucks, the black patriot who died for America's independence.

Looking back on my first two jobs, at which I was the only black person in the building, in fact in the neighborhood, sometimes I wonder what kind of toll that sinkhole of cultural/racial isolation has taken on me. Going through it at the time seemed like a natural experience, a kind of extension of my college life, one that had to be endured, overcome, triumphed. It had been happening since I was in elementary school. Had it made me stronger? Weaker? Arrogant? Oblivious? Compassionate? Angry? Some of all the above.

One of the first things I did with my Boys' Club salary was to buy Harold a grand piano, an old Bechstein. I purchased it from an elderly piano teacher in our building. I was elated to make a dream come true for Harold.

Boston was one of the first cities to undertake urban renewal. The Clubs' three sites were in renewal areas: Irish Charlestown, Irish South Boston, and black Roxbury. The renewal troops enlisted us in their cause. I went to meeting after meeting. The possibilities of making dramatic social changes made me swoon. I had a new dream to explore. Administration was okay, but planning was undoubtedly what I was meant to do.

While working at the Clubs, I enrolled in an urban planning course offered by the Harvard extension program. The first lecture and a glimpse of the reading list heightened the call. I aced the course and applied to the Harvard Graduate School of Design.

If anything, working at the Boys' Clubs made my sociology come to life. My job gave me an understanding of how institutions can help or hurt neighborhoods. From what I could see, the Clubs were valuable *in loco parentis* for some boys, but the key question was how to make them a necessary resource for all the boys in the community. In order to do that, the staff had to understand the dynamics, the politics, the social interactions of the neighborhoods in the restive atmosphere of the early sixties. That's where urban social planning came in.

In the fall of 1962, the United States discovered long-range missiles in Cuba pointing directly at the States. Not since Harold received his draft notice had such a pall hung over our lives. We called each other three or four times a day. Castro's Russian missiles were a palpable worry. Would we be incinerated at home, in the supermarket, on our way to or from work? Would there be any cities left to plan, any schools to be managed? We offered special prayers that Thanksgiving. The Cubans and the Russians had backed down. Life went on.

After four years of marriage I discovered I was pregnant again. The baby was due at the end of August 1963. This time we looked forward to the second coming.

Babies had never fascinated me. I had never babysat. Little children held no allure. Introspection about becoming a parent did not visit me. I was fearful of childbirth. Horrific scenes of pain and agony in the movies had marked me badly. Nonetheless, I looked forward to starting a family. I hoped I could be as loving to my children as my mother had been to me.

As our child was developing in the womb, the world was shuddering violently. Integration had become a national goal. The Civil Rights Movement dominated the evening news. The opponents used water hoses, police dogs, and tear gas. Images of doused bodies, bitten limbs, and prostrate children seared my brain, hurt my heart, and damaged my soul. I vented by swearing at the television, swearing at the South, swearing at the rednecks. Those were some of the first words the child inside of me would hear.

Harold traveled a great deal during my pregnancy, while Vietnam began to compete for attention in the news. Body counts of American advisors were posted like grocery lists. Would Harold be called to the front? Also making me nervous and edgy were the random killings of the Boston Strangler, a serial killer who viciously attacked women alone in their apartments. One of his victims had been found in Cambridge, not too far from our apartment.

When Harold was out of town, I kept milk and soda bottles by the porch door as an alarm. One day, I knew the Strangler had avoided the makeshift sentries. As I was talking on the phone with my mother in Connecticut, something strong and heavy gripped my shoulders. I dropped the phone and turned around. It turned with me. From a bookshelf behind my head, one of my large Maine coon cats had jumped on my back.

My mother came to stay for a while. She thought I needed her to help worry about the Strangler.

I worked until the seventh month of my pregnancy. It had been uneventful. Still determined to look good, I put together a maternity wardrobe from the racks of Filene's Basement.

I was trying my best to find some way to get to the March on Washington. Harold said there was no way we could go. I had not accepted his edict yet.

The doctor put his foot down. Feeling fat, ugly, hot, and sorry for myself, I stood in the kitchen unpacking groceries on the weekend of the march. A sudden whoosh rushed down my legs, soaking my sandals. Clear liquid covered the floor. My water had broken. "Harold, call the doctor. Find out what we do now." This had not been covered in my prenatal instructions.

I had on a lemon-yellow linen tent dress that day. My bag had been packed for a few days. I was ready. Luckily, my dress had not gotten wet. I went to the front door to wait. Minutes passed. "Harold, where are you? The doctor said we had to come right over."

"Be right there." Muffled.

No sign of him in the bedroom. Water running furiously in the bathroom. He was shaving. I was astonished.

The terror hit in the examining room. What was going to happen? What would I feel? How could I possibly stand the pain? Would I have a breech birth? Would the baby be deformed, disabled, slow?

Labor was long. Hard. I was determined to be dignified. No cussing and denouncing of my husband. My resolve held. After a night of numbing pain, in a haze I heard the doctor tell me he was going to perform a cesarean. The baby was determined not to come down the birth canal. The infant and I were getting weaker. "The nightmare is coming true," I thought.

Harold held my hand. "It's O.K., it's O.K. You'll be great in a few hours." His worried face belied his words.

Our baby was born soon thereafter. The doctor told me it was a girl. I saw a serene sleeping face, chipmunk cheeks, wispy brown hair. The terror was over.

Like many starstruck mothers, mine had named me after Shirley Temple, the reigning child star of the thirties and early forties. The name

"Shirley" held no adventure, no mystery, no *je ne sais quoi*. Adding the double "e" made it a little more tolerable. (Following my lead, Patty had changed her name to Pattee.) When I was mature enough to be grand, I saw myself as a Solange, a Juliette. Romance still suffused my life. Our child would have a more felicitous name. Arielle, maybe.

We chose the name Deirdre. I had never known or met a Deirdre. Something subconscious in my gene pool must have nudged me. I knew the name was Gaelic. "Deirdre" conjured up a slim, beautiful girl, clad in gossamer layers. She sits on a vine-covered veranda, holding a camellia and gazing at a quarter-moon in a velvet sky, if we could find such a place. Until then, "Dee Dee" would reign.

Had Deirdre been born a few years later, she might have been called Amber, Imani, Ebony, or Africa. Perhaps in time I will have a granddaughter with the name from the continent that gave us all life.

*H*AROLD: Our wedding gifts were fabulous, but we couldn't set up housekeeping with half dozens each of butter knives, salad bowls, stemmed glasses, soup tureens, corkscrews, and pizza pans. We pressed Shirlee's footlocker into service as a kitchen table, proudly covered it with a new damask tablecloth, topped it with two tall candles in crystal candleholders, and used my unopened book boxes for chairs—for starters.

Although we liked the same music and the same food, knew the words of the same songs, had read many of the same books, wanted to see the same movies, and liked to dance the same way, I was shocked to discover that we also shared the same unspoken taste for decorating our place. After hours of roaming aimlessly past bric-a-brac, junk, and drastic markdowns in antique shops, discount furniture stores, fabric houses, yard sales, and department store basements, we invariably picked the same one or two items (out of thousands) we wanted to buy and live with.

Food was our first major dividing line. We liked the same foods and always enjoyed eating well. But Mrs. Taylor had done most of the cooking in her family, so Shirlee knew only how to poach or scramble eggs and do oatmeal, toast, bacon, and hot tea, while I had a full repertoire of meals dating from elementary school. A thoughtful soul gave Shirlee *Joy of Cooking* as a shower gift. Her experiments with *JOC* meat loaf, poached halibut, chicken and dumplings, roast duck, pot roast, and lyonnaise potatoes were original creations. I complimented her efforts nevertheless. I cooked some weekends, ate hearty lunches on my teaching job at Wellesley High School, and, when we had a few extra dollars, arranged dinner dates for two.

When Shirlee began working we became a two-career family and time became a critical issue. Even after a late night of fun, her body clock woke her up on time and spirited her through her morning routines: bathing, applying makeup, and doing her hair while having a cup of coffee in the bathroom; dressing while itemizing a market list for me; and making the bed before I dragged out of it. When bills came, she expected me to pay them the same day. Whenever we planned a social outing, she was ready half an hour before our planned departure time. If I said I'd be home by 5:00 and didn't arrive until 5:45, she had to know what caused the delay.

Writing notes and preparing to mail birthday cards or greetings for Mother's Day, Father's Day, or Easter, she reminded me of the number of days I had left if I wanted my greetings to reach Ma on time. When she cooked, she alerted me to the time dinner would be ready; when I was doing the honors, about every fifteen minutes she asked what time dinner would be ready. She wanted us to finish decorating the apartment—that is, me to finish the desk and bookcases I was making for the closet we called a study, me to set a date and time to shop for area rugs, me to refinish the antique dressing table, mirror, and bench we bought for her last weekend, me to solve the workspace and storage problems in our tiny kitchen. She left notes to remind me when our clothes could be picked up from the dry cleaners or what time she'd be ready for a ride home from her shopping spree in Filene's Basement.

My preference (even during the workweek) for 9:00 P.M. candlelit dinners with Johnny Mathis or Frank Sinatra crooning in the background, followed leisurely by coffee and then brandy, heated tableside, in a stemmed snifter, made her grumpy and sleepy, not romantic. And when not working, she slept longer than I did, often many hours longer.

On waking most mornings, while still in bed I needed to think about my day before getting up to start it. Prior to shaving and showering, I needed time to have my coffee without rushing; time to decide what to wear; time to iron a shirt; time to polish my shoes; and time to go over my commitments for the day, regardless of the hour. Going out socially, I rushed into the shower as Shirlee put final touches on her makeup and debated which topcoat to wear. When bills came, I put them aside until the fifteenth or thirtieth of the month to savor the power of money in the bank for a couple of weeks. My dinners were so inspired that I couldn't imagine anyone worrying about what *time* we'd eat. Most days, I signed the office roster at Wellesley High minutes before the bell for homeroom period, still grumbling about the inconsiderate old ladies and truck drivers who nearly made me late.

Time and again, Shirlee's annoyance with my apparent lack of concern about time, except as it concerned myself, became quite obvious. Alternately, she questioned whether this was my attempt to control others, or my defiant indifference to others, or my self-centered determination to have the world on my timeline rather than theirs. She reminded me that except for our first blind date, I had been late for nearly every subsequent one, and that had she not always insisted on getting back to Wellesley on time, I would have gotten her into great difficulty with her house mother over and over again.

I questioned her compliance to gain the approval of others, and her seeming to care more about ritual than substance, more about them than me. Although I vigorously disagreed with her views about time and me, after the heat of battles on this topic I privately wondered whether there might, in fact, be some merit in what she had said. I replayed her most troubling comments again and again. Somewhere in my private vortex, I admitted the possibility that because punctuality committed me to someone else's schedule and expectations, I, more than Shirlee, may have had the compliance issue. It was possible, I thought more than once, that I risked being late—and sometimes was late—to reassure myself that I had a right and the power to decide how to spend my time. To save face with Shirlee, I kept silent about this possibility.

Our heated discussions, tears, and tantrums went nowhere until, agreeing to disagree, we negotiated personal bottom-line time needs that the other would try to accept and respect. I promised to do everything in my power to be dressed on time and not to make us late for movies, parties, and dinner dates—especially when other friends were involved—and to telephone her in advance if I was going to be late arriving home from work. She promised to try not to assume in advance that I would make us late for every engagement and not to be angry when there was an acceptable reason for either or both of us to be late.

Being offered a full-time, permanent teaching position at the end of my internship was unusual in the Wellesley public schools, but I considered it a validation of my professional preparation, dedication to my students, and ability to raise their levels of enthusiasm and achievement. I also suspected, privately, that I may have been hired as a safe integration trophy to give the Wellesley school board and community grounds to boast of their liberalism—despite the economics and real estate steering that kept Wellesley a solidly all-white, wealthy Protestant community with few if any Jews and a peripheral nest of poor Italians.

When the Supreme Court handed down its historic 1954 *Brown* v. *Board of Education* decision striking down legal segregation of schools, I often wondered what impact it would have on the Negro teachers in D.C. public schools who had done so much for me and who, in integrated schools, would now compete with whites to keep their jobs in a white-controlled school system. And, knowing how deeply ingrained racism was, I wondered whether white teachers, so long accustomed to teaching only white students, would or could invest beyond lip service in the hard work of preparing mostly poor Negro students, like me a few years back, for college and careers. I was doubtful.

Then began my private dialogues with myself: What in hell was I doing in Wellesley—an all-white community in which I couldn't afford to live, even if I wanted to—investing so much time and emotional energy in preparing white kids for their future? Would white teachers at Wellesley or elsewhere be likely to devote one-tenth as much time or energy to the future of Negro students? Was I trying to deny racism in America? Did I think, for one moment, that anyone would forget that I was a Negro, regardless of how well I taught their white children? Was I voluntarily perpetuating post–*Brown* v. *Board of Education* slavery by exhausting myself teaching white kids?

In the midst of this angst, a bomb exploded in my life: without warning I received a draft notice advising me to report for induction in the U.S. armed services in sixty days. Panicked at the thought of leaving Shirlee alone while I went somewhere in Vietnam to kill, or be killed by, people I had no beef with, I sought help from every source I could think of: Reverend Taylor, Dunbar High School graduates working for the U.S. Department of Defense, my Harvard and Amherst deans and professors, Tom Herzog's parents. Nothing worked. I then made an impassioned appeal to the Wellesley School Committee, which voted to look into the matter. Shirlee wrote a letter to the president. Within less than ten days of the committee's hearing, I received a deferral notice based on the "urgency of my work preparing America's future military and civic leaders for the challenges ahead." White power can be awesome, I wrote in the invisible last sentence of my thank-you letter to the Wellesley School Committee. In my heart I hoped it was Shirlee's plea that had turned the tide.

After escaping the draft, I tried to keep the Vietnam War as far distant from my life as possible but couldn't. Newspaper headlines and nightly television newscasts cited war casualties and MIAs as justification for the president's sending more troops, mostly poor Negroes and whites, into battle. Victory for the United States and her allies would be imminent if only we could outfox and outlast the unyielding resolve of the Vietcong's endless army.

The injustice and immorality of thousands of Negro soldiers slaughtered in Vietnam defending a country that systematically denied them their constitutional rights became a flash point of resistance across disaffected America.

Toward the end of my third year of teaching at Wellesley High School, I felt compelled to become involved, and not to hide on the sidelines of my own life, uneasily safe in an upper-middle-class white cocoon, a token Negro in a community too genteel even to acknowledge the existence of a race or justice problem in the United States. And because I knew I worked hard, I became most unhappy that my diligence and excellence in teaching were not reflected in my paychecks. Teachers' raises were like birthdays: as long as we were still alive and meeting minimum requirements, the union contract guaranteed us a motivational pittance of $200 or $300 at the beginning of each new school year. I wanted to be rewarded for the value of my work in a form that I could spend or save.

I applied and was accepted for admission to the doctoral program in school administration at Harvard. I wanted to prepare myself to run schools and school districts rather than simply teach in them. But I needed a hefty scholarship, and Shirlee would have to agree to work for another few years before we started our family.

The important questions we had to answer went far beyond whether I should go back to school for a doctorate. We were existing from paycheck to paycheck with no savings in the bank, no security against emergencies. We nevertheless lived relatively well by making certain trade-offs: purchasing good-quality clothes at greatly reduced, off-season prices at Filene's Basement, although both of us wished we could enter any upscale store, any time, and buy whatever we wanted—regardless of the price. To control food costs, I checked the newspapers every day for supermarket sales, religiously clipped coupons, and planned meals so that leftovers could be recycled into something new, exciting, and good. To obtain the kind of decorations and ambience that we wanted in our home, I became a one-man cottage industry, turning the inexpensive junk we purchased at Goodwill stores and flea markets into pricey-looking antiques. And although after three years I came to hate the Dauphine with a passion because it had so little power and was nearly blown off the highway by every car that passed us, the fact that I could drive it to and from work and everywhere else for ten days on six dollars in gas made it my best friend, at least financially. Months later, when a teenager burning rubber in the parking lot of a supermarket accidentally broadsided the Dauphine on the passenger side and totaled it, my anger turned to silent gratitude as soon as the investigating police officer told me that the kid was legally driving his parents' car, which was fully insured.

My going back to graduate school on Shirlee's salary and as much scholarship money as I could get meant that we would continue living on the edge, with many dreams deferred, for at least three more years. Neither of us was happy about the short-term prospects of this decision. We believed, however, that a doctorate would increase my salary by more than I would have received in raises after three more years as a teacher. And we believed that after graduate school my job satisfaction and earnings potential would skyrocket, providing us enough money either for Shirlee to get her master's degree, or for us to start a family, or both.

We leased an apartment within walking distance of Harvard Square, and I plunged into intensive doctoral studies. For two academic years and two summers, I was again a wholly focused, almost compulsive graduate student. I limited my frivolity to one nonacademic outlet, as elected president of the Harvard Graduate Students Association.

At the end of my two years of study, I had two options: either to design a major research project, find more scholarship money, and remain a full-time student while writing the dissertation; or to find a job in which the real world could become the laboratory for my research and Harvard dissertation.

Working with the placement office and scouring classified ads, my network of contacts, and the Harvard/Boston alumni network, I interviewed for a job as Education Director with Action for Boston Community Development, Inc. (A.B.C.D.), an embryonic research and demonstration project staffed by scholar-practitioners from Brandeis, Harvard, MIT, and Boston University, and funded by the Ford Foundation.

Ours was a match made in heaven, consummated before the initial interview ended. A.B.C.D. was looking for an articulate, self-confident educator (preferably Negro) who was as comfortable in the streets and schools of Boston's poorest ethnic neighborhoods as in the all-white School Committee offices, corporate and political offices, and social service agencies downtown.

They wanted someone who knew poverty, schools, and schooling to interpret their university-based research and statistics and design education programs for impoverished urban children, families, and community organizations. My Deanwood to Amherst to Harvard to Wellesley High School sojourn, coupled with my growing need to connect with the civil rights movement and give back to poor Negro students what my Washington teachers had given me, convinced me to accept the new position.

When I joined the staff, the research data had been gathered. The future of the agency (and our jobs) depended on our ability to attract three-year Ford Foundation implementation grants. We were competing with poverty think tanks in Detroit, Washington, D.C., Philadelphia, Atlanta, Chicago, and Los Angeles for these grants. My job was to decode linkages between education achievement and family income, and to sell innovative school- and community-based programs that promised to enable poor children to achieve at the same levels as middle- and upper-income kids.

The prevailing point of view was that poor children did not succeed in school because their parents had not succeeded in life. They had chosen (consciously or otherwise) not to lift themselves out of poverty by their own bootstraps. Poor children and families were therefore caught in a family-determined cycle of poverty and school failure that renewed itself child by child, generation after generation, to the dismay of educators and social planners.

Our analyses challenged these shibboleths. We documented that through the end of grade three, there were insignificant differences in the school achievement of middle-income and poor children, but that from grade four through high school, the achievement of poor children fell behind that of middle-income children by an average of six months each successive year. Those who fell behind ultimately became the majority of students who dropped out or were pushed out of school.

Earlier research had already revealed that a majority of underachieving poor children were members of ethnic minority groups; that the school district annually spent far less money on teacher salaries, books and supplies, enrichment programs, building maintenance, and new school construction in schools with a majority of poor, minority students than in schools for the middle and upper classes; and that far more inexperienced and "problem" teachers were assigned to schools in poor neighborhoods than to schools in average and well-off neighborhoods.

Politically, we couldn't touch the bombshell issue of intentional, institutionalized race and income discrimination. We focused, instead, on poverty and programs to demonstrate that poor students were as capable of school success as middle-income students.

By day, I searched the ranks of school supervisors, principals, teachers, union reps, PTAs, and youth and human service agencies for brave souls willing to risk careers and job security to work with poor, disadvantaged, minority youth. Evenings, I worked the streets, politicians, community activists, youth groups and parents in Roxbury, the South End, and Charlestown to garner credibility and support for A.B.C.D.'s programs.

Over time, after many fitful starts, political obstacles, protest marches, threatened teacher walkouts, and shouting matches at school committee meetings, A.B.C.D. generated millions annually from the Ford Foundation and federal agencies to support collaborative, multi-agency programs.

The Boston breakthrough became so successful in raising student test scores, improving school attendance, reducing the dropout rate, and increasing parent participation that the Ford Foundation sent me to impoverished communities across the United States to encourage the development of similar initiatives. *Time* magazine called me "a modern 'Horatio Alger'"—a double-edged comparison that often made me uncomfortable. Vira mailed copies of the blurb to every living member of the Haizlip family. The Boston Chamber of Commerce honored me as its first nonwhite Outstanding Young Man of the Year.

Shirlee worked at the Boys' Clubs through seven months of her healthy pregnancy, allowing me the time, day and night, to be away from home, advocating A.B.C.D.'s goals, rationales, programs, and promises.

I had just begun shaving in the bathroom when Shirlee yelled, "It's time. It's time. Call Dr. Belson. Get me to Beth Israel Hospital. Fast."

Since we had done a lot of reading, I knew that when she began having contractions, they would soon subside and we would have ample time to telephone Dr. Belson, calmly get his advice, and follow it. We were prepared. Everything was ready. So I said, "Okay," and kept shaving, my adrenaline pumping a little faster.

Shirlee's voice became shrill. She yelled, "I've GOT to go to Beth Israel NOW. My water broke."

Running from the bathroom, I saw Shirlee with a blanket around her waist, standing at the door to our apartment, her prepacked suitcase in hand. There was a huge puddle of water on the kitchen floor.

I zipped across town to Beth Israel in zero time and, with Shirlee sitting on the front seat of the car, rushed into the emergency entrance, yelling for Dr. Belson, announcing to everyone that my wife's water had broken and that the baby was coming—in the car. A nurse calmly told me to bring my wife inside and have her take a seat and cross her legs until Dr. Belson arrived. I was apoplectic with disbelief. Nobody moved to help us.

While getting Shirlee seated, Dr. Belson arrived from nowhere, smiling brightly. "It's time, I assume?" he asked.

I was feeling woozy and perspiring everywhere. I was nervous. I could only shake my head.

An aide put Shirlee in a wheelchair and disappeared. Dr. Belson ushered me to a waiting room and suggested I read a good book.

Hours later, Dr. Belson returned, told me that the baby was not moving down the canal as it should, and asked my permission for a routine cesarean section procedure. Whatever questions I asked, I think he answered. I approved and signed. For the first time, I was afraid. It never occurred to me that something might go wrong.

Within an hour, the doctor returned, beaming. He congratulated me on the birth of my beautiful daughter and invited me to follow him to see Shirlee and the baby. I could barely walk and was still sweating from head to toe.

Shirlee was groggy but smiling. In her arms was the most beautiful baby I'd ever seen. She had big round cheeks, bright eyes, tiny fingers, and peach fuzz for hair. She curled her hand around my extended finger and held on tightly. She opened her little mouth and cried like hell. Shirlee and I hugged and beamed. As soon as I collected my wits, I ran to the nearest telephone and called Reverend and Mrs. Taylor, then Ma.

"Can you believe we have a beautiful, beautiful daughter who looks like a real doll with no hair?" I asked proudly. I could hardly believe it myself.

CHAPTER 6

Wading in the Water

𝒮HIRLEE: In those days, they kept you in the hospital for a week after a cesarean. Unless you asked, the medical staff told you very little. On the fourth day, I began to feel human again. I could enjoy our new daughter.

Everyone in the maternity ward was still talking about the March on Washington and King's "I Have a Dream" speech. It did not surprise me that a speech that would become as memorable as the Gettysburg Address had come from a Baptist minister. From my father, from Dr. King's father, and from his colleagues, I had been hearing such powerful messages all my life.

I was glowing about that *and* our new baby. Maybe the moral suasion of the preacher from Atlanta would do for America what Gandhi had done for India. Everything was about to change, I thought. The things I had been taught to believe about America would finally be true. How lucky Deirdre was to be born on the cusp of these wondrous new times in a land we could truly call "our" country without wincing at the word "our." In an almost rhapsodic afterglow of goodwill, I left the hospital.

My father came to retrieve my mother and meet his grandchild. In the new Boston rocker Harold had bought me, my father sat and rocked a fussy baby, singing her to sleep in a high, clear voice. It was a song he had sung many times in concert:

> Over in Killarney
> Many years ago
> My mother sang
> This song to me
> In tones so sweet
> and low,
> Tura, lura, lura
> Tura, lura, ly
> Tura, lura, lura
> It's an Irish lullabye.

My parents bought their granddaughter a handsome navy English pram. In one of New England's most beautiful Indian summers, I walked Deirdre through Harvard Square and up Massachusetts Avenue. We passed grand museums, small bookshops, excited students.

Sometimes we strolled up Garden Street or over to Brattle Street to gaze at the great houses and beautiful gardens in the neighborhood where George Washington had his headquarters and Henry Wadsworth Longfellow created his poems. What a civilized place Cambridge was. So far from the turmoil of the rest of the world. I was torn over whether I wanted to be there or with the Freedom Riders in the South. The protectionism of motherhood won out.

Mothering came naturally to me. Nothing seemed mysterious, forced. What I didn't know, I asked my mother; or I read Dr. Spock or talked to other friends who had young children. The only thing I had not realized was the full-time nature of the job. With my mother in attendance, I was luckier than she had been.

I suppose all parents want the same things for their children. I wanted to protect this child of mine, to keep her close, warm, and safe. I wanted her to know that she had two parents and a larger family that would love and cherish her no matter what. I wanted her to have a life even better than mine had been. One that would be completely free of racism.

We had been home for a week. Routines revolving around the baby were taking hold. My mother reigned. Within a day of my mother's arrival at our apartment, we cried. It was the Sunday morning a bomb had blown four little Sunday school girls to angel dust in Birmingham.

Sweet Deirdre, child, where could we go to be safe?

From the beginning, I never saw Deirdre as an extension of myself. I appreciated her as a separate and distinct little person. She started out auspiciously. She was a good baby, sleeping well and not fussy about foods.

Fatherhood cloaked Harold in patience and wonder. His entire mien changed when he cradled Deirdre in his large hands. He was anxious to do everything right, to be a good father. He doted. He cheerfully got up at night and in the early morning to do the requisite feedings. I think he looked forward to those silent times in the deep black velvet of night to be close to and cuddle this child, this daughter.

Three months after Deirdre's birth, we were preparing to go to Connecticut for her christening. The bulletin flashed on as I was putting clothes in a suitcase. The words knocked the breath out of me. My joints loosened. I felt as if I would fall. "This must be a panic attack," I thought. Panting, I held on to the side of the bed. An assassin had killed President Kennedy in Dallas.

I picked up my sleeping child and the telephone at the same time. The circuits burbled and buzzed and hummed. All lines were busy. Harold did not call. Finally I got through to my parents. Should we postpone the christening? My father sounded as if he had been crying. He said we would go ahead with the plans.

I kept packing and repacking the same things. I could not cry. The last time a president had died dramatically I was a little girl.

When Harold and I finally arrived in New Haven, joy did not meet us at the door. Television became the focus of the weekend. The house was full of relatives and friends all watching grayish-white images coming from Dallas and Washington. No one felt like talking, eating, gossiping, or even fussing over the baby.

Christening Day at Macedonia was not festive. Woefulness prevailed. The church was full. Sorrow squeezed in everywhere beside sinner and saved. Most of those who had been present at my wedding would bear witness to the baptism of my first child. My father presided. He offered blessings of joy for his grandchild and her parents. For the fatherless children and their mother in Washington, there were prayers of sorrow and promises of relief from pain.

He recalled Kennedy as he saw him on his last visit to Connecticut: ". . . a young man, full of vigor and the joy of living; a son who honored his parents; a husband beloved by his wife; a father who loved his children; a brother, close knit to his family; a friend whom to know was to treasure and trust . . ."

On our way out of church after the christening, we heard that Kennedy's accused assassin had been shot. The good Christians on the church steps spoke out, "Good, they got him." I didn't know what to feel.

Out of the blue, early that December of 1963, the head of the sociology department at Tufts University called with an invitation. The offer, a teaching fellowship and a spot in the department's Ph.D. program, would begin midterm. Medford, where the campus is located, was just a quick bus ride away.

To take care of the four-month-old Deirdre, I hired a young woman with a five-year-old child of her own. Guilt hovered in the background, as I laid out my child's needs to a woman who had to leave her own child for mine. I tried to make it up to her, letting her leave early, buying her daughter gifts. But the guilt did not go away. As much as I wanted to, I knew I did not have the power to rectify the situation. All I could offer were fair wages, compassion, and empathy. I gave all three.

The night before I was to begin, I lay in bed, my mind whirling like a carousel. I ran through a litany of supposes. Suppose they asked me a question I didn't know? Suppose some of them knew more than I did? Suppose they saw me as lacking in authority? I shook Harold awake and asked him what to do in each case. "Look," he said, "you know more than they do. That's why you were hired."

On my first teaching day I felt as if I were giving a carefully scripted and choreographed performance. After what seemed like just a few minutes, the bell rang. I finally exhaled. Harold had been right, again.

Teaching was a blast. The students and I loved each other. Something I had never thought of doing was turning out to be a bright spot in my life.

On another score, I was not so sure. Not a day went by when I didn't wonder if working was the best choice for Dee Dee and for me. But she seemed to be thriving under her babysitter's care. She was healthy and accident free. She welcomed her sitter each morning as much as she welcomed me home in the afternoons. The part-time nature of my job allowed me to have considerable time with her. Each day I could still guide her carriage to our favorite haunts. It was, I decided, a good situation.

That summer, the letter of my acceptance came from the Harvard School of Design. Harold said, Go, by all means go.

We broke into preassigned teams for each project. My teammate, an intense young bachelor with dark hair, wondered why I was putting on weight. When I told him I was pregnant, he stared at me, mouth agape. He thought I was getting fat around the middle from spending too much time in Harvard's various libraries.

This time, the doctor told me when our second child would be born. The rule then was once a cesarean, always a cesarean. I would be permitted to take my final exams late, to allow for the birth of the baby.

This time, birth demons did not lurk in the shadows. I knew what to expect. Melissa Morris Haizlip was born, looking like a deeply colored anemone. We gave her my middle name, the name of my mother's missing family. We would not know what an irony that would be until thirty years later.

At first, Missy was a fussy infant, waking up at night more often than most. She would not go back to sleep until I cradled her and sang a song. Sometimes I was so tired I didn't want to do it. But I always did. I sang every song I knew, show tunes, spirituals, pop, blues, ballads. Her favorite was one that I had heard my father sing often at that time of day when the blue sky becomes the purple evening:

Sweetest little baby
Everybody knows
Don't know what
To call her but
She's mighty
Lak a rose

We added a jump seat to the pram, and Missy's first views of Cambridge's sky and Harvard's trees were partially obscured by her sister's back and head.

Caring for two babies eighteen months apart was no easy feat. Both were in diapers. Both needed constant supervision. I was exhausted all the time. I asked my mother when I would get enough sleep again. Her answer: "Not until they are in college."

A few weeks after Missy's birth—April 30, 1965—Harold received his Ph.D. in educational administration and job offers at the University of Chicago Laboratory School and Xerox in New York City, and I handed in my final exams for my term at Harvard. We had time to weigh the choices while luxuriating in a Pillsbury heiress's mansion near the Lake of the Isles in Minnesota. Harold was teaching a summer session at the University of Minnesota.

We had acquired our summer home through Jewelle, who had moved to Minnesota to take a job at the Pillsbury Corporation. Jim had taken a teaching position with the university. Unfortunately, Jewelle and Jim moved on, first to Liberia for a year and then to Stanford as we arrived in Minneapolis.

After living in that large house for two months, I knew I had been spoiled for life. We padded around in spacious bedroom suites, formal living and dining rooms, a solarium, library. There were multiple fireplaces, wainscoting, leaded windows, all in quiet good taste, rich taste. I could never be satisfied with uninteresting, cramped surroundings. Space, and plenty of it, is the main difference in the way the rich and the poor live.

Our hearts and minds were leaning toward New York City. A stay in a kingly suite at the Pierre Hotel—sans children—helped make the decision. After the bellboy left the room, Harold and I took off our shoes and jumped up and down on the featherbed like bad children. We could not believe our grown-up good fortune.

As I thought about leaving Cambridge and Boston, I knew that Harold and I had grown together in ways that would sustain the move. Our marriage had gelled. Faith and trust in each other had become integral parts of our marriage. I knew that I could rely on him and that in the great unknown of New York City he would keep me safe. I also knew that I wanted him to have the best job he could find, although sometimes I wished he had the freedom to explore as many career paths as he made it possible for me to do.

It didn't bother me that I had no compelling "calling." There was no doubt in my mind that I would once again discover something special. Besides, there were the girls. They needed me. Having the experience of a mother always at home, I didn't want someone else to raise my children. Yet I knew that I wanted and also needed a life of my own.

It's true I was not helping the poor, uplifting the race, or solving the other problems of the world. But even though I was a young mother, I was still growing, still finding myself. The collection of events I called living mattered then only to me, my family, and a few close friends. I loved my life then; it was lighter than air, brighter than the sun. It was still unexplored terrain.

HAROLD: When I began working at A.B.C.D. in the early sixties, the management team was white except for a Negro woman, one other Negro man, and me. No one talked openly about a race problem. It was understood that whites had problems with Negroes and kept them at a distance in jobs, housing, schools, personal relationships, clubs, churches, and marriage. And Negroes understood that many of their problems were, in fact, perpetuated by whites.

In public discourse, this known reality was a nonissue. Under the bemused and sometimes restraining influence of the Boston Brahmins, the Irish inherited and ran the city for their own benefit, with the unspoken divine right, blessings, and power of the Catholic Church, which claimed many of the city's business and political leaders as members. As the Italian population grew in both number and political sophistication, they further extended the reach and influence of the Catholic Church, since most Italians also were Catholic. On the other hand, the majority of churchgoing Negroes attended Protestant churches. On Sunday mornings, worshiping with one's own kind was a given.

We didn't discuss race, or religion, or their confluence at A.B.C.D. Our euphemism was "disadvantaged." Through our research and analysis, we documented correlations between low income, no income, and/or poverty, on the one hand, and all other categories of social problems, on the other: unemployability and unemployment; family instability; unwed motherhood and single-parent families; welfare dependency; school underachievement; the dropout problem; gangs and juvenile delinquency; and substandard housing. While it was obvious that a majority of the poor were Negroes, white people's negativity toward their African slave heritage was not cited as contributing to their condition.

To the concept of America as the Land of Opportunity we added the phrase "if you are not poor" or "if you can overcome your poverty." But from my own life, my own experiences as a Negro child and young man, and from my evolving Negro adult perspective, I knew that race and racism also were powerful, causal factors in the undermining or, all too frequently, downfall of a majority of Negroes.

I convinced myself that in the big game of long-term human engineering and social justice, I was in fact no more than a warm-up act being paid well to promote poverty as a socially systemic disease needing the treatments I espoused. Someone else, I thought, would soon enter the ring and promote race and racism as the main event. I knew for a fact that whites held power over Negroes in Boston at the time: power to terminate employment without a trace; power to deny or cancel mortgages; power to deny employment despite qualifications; power to provide or withdraw welfare benefits.

Among people with whom I worked, both Negroes and whites were keenly aware of and fearful of this power. My greatest challenge in getting white administrators and teachers to endorse or work with A.B.C.D. programs was overcoming their terror at the possibility of retaliation from the top in the form of denied promotions, denied tenure, reassignment to the boonies, or job elimination. The system could turn against anyone at will.

Louise Day Hicks, chair of the all-white Boston School Committee, had achieved national and local infamy as an avowed racist reelected by huge margins to protect "our innocent little [white] children in our safe [all white] schools from the organized, destructive onslaught of unqualified Negroes" demanding school integration. Her oft-repeated slogan, "You know where I stand," was backed by a solid majority on the School Committee and evoked images of a female Governor George Wallace defying at once the National Guard, the U.S. Attorney General, and the president of the United States.

Her gofer, the handpicked superintendent of schools, was a tired, career-service former gym teacher and football coach eager to please the School Committee and protect his substantial salary and pension until he could retire. A benign and not too bright racist, he appointed himself as the collaborator/partner to implement with me the innovative A.B.C.D. education agenda I was developing for the poorest schools. He stepped deftly into this uncertain role, in his public statements always signaling to the School Committee, school administrators, teachers, and union reps that he remained allied philosophically with them and was simply accessing Ford Foundation megabucks for them by playing ball with A.B.C.D. until the money dried up.

To my ears, the drumroll for the main event began softly in the distance at the Woolworth lunch counter in Greensboro, reached a dramatic crescendo at the March on Washington, and commanded national attention when, shortly after the march, a racist's bomb took the lives of four innocent Negro girls. Our nation's primary issue quickly became race and racism.

Because our baby was due at any moment, Dr. Belson forbade Shirlee from traveling to the march. Knowing how important I felt it was to be there, Shirlee urged me to go for both of us. I wanted to do so—to reaffirm my entire life up to that point, to stand with my people, even if participating in the march subsequently cost me my job at A.B.C.D. But no scheme that I thought of allowed me to feel comfortable about Shirlee giving birth to our first child alone in Boston while I marched on Washington.

Shortly after I met Shirlee, I instinctively wanted to protect her—because in my mind that's how men respond to something/someone they cherish. My greatest worry was that I could not shield her from the ravages of racism and that, because I was much browner than she, I most likely would provoke the very racist attitudes and behavior I wanted to protect her from. Deirdre's arrival intensified this angst. When I first held her in my arms, she was so fair, beautiful, tiny, innocent, and helpless that I shuddered at the unknown fatherly challenges I would face protecting my baby daughter into adulthood.

My first challenge, I decided, was helping Shirlee welcome the new little person in our lives. We had already purchased a white wicker bassinet, so during Shirlee and Deirdre's week at Beth Israel, I bought yards of soft pink tulle, borrowed a sewing machine, and covered the bassinet with a billowy pink skirt. For Shirlee's quiet moments with Deirdre, I found a Boston rocker whose soothing rhythms would comfort their souls. I purchased the baby formula Dr. Belson recommended and signed a diaper service agreement. When it was time for mother and child to come home, I filled the entire apartment, including the bathroom, with Shirlee's favorite flowers.

Lying on her back, gurgling and drooling as her tiny hands and feet jabbed the air from her oval sea of pink tulle, Deirdre seemed as curious about me as I was about her. Her big eyes seemed to look right through me without blinking, searching for information. I wondered if she knew I was her father, if she responded to my name, if she wanted to look at the flowers. What was she trying to see?

Me? A father? Of this cute, scriggly, bald little thing? Looking at her, I saw the love that Shirlee and I had known since we met, the oneness of our spirits. I saw my dad looking at me when I was Deirdre's age and pleaded with God to let me continue to be her father long past her tenth birthday; a good father to her, every day, every year, for the rest of my life.

What an awesome task this would be. I wondered who she'd become as an adult and how I'd influence her life. I remembered how as a child I had wished I could convince Dad not to be so demanding, so seemingly unkind, and so seemingly unloving in his tone of voice—even if he meant well—to my sister, Vira. I swore that I would never treat Deirdre that way because I knew the pain lasted a lifetime. And I wondered when and how I could ensure that she would become a positive, cheerful, and accomplished woman—fortified with understanding and self-confidence to remain so—despite the racism, sexism, and second-class citizenship she would encounter. I would do everything to avoid crippling her with the emotional bruises and scars I carry from the battles I've fought, won, and lost in these wars in my own lifetime.

In the aftermath of the March on Washington, my office was somber and tense, like the awkward silence of still-grieving family and friends gathered in the living room of a loved one they've just buried. There were a lot of people, as usual, but no one was talking or moving. Imprinted in their memories forever were the sheer magnitude and power of the march. It was likely that no one would forget the sight of throngs of people—Negro and white—together in protest, and the sounds of the cadenced rhythms of Reverend Martin Luther King, Jr., echoing from the Mall to the White House to every television set around the world. Black and white co-workers looked at each other differently, as if friends had become strangers meeting for the first time across a chasm called racism, wide, deep, and treacherous.

Everyone knew that I was returning from a few days off because of the birth of our first child. Brightly wrapped baby gifts and "Harold and Shirlee" envelopes covered my desk. Numerous photographs were in my briefcase, ready for my Proud New Father routine. But nobody wandered in. Nobody called on the intercom. Boston's War on Poverty generals were reconnoitering, I supposed, to review the research and run the numbers on a new plan: to combat racism—in addition to poverty. Because my education programs engaged so many across the city, I knew that I would soon find myself at the center of a firestorm of race issues ignited by the march and Dr. King, with Louise Day Hicks circling the wagons and surveying the landscape for enemies within.

The March on Washington rescrambled the philosophical and political playing fields of my world of educational and social activism and slowly but surely launched a paradigm shift. As blacks and sympathetic whites came to see malevolent, intentional, and deeply institutionalized racism as the the root cause of a myriad of problems, the search for solutions began turning away from A.B.C.D.'s agenda.

Instead, new strategies were proposed to change the entire system. School integration began to reemerge as a means of ridding American society of all race-based barriers to equality.

I knew that this strategy would prove disastrous in Boston, where poor communities like the South End, Charlestown, and the North End were essentially ethnic encampments, each group wholly and irrationally committed to their own kind. At stake was the sanctity of their schools, elected political leaders, churches, restaurants, bars, and neighborhood boundaries. As if honoring an unspoken armed truce, outsiders—including myself—wandered gingerly through these neighborhoods during weekdays but were nowhere to be found at night, on weekends, or on Sundays, except at their own peril. There was no doubt in my mind that the idea of the federal government forcing these communities to allow Negroes to live among them and to enroll Negro children in historically white schools, and white children in historically Negro schools, would inflame and incite most ethnically centered Bostonians.

Racism, Boston's leaders would soon argue, was a southern problem, and therefore such draconian proposals as school and community integration were appropriate for the South, not the North, where places like Boston's harbor and historic Bunker Hill had established this city's reputation for all time as a welcoming home of the brave and the free. The exercise of individual rights in choosing where to live and where to send one's children to school was established in and protected by the U.S. Constitution and must not be tampered with by misguided, social activist hotheads.

The millions of dollars flowing from A.B.C.D. through the school system's central offices and into predominantly minority schools and neighborhoods—coupled with my being black—inclined Louise Day Hicks and her compatriot guardians of the status quo to suspect that I might be fanning flames of racial discord in Boston's minority communities. For more than a year, she had slowly set the stage for a direct, public attack on A.B.C.D. in general and me in particular.

After my reports at monthly school committee meetings, she invariably shouted, "Point of order! Point of order!" Rising from her seat as if weary from a noble battle not yet won, she reminded the (white) staff, (white) parents, and (white) media of her ". . . deep concern, as a School Committee member elected at large to represent ALL of the good [white] people of the great city of Boston, that A.B.C.D.'s funds and programs were not benefiting ALL of Boston's children, equally." As the applause subsided, she intoned with feigned exasperation, "You know where I stand."

Deirdre looked as cherubic as ever, but Shirlee's face was flushed and her eyes red and teary as I flung open the door of our apartment ready to offer a litany of reasons for being late and not calling ahead to explain. "Oh, hon," I began, putting my arms around both of them, "I'm really sorry. I was stuck in Melrose with the superintendent, and my time got away from me. I'm really sorry. Rather than stop at a pay phone, I rushed home as fast as I could."

"You haven't heard?"

"Heard what?" My pulse quickened. I feared an accident or injury in her family or mine.

"President Kennedy was assassinated today. In Dallas." She began sobbing again.

We had been closeted in an emergency meeting all day with strict orders not to be interrupted for any reason. "Are you serious? What happened? Who? Where were the bodyguards? What time did this happen? Where in Dallas?" Deirdre's unblinking eyes fixed first on Shirlee and then on me, trying to comprehend the excitement. I rushed toward the TV in our bedroom and sank heavily on the bed. I watched in horror, shaking my head slowly side to side, hoping I'd awaken soon from this nightmare.

In my scheme of things, I worked for President Kennedy as a foot soldier in his army. I felt I knew him. We shared similar principles and priorities. I knew that he fought the right causes, that he wanted to make a place at the table of opportunity for all Americans, that he spoke honestly about issues of race and racism. I couldn't believe that the leader I knew I would one day tell in person "what I had done for my country" was dead.

With my commander-in-chief slain in battle, my sixth sense was that Hicks would feel empowered to have a field day at my expense. If she could pull it off with impunity, she'd assassinate me herself, mid-report, at the next School Committee meeting.

Watching and listening to Lyndon Johnson take the oath of office, I decided I would have to find another job. As much as I loved and enjoyed most of my work, and although I had heard he was a liberal, I could not work on the slave plantation that flashed into my mind whenever I heard his drawl. I knew he had a reputation for being sympathetic to black issues, but his southernness inevitably touched a raw nerve in me and refreshed the ill will I harbored toward everyone who participated in and benefited from slavery in the United States. I knew it was not his fault, but I could not separate him from my bad feelings. I had to get out.

But not before finishing my doctoral research, writing my dissertation, and getting my degree from Harvard. These were my primary objectives after Johnson became president. Restructuring my time and workload to accomplish these goals, I buffered myself from Louise Day Hicks.

She remained focused in her opposition, but less on me, personally, and more on A.B.C.D., just as Boston's political winds began shifting. As our three-year funding began drying up, we had difficulty securing replacement funds from the city and state, a major commitment we had made to both the Ford Foundation and the federal government. Relationships between our Executive Director, the mayor, and several of his department heads began to sour as a result. Vigorous fund-raising efforts in the private sector fell far short of our goals. We began developing Plan B. The wind was slipping out of our sails.

Shirlee was extremely happy—but uncomfortable. We were expecting our second child at the end of April. We had been thrilled at this news because we both wanted more children. But we were concerned about the demands on Shirlee at home alone with two children in diapers. I vowed to help as much as possible and to hire help if we needed it.

We moved to a beautiful, two-story, old New England house off Brattle Street, a few blocks from the Radcliffe Commons. At the end of April, after Mrs. Taylor arrived from Connecticut to take care of Deirdre and me, we checked Shirlee into Beth Israel Hospital for Dr. Belson to deliver our new baby. By then, I was an experienced, take-charge dad.

Melissa was perfect, almost doll-like. Her big, bright eyes, round face, and plump cheeks created an appearance of innocence and curiosity. When I first picked her up, she stared quizzically at me for a long while. In a flash her mood changed and she frightened herself and us with the huge wail that erupted from her body. As if looking for the source of the noise, her eyes darted back and forth. She wrapped her tiny fingers around my hand and my heart and has been holding them tight ever since.

"I'm outnumbered," I joked.

"And very lucky," Shirlee added, "because you'll be surrounded by not one, not two, but three beautiful, adoring women for the rest of your life."

"And I'll have to wear earplugs when they become teenagers," I replied. "And I don't want to think about all the clothes we'll have to buy for two teenage girls. Let's pray they have similar taste."

At home, I tried to explain to Deirdre that she had a new sister named Melissa at the hospital with Mom. She was uninterested and unimpressed. Mrs. Taylor provided a dramatically expurgated version of the birds and bees story, to no avail. Deirdre was more interested in the fact that I had recovered *her* bassinet in white eyelet cotton and lace, placed it in our bedroom, arranged bouquets of flowers everywhere, and attached a toddler seat to the rear of her Princess Pram.

With the special honor of being a Harvard commencement marshal, and with my crimson cap, gold tassel, crimson doctoral gown billowing in the wind, and a smile from ear to ear, I proudly led the colorful procession, carrying the marshal's baton. For a few seconds I held up the entire parade when I reached my family's row, enabling Shirlee to take a few candids.

Because thousands attended the commencement exercises, tickets were scarce. I managed to barter an extra one so that Shirlee, Ma, Reverend and Mrs. Taylor, and Vira could have reserved seats and share Deirdre and Melissa among them. This was the day I had been working toward for years, the day that would give me a document, a badge, as it were, validating my ability to compete successfully with the best minds in America. This was the day I would get the prize that could heal the wounds and pain I had endured during the race.

Commencement was a blur: music, a speech, honorary doctorates, special student awards, conferral of the degrees, and the recession into the arms, tears, and cheers of family and friends. Despite being barely out of the maternity ward, Shirlee hosted a celebration for family and friends in the garden of our new house. Ma's tears flowed intermittently all evening. Shirlee had paid her own high price, however, by deferring her dreams of a professional career to raise our infant children and help finance the last leg of my doctoral studies.

That summer, in Minneapolis, I thought my job offers over carefully. The University of Chicago Lab School is a venerable institution. I'd been asked to be headmaster—a wonderful leadership opportunity for any educator. But after talking privately with current and former Lab School administrators, faculty members, students, and parents, as well as with the president and education professors at the university and Harvard friends in the Chicago area, I came to view the headmaster's position as being similar to the head of Hydra. The competing demands of administering the school as the private education preserve of the children of the university family; as the laboratory for the varied research interests of university faculty members who must publish or perish; and as a traditional institution with obligations to students and parents made this an almost impossible job. Moreover, it was purely administrative: to keep the parts of the machine in sync. A job limiting me primarily to maintenance of the status quo was not for me.

By any measure, the Xerox job, where I had some history, was better. While in graduate school, I had taken several educational psychology courses on behavior modification with behavioral psychologist B. F. Skinner. I became fascinated with the possible applications of conditioning and teaching machines to the improvement of teaching and learning in elementary and secondary schools, and in any other environment where learning took place.

Several students in Professor Skinner's classes worked part-time for Basic Systems, Inc., a new business venture in Harvard Square created by J. Sterling Livingstone, a Harvard Business School professor. His goal was to develop innovative commercial applications of Skinner's theories. I accepted the offer of part-time work as a member of the team developing a self-instructional program that would, in record time, teach all employees of Volkswagen of America, Inc., to build a new Volkswagen from parts and thereby become the best Volkswagen repairmen on the planet. My bartending days were over.

While working for A.B.C.D., I moonlighted at Basic Systems as often as I could, more for the intellectual challenge than for the money, although the money was important. The success of our Volkswagen project attracted a contract with the U.S. Department of Defense. J. Sterling then sold Basic Systems to Xerox Corporation, which viewed the brainpower and creativity of the Basic Systems staff as a great asset for the new Education Division it was establishing. As Basic Systems folded into the Xerox Education Division, my Basic Systems colleagues convinced Xerox to recruit me away from A.B.C.D. for a senior position to legitimate the corporation in the education community and help identify and define business opportunities in this field.

The corporation felt that schools represented a potentially huge market for the newly emerging technology of xerography and wanted to explore ways of assisting public education. In addition to my Basic Systems colleagues, on the payroll of the new Xerox Education Division was an array of bright and experienced educational specialists. To complete this group and provide direct access to school systems and school leaders, plus know-how in resource development through foundations, government agencies, and private funders, they needed a person with my background. Because I welcomed the prospect of working with so many gifted, socially conscious people and envisioned the power of directing tremendous corporate resources to seemingly intractable problems in education, I signed on.

I anticipated that I would learn a great deal about corporate America and make valuable business connections that could only enhance my career potential in the years ahead. Most education leaders had no hands-on, real-world experience in business. Equally important, Xerox offered me more money, security, and perks than did the Lab School.

With some trepidation but much excitement, we left the environs of the colleges, universities, and communities that had become so integral to our lives. We left the nest we had created for ourselves. We had each other and the girls and confidence that we could make a place for ourselves in the biggest city in the world.

———

Under any circumstances, finding an apartment in New York City was a tremendous challenge. Finding one in Manhattan (we had decided not to live in Brooklyn, Queens, or New Jersey) with the space we needed, in a price range and neighborhood we could afford, was exponentially more difficult.

After looking at scores of apartments, I found one on West End Avenue at Eightieth Street that I liked. The tenant, a blacklisted Hollywood screenwriter leaving for Paris, wanted to sublease the apartment for a year, immediately.

I told the screenwriter that I knew my wife would like the apartment and that we would take it but that I wanted her to see it before signing the lease. I asked him to telephone the building manager and arrange an appointment for me the following day. The building manager readily complied. At the appointed time, I arrived dressed to impress in one of my new Madison Avenue suits. Before I could identify myself, the building manager told me there were no vacancies and proceeded to close the door to his office, saying he had an important appointment with a tenant.

"I'm the new tenant you're waiting for," I said, standing in the doorway so he could not close his office door. "I'm Dr. Haizlip. We have an appointment now regarding Apartment 11A."

"You're Dr. Haizlip?" he asked, looking incredulous and uncomfortable. "Well," he said, "you're an hour too late. I've already rented the apartment and don't have any additional vacancies. A couple who saw the apartment last week came back earlier today and gave me a deposit, so it's been taken."

I reminded him that as of the preceding afternoon, when the current tenant telephoned him and set my appointment, there were no other persons ready to sign a sublease and that, based on the telephone conversation, I had come to our meeting, on time, prepared to sign the sublease agreement and pay the necessary fees.

"That was a mistake," he said. "The apartment has been taken."

"If I don't lease this apartment, nobody else will," I said angrily. "You'll hear from me tomorrow. You're fooling with the wrong person." I held my tongue before adding, "Racist bastard."

Grabbing a cab, I went directly to my new boss's office, walked in without an appointment, and demanded to see him immediately. He was gracious but uncomfortable as I defied all protocols. As calmly as possible, I reminded him that in accepting the job for which he had recruited me so eagerly, I had given up my house in Cambridge and located an apartment in Manhattan after a concentrated effort and that, as he and I had agreed, I was ready to settle in and begin working within two weeks. I told him that I had encountered a problem most likely unfamiliar to him but all too familiar to me: housing discrimination by a white landlord and building manager. "My wife and I have decided that we want to live in Apartment 11A at 420 West End Avenue. We are not willing to consider other apartments."

Writing down the name, telephone number, and address of the building manager and the tenant, I told him that I was returning immediately to New Haven and would come back to Manhattan after Xerox's lawyers had resolved this problem. Not waiting for his response, I thanked him for seeing me and left for New Haven.

The following day, a corporate attorney telephoned to say that they were handling the problem immediately and would contact me within a few days. They sent a white couple to inquire about the apartment as testers, and the building manager not only had shown them the apartment but was eager to have them sign a sublease immediately. It was an airtight case, and they were sure of a successful outcome. They wanted to know if we knew any of the tenants or other prominent people in the neighborhood who could be called upon to pressure the manager to offer us a lease immediately rather than engage in litigation.

We recommended Judge Constance Baker Motley, a friend of the Taylors. She knew James Wechsler, the well-known columnist for the *New York Post* who lived on one of the lower floors in the building. Wechsler made some not too discreet inquiries, signaling a piece in the *Post,* and Judge Motley made a few well-placed phone calls. The Xerox attorneys then served the manager with notice of litigation and a trial date.

In less than a week, the attorneys arranged an appointment for me to meet with the manager to sign the lease and pay my fees.

We moved into our apartment the following week and lived there for more than five years. The building manager never acknowledged any difficulties in our securing a lease. And after we moved out years later, he came to visit us, unannounced, in the Virgin Islands. I took his call but did not oblige him with the tour he requested of St. Thomas.

CHAPTER 7

❧

Regards to Broadway

*S*HIRLEE: We quickly made friends and babysitting arrangements with many of the young couples who lived in our building.

A redheaded pre-Raphaelite–looking young woman, Bunny Dell, became my close companion. She was a high school art teacher who had moved from Los Angeles to New York, looking for a job. Her husband Jeff, a filmmaker, shot a film in Riverside Park about children and racial attitudes. For actors he used his daughter and Dee Dee. He intercut their playing in a wooden playhouse with scenes of dogs attacking civil rights protesters in the South. The piece won best short at the Montreal Expo World's Fair of 1967.

Our avocado green treasures and brown teak went into basement storage. Our new apartment took on aspects of a European salon though we had never been to Europe. All that we knew was we favored an eclectic look, mixing styles, periods, and fabrics; a far cry from our first apartment, but not at all a long way from what we were confident we would someday have.

We brightened up a dark dining room by lining its walls with a collection of mirrors we had found in Maine and Vermont. At auction at Parke Bernet we made the winning bid on an oak refectory table that had belonged to Helena Rubinstein. We installed it in the dining room.

147

The tenant-writer left behind a number of beautiful pieces of furniture, including a daffodil-yellow silk sofa. We filled up the living room with favorite things, found a nook for our Bechstein piano, and began to call New York City our home.

Sometimes in New England I felt like a bird of paradise trying to camouflage myself as a little brown sparrow. The dowdiness quotient of Boston and Cambridge was a good-natured fact of life. It had no relevance to the mathematics of New York appearances. In the sixties, New York women wanted to look good all the time. They chased after Twiggy's eyes, Vidal's hair, Susie Parker's lips, and Pucci's dresses. To be fashionable was to be in.

In my first months in New York, I was reluctant to go around the corner to Zabar's without eye makeup. I purchased false eyelashes. The first time I wore them, Harold kept squinting at me as if to get my face in focus. Finally, in a crowded elevator, he blurted, "Shirlee, your eyelashes are on upside down. They look like fringes of a lampshade curling inward toward the lightbulb."

In due time I came to my senses. Zabar's and the rest of my neighborhood saw me with a washed face and whatever I could manage to throw on.

One of the first to welcome us to New York was Ellis. We had not seen him since our engagement party. Wearing an oatmeal-colored linen suit, a cream-colored silk shirt, handsome loafers, and no socks, he showed up one day, armed with an enormous bouquet, the latest gossip, and a list of the people we should meet, the places we should go, and the things we must do. From that time on, the three of us became inseparable. He reveled in his new role as our daughters' enchanted and enchanting "Uncle Ellis."

Slender, dark, and owlish-looking, Ellis spoke with a nonidentifiable accent. Some thought it was British, others, Caribbean. Still others said it was southern, gothic. Educated at Howard and Yale, Ellis had an uncanny knack for spotting new talent and understanding trends. He had been busy since we had last seen him. Producing Off-Broadway plays, taking James Baldwin's plays to Europe. Producing and managing European dance tours for Donnie McKayle's

ABOVE: Nellie and Allen Haizlip,
Washington, D.C., circa 1942.

RIGHT: Shirlee at six.

BELOW: Harold at twelve.

ABOVE: Margaret and Julian
Taylor in the parsonage,
Ansonia, Connecticut,
circa 1942 *(DeWitt Keith, Jr.)*.

BELOW: Harold at seventeen.

ABOVE: Shirlee at seventeen.

RIGHT: Shirlee and Harold's engagement photo, 1958 (*DeWitt Keith, Jr.*).

BELOW: Shirlee graduating from Wellesley "as a Taylor," 1959. Left to right, Jewelle, Julian, Shirlee, Margaret.

ABOVE: Shirlee at twenty, "the Wellesley Wonder."

BELOW: Harold translating Homer at Amherst.

CLOCKWISE FROM TOP LEFT:
Shirlee, the bride, with, left to
right, Pattee, Margaret, and
Jewelle Taylor, June 1959 *(Edwin
Hardy, Jr.)*; Margaret, mother
of the bride, with son-in-law
Dr. James Lowell Gibbs, Jr.
(Edwin Hardy, Jr.); bride and
groom at the country inn;
Rev. Taylor, father of the bride,
conducting the rites in Yale's
Dwight Chapel *(Edwin Hardy, Jr.)*.

ABOVE, CLOCKWISE FROM TOP LEFT: Harold with his first-born in Cambridge, 1963;
Shirlee with Dee Dee in their Cambridge yard, 1964; Harold with Missy, 1969 *(Hella Hammid)*;
Ellis Haizlip beguiling Missy and Dee Dee in New York, 1968.

BELOW: The Haizlips enjoying spring in Central Park, New York, 1969 *(Hella Hammid)*.

ABOVE: As mystical beings in 1976 Carnival on St. Thomas.

RIGHT: Conferring as co-chairs of Natural History Museum event, 1969.

BELOW: Señor and Señora Haizlip, Carnival, 1977.

ABOVE: Shirlee posing at disco Arthur for *Ebony*'s 1967 Best Dressed List (*Moneta Sleet*).

BELOW: Shirlee as a television journalist with England's Prince Philip on Tortola.

RIGHT: Nellie and
Vira at home in
Washington, D.C.

BELOW, TOP:
Shirlee at WNET
with James Baldwin,
Toni Morrison,
and Howard
Rollins, 1984.

BELOW, BOTTOM:
Deirdre (center
first row) as a Yale
cheerleader, 1985.

ABOVE: On the stairs of our
"haunted house," St. Thomas,
1974 (Stevenson Photos).

BELOW: Melissa with Baryshnikov for Gershwin television
special taped at the Brooklyn
Academy of Music, 1987.

CLOCKWISE FROM TOP: After winning *Glamour* magazine's Best Mom Contest, Shirlee and Deirdre at home in the garden, Los Angeles, 1993 *(Blake Little)*; The Haizlips return to St. John for a nephew's wedding, 1995; Melissa starring as Josephine Baker in *The Dark Star of Harlem*, La Mama Theater, 1990; Shirlee with her "new" cousin, Carol Battles, from Shirlee's "lost" family, Ohio, 1995; Deirdre receiving her law degree from Fordham Law School, 1990.

Harold and Shirlee after the rain on their twenty-fifth anniversary, 1984.

troupe. Establishing himself as the black Sol Hurok.

He was able to introduce us to the delights of the demimonde and of haute couture. Among his friends were performers, artists, socialites, hangers-on, producers, and financiers. He treated all equally to his outrageous view of the world and wickedly funny sense of humor. His circle included James Baldwin and Maya Angelou. Nikki Giovanni was a protégée. On any given night he might show up at our apartment for coffee or oatmeal with Judith Jamison or Melba Moore in tow. Sometimes he would take us and a group of twenty or so out to dance at the disco Aux Puces uptown or to eat sweet potato pie at the Pink Teacup downtown.

He turned over to us his highly valued Monday night season tickets to the Metropolitan Opera because he had become bored with the Met. He did the same thing with his New York City Ballet subscription. Eurocentric art forms were passé, he told us. It was the first time anyone I knew used the word "Eurocentric." I barely knew what it meant. I thought *he* was being eccentric. Instead he wanted to devote a block of time to the development of a new dance troupe run by an old pal, Alvin Ailey.

Harold continued to travel, almost every week. His main route was between New York and Huntington, West Virginia. I hated the fact that he was away so often. Nonetheless, it never crossed my mind to look for the romantic company of other men. Harold was my partner. I just wanted him home more. Mostly I resented having to be the primary parent. I believed taking care of children was a two-parent job. It was up to each parent to find a way to participate equally. Harold, I thought, was out furthering his career, having a good time while doing so. I was homebound with two toddlers. It wasn't fair and I wasn't quiet about my dissatisfaction. He kept saying it would get better.

Ellis and his friends came to my rescue. He introduced me to the subculture of homosexual life in New York. At that time, he was one of its centers. Hip, charming, and well turned out, Ellis and his coterie escorted me around town. They babysat for the girls and took them to Riverside Park. Ellis saw to it that I went to the Viennese Opera Ball with a gay descendant of an Austrian count and to the Off-Broadway introduction of a new actor, Al Pacino, in *Does a Tiger Wear a Necktie?*

Sometimes, late at night, sitting in the girls' small blue chairs in the tall white kitchen, Ellis and I would gorge ourselves on oatmeal and cream talking about what it meant to be black and female or black and gay.

Among the men who ferried me around town was Maurice Noel, a blue-eyed blonde from Iowa. Maurice was a recreation supervisor by day and a playwright by night. In a broad midwestern accent, he called me "Hon." Quiet and soft-spoken, he had a way of covering his mouth and widening his eyes when he said something devilish, as if to block the words. Poetically handsome, he kept a trunk of women's dresses and shoes for his special parties, which I heard about but was never invited to. Sometimes he consulted me about what to wear.

Richard Palan was Maurice's best friend. Richard was as dark as Maurice was light. Black hair, dark eyes, and elegant hands made him look like a character out of an Oscar Wilde play. He had a wide smile, like Dr. Seuss's Cat in the Hat. He designed costumes for the Metropolitan Opera. His side business was creating angels and animal dolls, which he dressed in the opulent scraps from his costumes. Another business was designing extravagant costume jewelry that he sold to Bergdorf Goodman and Neiman Marcus.

Whenever I talked with Richard, he said he had to rush back to the ladies who were working with beads in his kitchen. He never made much money on his beautiful designs because they were so labor intensive. To charge what they were worth would have made them unrealistic for the market.

Joe Dennis, a producer and jack-of-all-trades, had them all beat when it came to looks. Sort of a black Cary Grant. Tall, sophisticated, with planes on his face like those of Marvin Gaye, Joe made all the ladies swoon. I loved being on his well-dressed arm. Female heads actually swiveled on their necks when he walked by. Men smiled at him as they passed.

Joe designed a voluptuous small apartment on West End Avenue. African, batik, and Indian patterns created a mélange of cultures in his sensuous space. He jammed art and artifacts collected in his travels against tapestried walls, elephant tables, and Persian rugs. His apartment was like a Middle Eastern souk. Ever-burning incense sealed the illusion.

Tony Rhone came around often. A gray-eyed Billy Eckstine look-alike, Tony worked at WNET television as a production aide. Ellis got him the job. Small and limber, Tony was best for gossip and dancing. He knew all the latest steps. He told me what I should wear and what I should throw out of my closet. His impish behavior garnered continual attention.

Another fashion advisor was Bernard Johnson, whose theatricality was outrageous, "beyond the beyonds." Every gesture, every word was designed for maximum effect, even if the audience was only one person. He had had a varied career, including acting, dancing, choreography, teaching, and dress design. His pants for dancers were some of the most coveted on Broadway. Sometimes Bernard would loan me an extravagant item he had designed for one Broadway diva or another. Once, a completely transparent blue chiffon tunic and pants. I had to be ingenious to figure out how to wear it. Another time, a forest-green knit pants dress trimmed in blue and green bugle beads. He said he made it for Leslie Uggams. With his hand on his hip and his chin jutting out, he'd say, "Now you know I have to have it back in a week, because Miss Thing will be looking for it."

It was lovely to have a group of flattering, handsome men with whom I could discuss the latest fashions, movies, plays, and exhibits, all with Harold's blessing. Men who were like my sisters. We never discussed their sexuality, nor did they discuss mine. At least not in my presence. The time had not yet come when we could do that with freedom and comfort. But we adored each other, and I had a wonderfully eccentric extended family upon whom I could rely for emotional, spiritual, and just being there support.

Except for Ellis, for most of them there was a common denominator: the absence of demonstrated family love in their lives. Ellis and his friends taught me a lot about generosity. They gave of their time, their money, their knowledge, and their skills. More important, they deepened my kindness quotient and helped me enjoy my children more.

Toddlerhood in our household was marked by the discovery that Missy was prone to asthma and allergy. We learned the hard way. Nuts caused her eyes to swell and her trachea to close. A visit to Lenox

Hill's emergency room brought her back to normal. A winter cold returned her to the hospital when once again she could not breathe. This time she went under an oxygen tent. I was afraid. "Standard operating procedure," the pediatrician said. "You can do this yourself at home. Anytime she has breathing problems, take her into the shower and the steam will open up her lungs." Many times I sat on the edge of the bathtub, shower running full blast, singing away her discomfort and my fears.

Riverside Park was our main hangout. Young mothers from my building clustered together, exchanging homey advice and unfulfilled dreams. One day, Dee Dee was playing near the swings and Missy was in the sandbox, building a structure with an older boy. My neighbor Bunny and I were comparing notes, mostly about the civil rights movement. This is what we talked about more than anything else.

Dee Dee came up to me and said quietly, "Mommy, a little boy is choking Missy behind those bushes." The bushes were twenty feet away and within my eyesight. I ran over and saw the six-year-old boy from the sandbox squeezing two-year-old Missy's neck. His hands could not quite close around her throat. It took all of my willpower not to smack or beat that boy. Instead, I gathered up the crying Missy, grabbed the boy by his elbow, and told him to take me to his mother.

I had seen her often in the park. She did not live in our building. My voice was shaking in rage as I told her what had happened. She looked at me with wide, frightened eyes. Then she took her son and talked quietly to him as they walked out of the park. They returned the next day, but the mothers in my group gave them a wide berth.

The incident left me feeling guilty. Was I for just a few moments a bad mother? I convinced myself that I was not bad—inattentive for a few seconds, perhaps. A few seconds too long. I resolved to be more vigilant. I made the spot behind the bushes off-limits to both girls.

I sought out other black children in Riverside Park. In our area, I could find only one. She was a pretty little girl between the ages of Missy and Dee Dee. She was shy, serious, with lovely manners and beautiful clothes. Her name was Sumayah. The girls played easily together. I struck up a friendship with her mother, Sharifah, a gorgeous woman who lived on Riverside Drive. Her last name, Jamal, was Islamic. She and her husband were practicing Muslims. The first Black Muslims I would meet.

A few weeks later, she introduced Harold and me to her husband, Ahmad, a jazz pianist. Ahmad was small, dapper, and handsome. I was struck by the beautiful shoes he wore on his small feet. His private persona was charming and warm. We became lifelong friends.

Across the street from our building was Calhoun, a small private school. Although both of us had done well and believed in public schools, there were no public nursery schools then. We knew at some point that we would make sure our children had a significant period of time in good public schools. But now we were dealing with a three-year-old and a highly touted school right across the street. The location was too good to be true.

So few blacks applied to or could afford to go to private schools that there was no fight to gain admission. In fact, our child was greatly sought after. We visited the school and decided to enroll Dee Dee in its nursery program. She did not scream or cry when I left her during that first week, but she looked anxious as I waved and went out the door. It was a look that said, "Please make sure you come back."

Dee Dee was the only black child in the class. To remedy that, my black friends and I planned joint outings for our children. We ferried them back and forth to each other's houses, from Harlem to Greenwich Village, from Teaneck, New Jersey, to Mount Vernon. We wanted them to have balanced lives.

So much of New York is a gigantic, dazzling playground for children. Beautiful days found us at the carousel and zoo at Central Park, the Museum of Natural History. We never knew what or who we would see when we went around the corner to Broadway. From there we would stroll down to Lincoln Center and sit in the sunlit plaza, feeling the cool spray of the giant fountain.

Sometimes we visited our friend Richie Havens, an upcoming folksinger. Bushy-haired and lean, Richie lived on a boat at the Seventy-second Street Boat Basin then. Dressed in flowing tie-dyed shirts, full pants, with braceleted wrists and silver rings on every finger, Richie told the girls stories about talking to whales and swimming with porpoises. Sometimes he sang "Puff the Magic Dragon" as little wavelets from the river lulled the girls to sleep on the gently rocking boat.

The girls loved to hear me read. Except for *A Snowy Day,* there was little in their storybooks that related to their color or culture. Often I made up stories to keep them amused. I even wrote one, about a little black girl from Striver's Row in Harlem. *The Little Girl Who Lost Her Smile* was the tale of a child who woke up in a bad mood. Her mother decided to take her out for the day, to see if she could find her smile. They went to black stores, black museums, black offices, and a black doctor. On the way, they saw the varied faces of Harlem. Bob Bernstein, then the publishing chief at Random House, heard about the book at a dinner party he hosted. He asked me to send it to him. He thought it was charming, but he said there was no market for it.

One of the ways to make friends in a big city is to join a club. I belonged to two, the Links, a national black women's service organization, and Liaison, a local New York service group. My mother had been one of the founders of the New Haven Links chapter and I had become a Link in Boston, joining a chapter of women her age or older. The Links took on worthwhile projects in education, art, and culture and gave hundreds of thousands of dollars to the United Negro College Fund. Locally, they awarded college scholarships to black scholastic achievers.

Liaison was formed as an activist group concerned with child development and civil rights. Eleanor Holmes Norton, who would later become a congresswoman, and Alma Brown, the wife of future Commerce Secretary Ron Brown, were in the group. We took pride in breaking new ground. Bringing black designers to Bergdorf Goodman or children's rights forums to Harlem was our métier. The Northside Center for Child Development, the brainchild of Drs. Mamie and Kenneth Clarke, was the frequent beneficiary of our good works.

Those were dissonant times. Our lives often separated us from other black people. Although we made constant efforts to keep those ties, we pushed another agenda: integration, integration, integration. I became part of the Women's Committee of the Museum of Natural History. The committee was composed of the wives of trustees and officers of the museum. The first time the museum's president, Gardner Stout, invited us home to dinner, I felt as if I had become part of a thirties movie. They lived in a lush apartment on the East Side. Clare Stout, a tall, patrician woman, the kind some describe as "handsome," walked toward me with an athletic stride. For entertaining at home she wore an ecru satin hostess robe trimmed with mink cuffs and collar. She looked perfectly at ease in it. Gardner had on a velvet smoking jacket. I didn't think people dressed like that anymore. Harold came to the dinner in a business suit from the office, and I, a "little black dress."

Antiques, art works, and Persian rugs filled the huge apartment. Good taste, old money taste, was everywhere. A butler took our coats and served drinks. We were the only guests. The Stouts were an easy couple to know, without airs or pretension. We developed a healthy friendship. She was as politely curious about the story of our lives as we were about theirs. We saw them often, at their house and ours.

Mayor John Lindsay invited me to join his special events cadre. Special events was the unit that planned all the city's social activities for visiting dignitaries. The mayor wanted to add more "color" to those events. The group was another of New York's doorways to the lifestyles of the rich and famous. A way for the privileged who really ran things behind the scenes to entertain each other in a socially validated way.

I jumped right in, sitting next to the ladies who lunched and planned menus and protocol for royal highnesses and rich sultans. It was through this group that I dined and chatted with the queen's cousin, Princess Alexandra, who opined that Richard Palan's beaded earrings and necklace were "smashing." Royal chitchat at Gracie Mansion.

We lived our lives on so many different levels. Nights at the museum or Gracie Mansion or the Metropolitan Opera, days in the streets, protesting, chanting, "Hey, hey, LBJ, how many kids did you kill today?" No one told me then that I was strolling across the path of history.

Hair had come to Broadway and real life. Wanting to have it all ways, I bought a waist-length braid, a long fall, and the largest Afro wig I could find. Harold let his hair grow longer into a dignified Afro. For a while, he wore sideburns, which I never particularly adored.

The fashion advice from Ellis's coterie came home to roost. *Ebony* put me on its 1967 Best Dressed list. New York's black newspaper, the *Amsterdam News,* included me on its Most Elegant list. I wore my long fall and a black sequined jumpsuit from a Donnie McKayle production for the *Ebony* picture. For the newspaper, I was more conservative: a blue velvet cape and a white satin ball gown.

The *Ebony* shoot took place in Arthur, one of New York's first celebrated discos in 1967, under the watchful eye of the manager, another Ellis friend. *Ebony* photographer Moneta Sleet, who the next year would win a Pulitzer prize in photography for his picture of Coretta King holding her daughter at Dr. King's funeral, coaxed me into relaxation and a usable picture. As far as I was concerned, the episode was a romp. The best part was working with Moneta, a humble, congenial genius. Thereafter I would see him everywhere, at all the "big scenes," quietly orchestrating a legacy of memorable images.

Much to the chagrin of many of my friends, who thought that Afros were too militant, too nappy, too declassé, my Afro showed up full bloom in a profile *The New York Times* published on its then society page. I was chairing a benefit for Jazzmobile, a group of eminent jazz musicians founded by my cousin the jazz pianist, Billy Taylor. In the summer, Jazzmobile gave free concerts around the city. Wearing the Afro in the picture was an important choice for me. I knew that my skin often photographed quite light. I wanted there to be no mistake as to what culture claimed me. It was also another way of getting as close as I could to the radicalism of the times.

In a Christmas letter, Harold looked at the year as a time of growth.

December 25, 1967

Dearest Darling,
Again, and with ever more love and feeling, Merry Christmas to you. . . . what a beautiful thing our relationship can be—and is—even after nearly ten years.

In sum, 1967 has been a good year for us. We have had our share of sickness and happiness, of sadness and unlimited pleasure. Our children are growing beautifully. My job only recently has become a source of some pain and dissatisfaction. We've done a great many things and gone lots of places—and had fun.

I hope you feel that I have improved upon my attempts to share everything I think and care about with you, this year. I hope, also, that I will continue to share in this way.

Be happy, Darling, this Christmas. You are my life, my love and my happiness. Please know that as always, I love you more with each passing second.

Merry, merry Christmas to you, my love.

> Love always,
>
> H.

*H*AROLD: Because of my penchant for romantic dinners by candlelight, on one trip we picked up a huge nonelectrified chandelier with long, elaborately carved arms extending several feet in all directions. With the help of friends, I installed it in the dining room. Somewhere in the Village, I spied eight Spanish wall sconces and mounted those around the room. In Vermont, I discovered a candle factory and arranged to have dozens of honeycombed beeswax candles made to order for the chandelier and wall candelabra and shipped to New York. *Voilà!* A dining room lit entirely by candlelight—overhead, around the room, and down the center of the table, all reflected in the gold framed mirrors.

The effect was exactly what we wanted, but the candles became a real pain in the ass. If we opened any windows, melting wax from the overhead chandelier dripped onto the flower centerpieces and Shirlee's tablecloths; onto plates, food, and people. From the sconces, it cascaded in free-form patterns down the walls and coagulated in puddles on the carpeting. Whenever our entrance door opened or closed, cross-drafts sped up the dripping or blew out most of the candles, sending spires of smoke throughout the apartment. With the windows closed, the dining room quickly overheated—especially during dinner and dancing parties. We finally compromised and added a dimly lighted floor lamp, covered in dark rust-colored beads, for "emergencies," and lighted the candles just minutes before our guests arrived to savor the romantic ambience.

Ellis (now pronounced "Ehlll-isss") became a beloved "brother" to both Shirlee and me, and favorite guru, uncle, babysitter, and everyday Santa Claus to Dee Dee and Missy.

Expansive, spoiling, and vastly loving, Ellis talked with Dee Dee and Missy as if they were grown-ups, and they loved it. He catered to their most outlandish whims, preparing oatmeal with fresh strawberries and cream for them or having their favorite Chinese food, M&Ms, and watermelon delivered for the breakfast the three of them decided would be better than the bacon, eggs, and toast that Shirlee was preparing in the kitchen. He took them on impromptu dates—to lunch at Tavern on the Green, to a Leroi Jones poetry reading.

He invariably arrived with an entourage, all laden with shopping bags of fancy takeout food, juice, flowers, toys, and wine, ready for a gourmet feast and party at which Dee Dee and Missy were the center of attention. He allowed the girls to set the musical agenda for the evening, asking whether they would rather hear Elvis or the Dinizulu Dancers; The Temptations or The O'Jays; or listen to the latest Aretha Franklin album. The gentle and kind but formal British babysitter we regularly used suffered by comparison. She was "boring," they said; she would read only the books they already knew by heart to make them go to sleep. From the moment they learned that we were going out for an evening and that this woman would babysit, they pitched royal tantrums until we closed the door behind us. Sometimes they told her that she need not take her coat off because Ellis was on his way to sit with them.

I understood how the girls felt but couldn't say so, because we would never have gotten out of the apartment for our own fun, often with Ellis. My Xerox job was challenging and stimulating but boring by comparison to the evenings and weekends we spent in Ellis's company. We usually capped these evenings when his limousine dropped us at Aux Puces, a very "in" disco–cum–antique shop owned by one of Ellis's friends. We sat grandly on aging velvet sofas and chairs in rooms enclosed by antique, heavy brocade curtains, amid old theater props, chandeliers, life-sized stuffed giraffes, horned toads, (with outrageous price tags attached), sipping cordials and discoing until dawn.

After touring Langston Hughes's *Black Nativity* around the world for a year, Ellis produced international tours of the Donald McKayle Dance Company's *Black New World,* Eugene O'Neill's *The Emperor Jones,* and James Baldwin's *The Amen Corner,* directed by Lloyd Richards. Upon returning to New York in 1966, he moved in with us for a year and a half. Dee Dee and Missy were ecstatic because our apartment became Grand Central Station as Ellis invited a parade of performing artists, writers, producers, and directors to social or business sessions in our living room. The elevator operators in our apartment building automatically brought every black person entering the lobby to our eleventh-floor landing, without asking questions.

At the new Xerox Education Division, we were talent and creativity looking for business opportunities in education. For a while, we dreamed of voiding or finding a legitimate loophole in U.S. copyright laws and placing a Xerox copier between every two classrooms in schools throughout America, thereby putting the textbook publishing industry out of business. But when the corporation (by virtue of its technology) became second party to costly and protracted litigation in a major copyright infringement case, we quickly abandoned this dream.

In collaboration with the American Academy for the Advancement of Science, we developed a prototype K–12 learner-centered science education program, in which students became their own teachers as they pursued their science interests from one level to another and one subject area to another, after mastering benchmark, self-instructional competency exams. Expanding the application of Skinner's principles of behavioral science, we developed and field-tested an innovative, self-instructional reading program for the elementary grades. Threaded through all of these ventures was our objective of freeing teachers and students from the traditional lockstep method of textbook-guided whole-class teaching, day-by-day. We provided teachers with a master copy of many different learning exercises and homework assignments. With her handy Xerox machine, the teacher could individualize class instruction and homework for each student, a major goal of the education community.

We competed successfully against IBM and other "socially conscious" corporate giants for multiyear Great Society funding to establish a residential Job Corps Center for eight hundred disadvantaged
young women in Huntington, West Virginia. The program featured
applications of our teaching and learning technologies to reduce the
time and cost of equipping underachieving girls and dropouts with
basic education and entry-level skills for the workforce. As the corporation's expert on disadvantaged youth, I spent a great deal of time
setting up our Job Corps operation as a twenty-four-hour-a-day residential program. This was no theory, no study. This was real life.
Though only sixteen years old, many of the girls already had one or
more children somewhere back home. Most had no marketable job
skills, no work ethic, no basic education, and no thoughts about a
future for themselves or their children. Our Job Corps program was
a government-sponsored vacation from the hell they had lived at
home. We added counseling, instruction in personal hygiene, sex education, child growth and development, grooming, and makeup, and
other services, barely remaining within budget.

The challenges were enormous. But with each graduating class, I
was deeply gratified and rewarded—almost in a spiritual way—to see
how significantly we had altered the future of these young women
who had come to us for a last opportunity to turn their lives around.

Because I spent so much time at the Job Corps Center and in
meetings around the country, Ellis and our extended family rallied
around Shirlee and the girls. For a while, I enjoyed the heady excitement of jetting around the country in expensive three-piece suits for
quick-paced, no-nonsense executive meetings. I reveled in picking up
the tab for lavish power lunches to impress school people unaccus-
tomed to business perks, and I looked forward to the camaraderie of
belting down scotches with "the guys"—the team—after intensive
workdays in city after city.

Over time, however, the sweet scent vanished from the rose as I
began to feel like a weekend guest in my own home. I acknowledged
that there was no way to recover lost time and involvement with my
wife and children, despite gifts and whirlwind weekends with Dad. I
decided that in the long run I would pay a much too high personal
price for the money and prestige I earned from the corporate lifestyle

I was leading. My challenge was to find significant ways to travel less frequently, without compromising my work or future at Xerox.

I had been working at Xerox for two and a half years when the corporation decided to redirect the Education Division into the more profitable and predictable business of book publishing. This was purely a business decision. Although we had developed high-quality instructional materials, curricula, and programs and in pilot programs had demonstrated their effectiveness, we found that despite our best advertising efforts the education community was slow to move away from deeply entrenched traditions, some of which were mandated by local or state law. In the largest states, for example, state laws required local school districts and individual schools to purchase new textbooks and other educational materials only from lists approved by the statewide textbook adoption committee.

Xerox sought a shorter turnaround and quicker profit on its investments. It decided to acquire major textbook publishers whose books were already on most state adoption lists. These annual sales were more predictable and profitable in the short run.

Not interested in becoming a textbook agent or salesman, several months later I returned to my first love, schooling and direct involvement with kids. I accepted an appointment as headmaster of the New Lincoln School in Manhattan, the pre-kindergarten through grade twelve private school at East Eighty-second Street and Fifth Avenue, opposite the Metropolitan Museum, and on Central Park North at Fifth Avenue.

New Lincoln was originally established by John Dewey as the Laboratory School for Teachers College, Columbia University. It separated from Columbia and became a full-fledged Manhattan private school successfully competing with such schools as Ethical Culture, Walden, and Dalton. Offering an innovative, creative, student-centered philosophy and program of study, New Lincoln catered to bright, creative, nontraditional kids and their parents. Eleanor Gimbel, of the department store Gimbels (and Macy's), was chairperson of the board. Ethel Epstein, whose husband was executive director of the Anti-Defamation League, was vice-chair. Steve Ross, soon to become president of Time-Life and Warner Brothers, was treasurer. Dr. Hugh

Butts, a well-known black psychiatrist at Harlem Hospital, Stuart Levin, owner of Le Pavillon, then New York's most upscale and fashionable restaurant, and a host of other successful, high-profile New Yorkers were active, contributing board members with children enrolled in the school.

Leading a school was a more than full-time job requiring oversight of everything from the board of directors to students. While raising funds, I had to keep faculty and parents happy, involved in their children's education, and supportive of our school and mission. In addition, New Lincoln was firmly committed to integration. Over time, the board, faculty, and parents decided to increase the minority presence in the school beyond a token level and set fund-raising priorities and targets to make this possible. Through collective efforts we achieved this goal while enriching our curricular offerings and attracting the best bright lights in the teaching profession.

The sixties were years of great change in America and of fundamental shifts in attitude toward government, politics, politicians, and the system. Young Americans, in particular, became ever more skeptical of the motives, veracity, and actions of the country's leadership and rejected the alleged necessity, purposes, and costs of war; the empty rhetoric about equality among the races and sexes; and the power of the system to deny individual freedoms.

The first time I saw I television reports about Haight-Ashbury and hippies, I thought the lunatic fringe were being accorded their sixty seconds of fame and would soon disappear into oblivion. They didn't. Instead, they touched a nerve, they connected with people's alienation and disaffection, they galvanized the morally disheartened, they encouraged passive resistance and withdrawal. Marijuana and pot were their escape vehicles. This was a U-turn I could not personally navigate, although I understood and often agreed with their sentiments and reasons. In my own way, I was still struggling for a place at the table of life and could not fathom starvation as a better alternative. As an educator entrusted by parents with the awesome responsibility of acculturating young minds and aspirations toward success in the system, I could not simultaneously debunk it. To be true to myself, I had to find a middle ground comfortable for me.

Ellis was among friends sharing Thanksgiving dinner with us in 1967. We were guffawing at Novella Nelson's dramatic story about a moose biting her husband in Yellowstone National Park when a friend of Ellis's toppled headfirst into his plate, upended glasses and candles, and slid sideways to the floor. I suspected a heart attack. But he was much too young to be a likely candidate.

Pandemonium erupted. We cleared the dining room and opened the window. Shirlee got ice cubes and a towel. Hugh Butts checked his pulse, said he was still alive, and urged getting him to emergency immediately. I had a flash of three black men holding a white corpse, frantically flailing at vacant taxicabs whizzing past on West End Avenue. We piled into my car, rushed to St. Luke's, and placed him on the first available gurney. Half a dozen glossy yellow capsules rolled out of his pocket as we waited for the emergency team.

"Go home, Harold. This second," Ellis commanded urgently. "Get going. We can't have the headmaster of New Lincoln implicated in a drug overdose. Leave. Now," he insisted. "We'll return as soon as we can."

Ellis's friend survived a deadly combination of alcohol and drugs. I unwittingly survived a potentially serious threat to my career and received a wake-up call on the need to distance us from the growing popularity of drugs, which I knew nothing about and had no interest in. Our roast piglet and turkey survived Thanksgiving Day virtually untouched.

Although I kept my hair short and neat and wore conservative three-piece suits, button-down shirts, navy blue blazers, Rep ties, and Brooks Brothers wing-tipped brogans during the day, for evenings on the town or parties with Ellis and our theater friends I commandeered Shirlee's hair dryer and blow-dried my hair into an Afro that put Jesse Jackson's to shame and made me look like Balthazar with an aerated, six-inch crinkly halo. I dressed from a collection of high-style, brightly patterned, gold-chained leisure suits, huge bell-bottom pants, see-through shirts open to the navel, dangling chain belts and beads from Shirlee's jewelry collection, and gleaming patent leather, high-heeled platform shoes that added a full two inches to my six-foot height—in addition to my six-inch halo.

Shirlee was equally hip. Her long dangly earrings and gauzy

Indian-print pants suits, fringed everywhere and overlaid with rows of multicolored beads reaching below her waist, made her a study in perpetual motion, her softly tingling bells and chains a constant reminder of her whereabouts. Sometimes she wore wildly colored, tie-dyed sunburst combinations that were eyepoppers and show-stoppers, or sexy see-through ultra-sheer blouses and matching pants, bras, and panties that focused my attention all evening on the great figure underneath.

And for a long while, she wore a stylishly bouffant Afro that reminded me of Angela Davis, without Angela's perpetual grimace. If she'd had her hair straightened but needed an instant Afro-look for the evening, she pinned her hair back and popped on a huge Afro wig larger than my halo. For mixed, upscale society events on bad hair days, she sometimes donned her Diana Ross wig, which made her look like Cher with hair long enough to sit on, and dark eyeliner, eye shadow, and inch-long eyelashes that, together, reminded me of Elizabeth Taylor in *Cleopatra*.

At home and at private parties we were safe. When we made our entrances at restaurants, dances, theater performances, and other public events decked out in our contemporary finery, however, I prayed to God that none of my New Lincoln parents would dash through the crowd to complain about a math teacher's unfair grade and gasp with amazement, midsentence, that the bare-chested plat-formed hippie with halo, bell-bottoms, and chains was, in fact, their school's buttoned-down, Ivy League headmaster.

In 1967, Ellis joined the staff of the Educational Broadcasting Corporation (WNET/Thirteen) and became executive producer of *SOUL!*, an Emmy Award–winning television series that became a focal point for the black empowerment movement. *SOUL!* was a daring, uncertain, and, to a majority of PBS's family of stations, a risky and boundary-breaking venture. In the wake of the March on Washington, the War on Poverty, and growing civil unrest over race issues, it was a program by, for, and about blacks—produced through the beneficence of white money. As one of the arbiters of black culture in New York and nationally, and as producer of *SOUL!*, Ellis insisted upon total control of the show's content, script, performers, tone, and message. In television history, *SOUL!* is credited with single-handedly raising the collective consciousness of the American public by providing exposure of promising and potentially influential African Americans via the written word, dance, and song.

After much cajolery from Ellis and his minions, I agreed to succeed Alvin Poussaint, *SOUL!'s* first host. My duties came naturally to me, seemingly because the experiences of my own life enabled me to establish a connection that lowered my guests' fences and got them talking openly and sometimes angrily about their professional and personal lives in ways that put American society as a whole on trial. And because classical and popular music—and especially black popular music—was such an integral part of my life, I loved introducing and interviewing The O'Jays, Patti LaBelle and the Bluebells, The Temptations, The Four Tops, Stevie Wonder, and others. I was having the time of my life.

My success as host of *SOUL!* for several programs generated positive response from viewers and frequent recognition as a TV celebrity, especially in the black community, but caused me great pangs in private. As headmaster of New Lincoln, a predominantly white private school with only a 25 percent minority student enrollment, I became concerned about how my being identified with the no-nonsense, sometimes angry, and pointed dialogues and interviews I conducted on race and racism in America might affect my job security and effectiveness. Could my New Lincoln constituents, I wondered, accept the duality of my private/public life? While I was thinking this through, PBS funders and administrators became increasingly concerned about the black tone of the show, despite its success; I became concerned about losing my job for being too openly and publicly identified with the struggles of black folks. Anxious and conflicted, I opted to keep my day job and advised Ellis that I could not continue to host *SOUL!* I told myself that I had not sold out. I still have mixed feelings about that decision.

After much resistance and discussion, Ellis decided that to keep the Haizlip name publicly identified with *SOUL!*, he would host the show himself. I thought he might consider asking Shirlee to take over, but he didn't. I did not pursue this possibility, even though I thought she'd be good at it. And then again, her light skin on a program about

blackness might have been offputting to some. At some level, I suspected that Ellis was committed to showcasing a black male in the
role of host of a national television show, breaking down yet another
barrier in the industry.

Shortly thereafter, *SOUL!* became the television show most eagerly
watched every week by a majority of blacks and a substantial number
of whites. Shirlee and I remained close to Ellis and to *SOUL!*, discussing and planning upcoming shows, guests, and themes and
attending tapings for moral support.

When *SOUL!* went off the air in the eighties, Ellis moved on to
produce Alvin Ailey's *Memories and Visions* and organized the Minority
Writers Conferences on Television Production. He chaired the Arts
Committee of the 1982 New York City Black Convention, was
appointed by the governor to the New York Task Force on the Arts,
and became deeply involved with the political campaigns of Jesse
Jackson and David Dinkins. As director of Special Programs for the
Schomberg Center for Research in Black Culture, he produced *A
Harlem Welcome for the Most Reverend Desmond Tutu*. He received numer-
ous awards but was most honored when the president of the Borough
of Manhattan proclaimed December 6, 1988, Ellis Haizlip Day.

Raising funds for New Lincoln garnered attention and an invitation
for me to become the first black trustee of the American Museum of
Natural History. Greatly honored, I felt obliged, before accepting, to
advise the board and the president up front that I did not have a
reserve of personal wealth from which to contribute money to the
museum (which I assumed was sine qua non for all trustees) but that
I was quite willing to use my contacts and powers of personal persua-
sion to tap contributions. My frankness and my willingness to go after
others' money were well received. I joined the board immediately,
with media fanfare about the long-overdue breakthrough into the
bastion of white Protestant money and power that controlled the
museum.

Two deeds established my firm place among the museum's
trustees and staff. During several monthly board meetings, I found
different ways to advise the museum that through its programs and
outreach activities it was continuing its tradition of appealing primar-

ily to middle- and upper-income whites. In so doing, I pointed out, it was missing a sizable number of fee-paying visitors and contributing supporters among middle- and upper-class blacks. Most of the board members responded with stony silence—except Gardner Stout, who asked me to develop my concerns into suggestions and talk with him personally about any recommendations I might want to make.

I talked at length with Shirlee, who had been elected president of the Greater New York Chapter of Links, and in 1969 we came up with the idea of having the Links co-sponsor with the museum a dinner dance and fund-raiser in the museum's capacious halls, featuring many of the never-displayed pieces from the museum's extensive African art collection.

In addition to guaranteed income from the sale of benefit tickets to the Links, their friends, and associates, we were confident that for a first such as this, we could secure new private and public supporters and funders for the museum. Gardner loved the idea and embraced it fully, requesting that Shirlee and I co-chair the event. We went to work. As the planning proceeded, the event took on considerable momentum and generated extraordinary excitement among the board and in the media. Hundreds of the city's black and white glitterati showed up, and every seat was occupied. With the staff, Shirlee had created breathtaking, theatrically lighted displays of large and small, strikingly beautiful artifacts and hangings. The guest list was half black, half white. Each table reflected the same proportions. The tables were resplendent with authentic African centerpieces. The band played music that brought black, white, and mixed couples onto the dance floor, obviously self-conscious and excited about the occasion, the ambience, the place, and the purpose.

Gardner, the trustees, and the staff were astonished at the elegance and obvious money represented among this turnout of potentially new museum supporters. The event garnered a full page in *The New York Times*, which hailed it "a first," pictures in *Women's Wear Daily*, and features in *Jet* and the *Amsterdam News*.

My second contribution was no less significant but much less spectacular. The Education Department at the museum had grown stale, uninteresting, and nonproductive of income—except from the busloads of schoolchildren rolling into the museum parking lot daily for their teachers' day of R&R. There were few new exhibitions planned, few if any special events on the museum roster to bring in more income-producing foot traffic, and little else on the department's ho-hum agenda. Gardner announced the search for a new education director with vision, energy, enthusiasm, creativity, connections to money sources, and the ability to reinvigorate and renew the department.

I telephoned Gardner at home one day and told him that I wanted him to meet privately with the new education director he was look-ing for. He was surprised but pleased, and we set a date.

A Harvard alumnus, a friend of Ellis's, bright and articulate, Malcolm Arth was deeply ensconced in national and international anthropology circles and highly regarded by all. He had traveled and published extensively, done field research around the world, loved movies, loved children, competed successfully for external funding, and was a raconteur capable of telling back-to-back true stories that left his audiences bent over with laughter.

When I told Malcolm about the education job at the museum and the private luncheon to meet the president, he resisted, citing his tenure at Adelphi University and his commitment to college and uni-versity teaching and research. But he agreed to have lunch. On the day before our appointment, I advised Gardner that he'd really have to pull out the stops to get a person like Malcolm to join his team—if he liked him and was impressed by him. The meal in Gardner's pri-vate dining room lasted nearly three hours. The two men talked like old friends. I watched Gardner as Malcolm chatted amiably about the kinds of programs the museum should be offering and how they could be funded and marketed to generate tremendous turnout.

It worked. Within a few weeks, Malcolm took a leave of absence from Adelphi and dug in as education director of the museum. He soon funded and launched the Margaret Mead Film Festival and rein-vigorated the world-class Hall of Man in Africa. Other new funds began flowing into the museum to support Malcolm's countless new programs. Within a year, the number of persons sampling the Educa-tion Department's exhibits and programs had risen dramatically. Mal-colm resigned from Adelphi and accepted permanent appointment as education director of the museum, a position in which he flourished until his death in the early nineties.

CHAPTER 8

Mule in the
Strawberry Fields

$\mathscr{S}$HIRLEE: In those years, it seemed that anything could happen. Life was an ongoing costume party, led by the Beatles and Elton John. At times we affected aspects of hippie dress. I had my share of fringed vests, mirrored shirts, beaded tops, bell-bottom pants. Even wore a headband. For his part, Harold enjoyed whatever was in style. Vests and bell-bottoms were made for his slender physique. Bernard Johnson, our designer friend, said to Harold, "Honey, you've got the body for these clothes. There is no one, I repeat no one, who looks as good as you do in these styles, child."

He designed some dressy knit bell-bottoms exclusively for Harold, who topped them off with a poet's shirt with flowing sleeves and a tricolor striped velvet vest that looked as if it had come from a Shakespearean play. Years later, our daughters would wear the vests and tops as Halloween costumes.

Pot and hippies were everywhere. We didn't smoke; we didn't even inhale. Smoking marijuana was not a moral issue for us. Its smell repulsed me, made me think of manure. Harold preferred his commercial cigarettes, not knowing then that they had already seduced him into addiction. Neither of us needed external stimulation to get high or feel good. We got our highs from our egos and love of life.

But there were no "real" hippies in our circle of friends. Hippies tended to be white. Most of our black friends were not attracted to the hippie lifestyle. It was so deeply antithetical to everything they had been raised to respect and admire. To affect free-form clothes, communal living, and drug consumption was a betrayal of black parents who had struggled to provide their children with Ivy League lives.

In our crowd, there had been one exception. One of our college friends, a member of my AKA sorority, let her hair grow into an Afro and moved in with her Afro-haired boyfriend. *Quelle scandale!* A few months later they married in a lavish traditional society wedding.

The black people we knew did not go to Woodstock, either. I was only mildly interested. Even though our friend Richie Havens was scheduled on the program, the idea of joining the crowds was none too appealing. With a searing version of "Freedom," a hoarse Richie electrified the gathering and achieved instant celebrity, later cult status. But in that widely filmed summer of love, few black faces could be seen.

New Lincoln board members, faculty, parents, and students turned out for the school's welcoming gala at Tavern on the Green. Feeling like a bride again, I wore a white silk A-line dress encrusted with iridescent pearls. But at the party, Harold, the groom, was the focus. I was merely "Mrs. Haizlip," window dressing on the set. We were following Harold's career paths, his needs. I had no doubt he would do well by me. And my time to shine would come. So I became a "head"'s wife; it was not a burden. In fact, at New Lincoln, the headmaster's wife had no higher status than anyone else. It was a benign place, a sort of utopia, where, ostensibly, status was irrelevant.

Among the new currents, feminism made few inroads into my life. I had no need for it. My father had always told his daughters they were as important as any man, and my mother reinforced that view. It never occurred to me that I was a lesser creature. I lived my life outside of the bell jar. I was part of that vast group of black women who were self-possessed because society forced them to be. Our take on feminism was radically different from that of our white counterparts.

But living comfortably in two worlds, I was also part of the group that had come to adulthood on the cusp of the women's revolution. Part of me was still riding on the back of my prince's steed; the other part was galloping ahead, confidently astride a horse of my own.

It's true I was still Mrs. Harold Cornelius Haizlip, not yet Shirlee Taylor Haizlip. I had no quarrel with that. It seemed supportive of my husband and appropriate, ladylike, fitting. All the things I thought I was. It had always been that way. It went along with white gloves, girdles, and the hats that I favored. I was the sum of the expectations of my parents, my family, my church, my community, my race. Now I reconsidered my freedoms: I was free in a new way—free to have expectations of my own. But what was the point of change? I was lying happily in the bed that I had made. Did I need a new set of bedding or a larger bed? Surely *I* knew who I was. Or so I imagined then.

We transferred Dee Dee to New Lincoln, and Missy began school there in 1968. Fortunately, they were in the lower school, on Eighty-second Street and Fifth Avenue. Their father's office was in the High School, on 110th Street, so they didn't have to feel the heat of his presence every day. The girls thrived at the school as their social life burgeoned. Parents encouraged after-school visits and weekend dates. We were pleased that our children were being exposed to good intentions and goodwill.

I was free for part of the day. It's ironic that living in one of the world's greatest cities had deadened my interest in city planning. I turned to planning events and informally assisting Ellis in the development of his television show.

Sometimes our life took on a surreal quality: chatting with Art Linkletter and one of the Vanderbilts in Art's Central Park West kitchen about how to meet Negroes who were interesting but not famous; being ignored by Truman Capote as he flirted with Harold at a dinner party. We were moving in all directions in the community. I suppose we were searching for "place." It seemed as if there were unlimited possibilities.

Someone who helped us find a place she thought we should be was Mary Richardson, a fabled Harlemite. Mary was old enough to be our grandmother and knew everyone. Some said that if Mary didn't know you, you didn't count. For many years she lived in the Hotel

Theresa, where she rubbed elbows with Paul Robeson, Duke Ellington, Cab Calloway, Lena Horne, the Cotton Club girls, and every black celebrity who came to Harlem. She was there when Castro and his chickens occupied the place. She invited him to one of her parties, but he was a no-show.

Tall, handsome, and silver haired, Mary was the color of a walnut. She had been married once but said she had no use for men. For a living, Mary sewed, doing alterations, mostly for celebrities and wealthy East Side matrons. Among her clients were Loretta Young and Faye Dunaway. For herself she created dramatic chiffon and silk caftans, flowing pants and long scarves.

Mary had a rule: If you left a dress at her house for more than a year and made no inquiries about it, she called you. If you did not come for it, she claimed it. Loretta Young left several dresses, which Mary gave me. Designed by the famous screen couturier Louis, the dresses became the stars of my wardrobe for a while. One was a tangerine ruffled crepe cocktail dress with tiny straps and a matching stole. Another, a camel's hair coat dress with a six-inch-wide belt. Loretta's dresses had a life of their own, swishing and whirling me around.

Mary's real talent was for orchestrating parties—more like salons, really. When we met her she was living in Park West Village, a large apartment complex on Central Park West in the nineties. Everyone wanted to come to Mary's get-togethers. But one had to have special qualifications to get in. Mary worshiped beauty and talent. On his ninetieth birthday, longtime friend Eubie Blake played for her. Opera stars sang. Actors did their monologues. If one was untalented and homely, it was unlikely one would find oneself at Mary's gatherings. She loved Harold for his brilliance and piano playing. She let me in because I could sing gospel and wear clothes well.

Although she was scrupulous about her guest list, Mary paid less attention to her provisions, often running out of food or liquor, or both. Nobody cared, though, least of all Mary. It was part of her charm.

For our daughters, Mary was like an Auntie Mame, babysitting, taking them on outings, and exposing them to her glamorous world. She talked to them like adults. "Now, darlings," she would say, "what fabulous thing shall we do today?" In turn, the girls loved to go to Mary's and stay in the bedroom during her parties, dressing up in the hats, coats, stoles, and gloves of the glittering guests in the other room.

A family celebration inaugurated 1968. Harold and I joined with my sisters and their husbands to give my parents a thirty-fifth wedding anniversary party. My parents had eloped. This was their first major party to celebrate their nuptials.

Pattee had married again and now had two sons. She worked for the Poverty Program in New Haven. Brother was living in Boston and working as a nurse's assistant in one of the city's hospitals. Jewelle and Jim had moved to California, where Jim was teaching at Stanford and Jewelle was beginning her studies at Berkeley toward a Ph.D. in clinical psychology.

We held the event at my parents' home, bringing together three hundred people from their past and their present. A string quartet from Yale provided tasteful, elegant music as grandchildren in pajamas peered down the banister at their grandparents and parents in formal clothes. Mother wore an aquamarine and lilac chiffon Grecian-styled gown, gathered softly on one shoulder. Dad looked immaculate in his gray silk dinner jacket. They seemed pleased they had reached this point in their marriage. We were grateful and proud; our family was still intact.

Three weeks before Melissa would turn three years old in 1968, life dragged me down a long corridor that I didn't know was in the house. It was sunset, and the girls and I were reading together just before their bedtime. Frantic banging on the front door interrupted our quiet time. One of the neighbors in our babysitting crowd rushed in with a flustered look on her usually serenely beautiful face.

"I knew Harold wasn't home and I thought you shouldn't be alone right now."

"What's going on?" I asked.

"You mean you haven't heard? Martin Luther King has been shot. God, I can imagine how you must feel."

"No. There's really no way you can know how or what I feel right now," I said, not unkindly. "I think I'd rather be alone. I'll call you tomorrow. Thanks for coming by." She turned and left with a puzzled expression on her face. I felt badly about that, but at that moment she had become the enemy: the wife, the mother, the daughter, the sister of the bigot who had killed King.

It was the second mind-numbing assassination during my life. This time I gathered two little girls on my lap, crying and swaying from side to side on a velvet ottoman. I told the children that someone very important in many people's lives had died. Mindlessly I watched the blood-red sun set over the dead brown river, crying into my daughters' soft hair. Where was Harold when I needed him? What was God trying to teach me at that moment? To be strong? To get a fleeting glimpse of the loneliness, the vulnerability of widowhood? I didn't like the lesson.

I was frightened. If the shepherd is killed, will his flock be far behind? As a minister's daughter I had always known safety and comfort in the homes and churches of my father's colleagues. Would collars, robes, Bibles no longer shield?

Shock numbed my father. This was the son of his longtime friend and colleague. He had seen the boy grow up in the Baptist Convention. He was at a loss to console me, knowing no reason could be made reasonable and platitudes would not work. Fury consumed my mother. She had known King's mother. They sat together, worked together at National Baptist meetings. My sisters were angry, hurt. I felt helpless, hopeless. Anger and disbelief vied with shock and horror among my friends. Some wanted to give up. Others wanted to leave the country. Some wanted to bear arms. Others simply wanted to pray. Visions of fire hoses and police dogs danced in our heads.

If this great, compassionate man could be brought down in an act of hate, what hope, what safety, what refuge was there for me? Were all my personal, if small, efforts for integration useless? For a while, I felt myself pulling physically and emotionally away from white people, friends and strangers alike. Was it not their fault? I knew the answer to that question, of course.

There was dread everywhere in black communities. What would happen next? A simple wagon, drawn by a single mule, carried goodwill away.

That was when I stopped wearing white gloves.

Now there is no doubt in my mind that the assassination of Martin Luther King dealt a major blow to my hopes for my country. There is no doubt that it raised my level of cynicism. There is no doubt that it killed some of my dreams. I lost the last of my interest in city planning. My utopias would have life in my mind only.

Fashion was a way to be creative, another means of escaping, warding off the unpleasantness of the real world. I opened a boutique with my sister, Pattee. Sunday's Child perched right next to my father's church in the ground floor of a building that he owned in Ansonia. My job was to select and buy the clothes, design the windows, and create the advertising. Pattee's assignment was to manage the daily operations, market the goods, and find out what the customers wanted.

As my godfather of fashion, Ellis was delighted with the idea of the boutique and introduced me to all the black designers he knew in New York, talented people looking for outlets for their work. Soon boxes began arriving from Willi Smith, Arthur McGee, Scott Barrie, and Bernard Johnson. There were designs from a black jewelry maker who worked for a major firm but whose offerings remained anonymous. In our shop, he got top billing. Richard Palan sent his creations with apologies that he wasn't black. We happily accepted his stunning pieces.

Excitement built up for the New York–style opening. Ellis commandeered a slew of limousines, inveigling a number of his celebrity friends to come. Bernard Johnson hopped out of one car, wearing a greatcoat and a fedora and dangling an ivory cigarette holder. It was perfect. Opening night was standing room only. We had a hit on our hands.

Sunday's Child was the town's first sixties-style boutique. It attracted attention in all the neighboring valley towns and as far away as Bridgeport and New Haven. Our stock included shifts, minis, tie-dyes, chain belts, bell-bottoms, halters, and vests. We developed a crossover clientele, setting the mood in the daisy-strewn room with incense and music from James Brown to James Taylor.

We pulled everyone we knew into the act. Friends and relatives modeled in our runway-style fashion shows, with the now-celebrity

Ellis as our emcee. Jack and Jill and the Links, black social clubs, booked our shows, their members buying, snapping their fingers to the music in the dressing rooms, and doing little dances like those they saw the models do.

Every Friday I ran to the New Haven train in Grand Central with the two girls, suitcases and clothing boxes in tow. Harold joined me after work. It went that way for two years.

The bubble did not last as long as we hoped. Business dried up as entrepreneurs ushered in the era of the malls with large parking lots and a cornucopia of products. Getting out while we were ahead, we closed the boutique and looked for new dreams. Our closets were the fullest they had ever been.

Although we were not making a lot of money then (educators rarely do), through the beneficence of position and patrons we lived as if we were rich. I'll never forget the first time I saw a triplex apartment. My eyes took in the carved moldings, the circular staircase, the marble foyer. It was incredible to me that people lived this way. Three whole floors on Park Avenue, in New York. As I absorbed what I was seeing, a wave of anger came over me. For a moment I felt like the Russian revolutionary in *Dr. Zhivago* who berated the wealthy family for having so much space. I remembered my father saying facetiously that some white people have their heaven on earth. Then I moved on.

Wanting to build my profile, Ellis had a friend at *Women's Wear Daily* photograph me at one of the city's fashionable parties. It was the time of radical chic, when Leonard Bernstein held parties for Black Panthers. For us there were weekend invitations to houses with ballrooms in East Hampton, dinners in art-filled duplexes on Fifth Avenue, sailing on a yacht off City Island, musicales in grand homes on Gramercy Park. White guests would ask me about poverty and the Black Panthers, neither of which I had ever known. In those situations, there was a mighty temptation to pontificate, to be an expert. My answers would depend on my mood, what had happened in the world on that day, or my sense of the ridiculous.

It was clear we were invited because we were "black, amusing and intelligent." The fact that we dressed well, spoke well, and looked acceptable did not hurt, either. From our point of view, we accepted because our hosts were white, amusing, and intelligent. At some level, it was a two-way game. After Robert Kennedy died, our lives seemed less focused on change. How many parties could we go to and talk about social change without change happening? When would we ever be able to stop explaining what it means to be black?

As an antidote to urban life, we took the children to Maine and Vermont in the summers, spending time in some of the hamlets of our honeymoon, driving along bumpy roads in a green Ford station wagon singing John Denver's "Country Roads" at the top of our lungs. Several years, we brought along teenage babysitters. Charlene was one of Harold's students. On scholarship, she was a poor and brilliant black girl who wanted to be a poet. How little she had, how limited her world had been, how great her dreams were took my breath away. And made me angry at a world that had so little regard for this beautiful dreamer. We thought we could change her life over the course of six weeks. When the summer was over, school was her only salvation. At least she realized part of her dream, writing poetry in her own apartment, where she would die mysteriously in a fire.

We did not think of ourselves as curiosities, yet we could not help notice the mostly friendly stares of the natives of those mostly white states.

One day, Ellis brought a new friend to our house, a shy young woman with high cheekbones and large, sad eyes. Ellis had begun squiring her around town. When I first met Betty Shabazz, the widow of Malcolm X, she talked little. But we found a link: both of us had daughters born in the same year and a mutual friend in Sharifah Jamal.

Despite her husband's fame or because of it, Betty had not been out in the world much. Ellis recognized something powerful in her and wanted to expose her to a broader group after the murder of her husband. He started with us. I had Betty over for lunch to meet my friends and my sisters. Ellis asked me to go shopping with her, to help her select some new clothes. She had favored simple navy, black, or brown suits that made her look dowdy.

In limousines that Betty grew to love, Ellis took her everywhere, to shows, dance concerts, movies, and dinner. Often we joined them as a foursome. Generally secretive, Betty confided in Ellis and considered him her brother, as I did. He became an important man in the lives of her daughters.

Ellis worked on Betty's self-esteem, telling her she was an important person, a public person who was beautiful and deserved to look splendid. She became his Galatea. He became her Pygmalion. She believed every word he said, and he made her laugh.

Over the years, Betty stayed in touch with Harold and me wherever we were. From time to time when she was with us, an endearing, piquant girlish quality popped out from behind the now well-rehearsed stately public persona, and we would giggle until tears ran down our cheeks. Whenever we got on the phone, we would usually talk an hour, rehearsing our lovely times with Ellis, in those days after Betty walked out of the valley of the shadows of death.

Suddenly, we had been married for ten years. I came home to find a large box with a red ribbon on our bed. Red floral chiffon drifted into a tent-shaped dress. The dress floated around me like a lazy parachute in the sky. The note read I was to wear it to hear Duke Ellington that night at the Rainbow Room.

Through my cousin Billy, Harold had obtained a celebrity table. Sitting knees away was Judy Garland, looking as pale and ethereal as the flesh-colored sequins in her cocktail dress. Dark circles surrounded her eyes. Furrows divided her brow into tiny shelves. I was surprised she was so short. With a half smile, she kept her head down as she moved through the crowd. She would die a few months later.

Billy had passed the word to Duke that we were celebrating. As we danced, Duke, resplendent in white tails, dedicated the "Satin Doll" number to me, "the lady in the red dress who surely fits the profile." Heaven. What could have been more heady for a young couple in their early thirties, dancing at a pinnacle of the world and saluted by an icon of their times?

It was a good time to take stock of our lives. I knew that we had had more than our share of what F. Scott Fitzgerald called "life's golden moments." But we felt as if we were being carried forward by a rushing stream, heading to an unknown sea. What did we have spiritually, materially then? A solid marriage, two healthy children. An extended family that loved us. A circle of caring friends. A need to make things better in the world, though somewhat diminished. A lovely apartment.

Where should we go from there? What about our pledge to uplift the race? Where would we be in another ten years? I think I had my first realization then that you can only make a rough draft of your life's plan. Fate or circumstances, luck or karma, prayer or preparation all come into play for the final blueprints.

Before school started, Harold made a trip to St. Thomas. An hour before he landed he wrote:

Sept. 5, 1971

Honey—

Sitting here on the plane, alone, I have been mentally drifting in and out of various scenes of our life over the last few years, and particularly the last summer. I want to share with you my thoughts.

First, I feel inordinately happy that you are my wife. Yesterday as I watched you dozing in the car on the way back to New York, I felt warm, proud and especially caring for you. You are a good wife, lover and mother; a treasure without price in my life. And I drove a little more slowly and carefully. . . .

Second, I want you to know that I really loved and enjoyed our summer in Vermont this year. For me it was a tender and touching moment to drive away from that house. We'd been very close and happy there, and I loved both the house and you for that experience. I need it and you more often, in that way.

What pleases me most about New York is that in addition to a lot of fun, growth, new friends and experiences, our own relationship grew. I feared New York once, because I thought it might hold out to us the attractions of anonymity and depersonalization which might have undermined our relationship and taken you from me, me from you, us from each other. I am happy that such has not happened, and that I have remained faithful to you without question. A tested marriage, I suppose, is a better one. Even without a test in this sense, ours is a good marriage.

Sixth, I want you to know that I consider you not only my good wife, but also my best friend. Good friends have been few in my life and so I cherish them all the moreso.

Seventh, you should know that I think you're doing a great job with the kids. Missy luckily seems to have inherited the most fortunate combination of your and my best traits, happy, loving, amusing, pleasant, sensitive and bright. There is no doubt she will be a beauty. Dee Dee has all of the same inherited characteristics and, in addition, will be a gorgeous and beautiful woman physically, much like her mother.

My time is up now, darling, since we're almost in St. Thomas. It's been nice having you with me, where, God help us, you should always be.

My love to you, forever and three days.

                                        H.

HAROLD: In something I read at Amherst, I came across the question, "What baggage should you take into the future?" The question was like a huge Stop sign on my life's journey. There, in eight simple words, was the question I had struggled to answer without ever recognizing or knowing exactly what the question was—ever since I was ten, when I said "Yes" to Mrs. Gregory's encouragement to do whatever was necessary to become the best student.

The question was imprinted deeply in my memory bank, popping up involuntarily and unexpectedly while I was driving to Smith College for a date; or choosing to deny, ignore, or pay a high personal price for the racism that was my constant companion at Harvard; or debating how to tell my family and Pam about Shirlee; or protecting myself from the pain of Bennie and Claude's decision not to be ushers in my wedding; or decorating our apartment without a hint of the home I loved on Sheriff Road; or forsaking for Shirlee my involvement with all the women I had known before her; or teaching at

Wellesley rather than in Roxbury; or dealing with Louise Day Hicks while advocating for A.B.C.D.; or rejecting my dad's way of rearing children; or living a rich life in the black community while aggressively cultivating and enjoying a different kind of richness in our white life. In my answers to the eight words in this question, I recognized the baggage choices that had made me me.

Unlike any other school I had been affiliated with, New Lincoln faculty and staff lived and breathed their philosophical commitment to each individual child in the school. While we sought to maintain our competitive edge with other private schools in terms of overall enrollment, waiting lists, special services and programs, facilities, promotion rates, IQ and SAT scores, and college placements, we put far less emphasis on students competing with each other. Instead we chose to identify, nourish, and tap the potential and talents of each individual, whether they were performing well or not. This belief that we could and should help individual students overcome their weaknesses—whatever they were—and discover their abilities, interests, and strengths. This, in a rigorous, rich, and supportive academic and artistic environment attracted students (and parents) who were fiercely independent yet filled with uncertainties, longing for answers to important identity questions in a society with radically shifting, sometimes contradictory, values.

With significant leadership, encouragement, and support from black staff members Mabel Smythe and Verne Oliver and board member and psychiatrist Dr. Hugh Butts, the entire New Lincoln community was light-years ahead of other private and public schools in forthrightly addressing issues of race, in all areas of the school's philosophy and operations, making it a free, warm, and welcoming place for white and black children, mixed children and couples, Hispanic and Asian students and their families. We were a mini–United Nations throughout.

This conscientious acceptance of the "other" and dedication to individual students as unique people—along with free tuition for my children as part of my headmaster's compensation package—led Shirlee and me to enthusiastically enroll first Dee Dee and then Missy in New Lincoln. While sisters, they had different personalities with distinctly different interests, and they looked different. Dee Dee had

Shirlee's fair complexion and Missy my chocolate tones. We were eager to find a school that appreciated their likenesses and differences equally. And I felt comfortable that the staff was so totally dedicated to individual children, regardless of who their parents were, that my daughters would be encouraged to find and define themselves as individuals, unimpeded by the shadow I cast as headmaster.

Gloria Steinem and the fledgling women's movement sharpened my concern for our girls' growth toward independence and self-confidence, and caused shifts in my attitudes toward Shirlee in particular and women in general. Somewhere along the way, in response to the women's movement's rhetoric and protests, a lightbulb flashed on for me, illuminating the unfairness and high personal cost of overt and covert discrimination based on gender. The luxury I felt at not having to prepare a son for the vicissitudes of black maleness was displaced by the urgency of recognizing and fighting discrimination against women and girls, to say nothing of double discrimination against minority women and girls. My commitment to my black wife and my black daughters, and the pain of racism I had endured and fought all my life, gave me no choice but to add "aggressive feminist" to my resume and values.

I started at home, with Shirlee. I knew that I had long ago passed the point at which my father had stopped growing in his relationship with Ma: when he died, she had never worked outside our home, seemingly content (until she discovered the Church of God) to be a housewife and mother. I had previously encouraged Shirlee's teaching stint at Tufts and her graduate study at Harvard. There was no problem hiring babysitters when she wanted to be free for a Links meeting or shopping spree on weekends. Because I was a neat freak and she was keenly interested in interior decorating but had no interest in housekeeping chores, we had hired a cleaning lady. She, more than I, had done an excellent job conceiving, planning, and orchestrating our highly successful Museum of Natural History evening, as well as other major events: at Carnegie Hall, City Hall, Lincoln Center, Northside Center. And I had come to appreciate over the years that she had wide-ranging interests and tremendous abilities that had nothing to do with being Mrs. Harold Haizlip.

My quandary was how best to support her in these new times. I was concerned not just for Shirlee or me but for our girls. I wanted no doubt about the clear messages that Shirlee's independence would send to them—about their mother, about their father's relationship with their mother, about themselves as blacks and as young women, and about the kind of relationship they would expect or require from the men they would allow to enter their lives.

I found no formula, no exemplar, no map. So we talked frequently about who she was, who she wanted to become, and what she wanted to do for herself, for her own reasons—independent of the girls and me. I plotted how to help her to get where she wanted to go, whatever the outcome might be. As a result, I think I deepened the friendship dimension of my relationship with her.

I recoiled in anger, disbelief, and pain when Martin Luther King was murdered on that balcony in Memphis. I was forced to acknowledge that despite his role as the conscience of America, if not the world, on issues of race and humanity, and as the galvanizer of black and white believers in his dream of a better world, there were people in this country who regarded him simply as an uppity, well-spoken nigger. If whites were free to do this, I should be free to fly to Kernersville and blow away Mrs. Mabe at her store on the road leading to Aunt Minnie's house; and then to Boston to wipe out Louise Day Hicks so everyone would know not where she stood, but where she lay; and from there to Cambridge, where there were professors and staff members, salespeople in stores, and waiters in restaurants who should be punished for the pain and anger I still carry.

Maybe, I thought, just maybe the real bottom line was that blacks and whites would never cross the chasm of race in this country. Maybe I was deluding myself by thinking that there would be any long-term impact or value for the students, the board, the parents, the faculty, or anyone else in the symbolism of my being the black headmaster. Maybe there was some kind of secret cabal at the power center of this institution. Maybe they were using my blackness and the school's integration for the public relations value conferred on their liberalism. Maybe they saw it as an edge I had over other headmasters in competing for financial support from corporations and foundations. Maybe they had their own business reasons to be allied with a racially correct institution. Maybe it was all just a game. Maybe I should take my marbles and return home to the black community and stay there.

I mourned for Martin Luther King and for myself. The dreams we shared from afar were unlikely to be realized. The only difference was that he had been ushered over the great divide ahead of me. When they sent Robert F. Kennedy to join his brother and King on the other side, I took his departure as no more than further confirmation of what I had already decided. "They" would get all of us, sooner or later. We weren't going to win the war of the races in our lifetimes. And I had begun to doubt that it would ever be won.

For a while we maintained our high profile as available integrationists, hosting power dinners in our apartment for white, monied investors that Ellis wanted to line up behind *SOUL!* or the black dancers that Ellis's associate Alvin Ailey was shaping into a dance company, and participating in a never-ending stream of tête-à-têtes at the homes and in the executive offices of New Lincoln board members helping me get the school on the benefactor list of wealthy New Yorkers.

More often than not, we were the only blacks at these events, well-dressed entertainment, novelties who had been places and done things prized by the majority—proof that the outcome of integration would be worth the costs, and that our hosts were well ahead of the curve. We were always assured future invitations from like-minded guests who wanted to share the message—and be identified as its purveyor—to ever-enlarging circles.

The more we traveled in these circles, the more I realized how wide the gulf was between haves and have-nots in this country, physically, financially, emotionally, culturally, and otherwise. Financial security gave haves the freedom to be masters of their own universe, the power to make decisions that would be implemented, the readiness to confront successfully any problem (short of death) that life would hurl in their paths, the self-confidence that they could do whatever they wanted.

I came to understand and unwillingly accept that I might never know in my lifetime the freedom they enjoyed because mine—ours—was a more dependent life. Our security depended on my keeping my job or soon finding another. It depended on having credit. It depended on our continuing to act as if we believed what we knew not to be true. It depended. Freedom was an illusion. We were not free. No black people we knew were.

Hundreds of visitors trekked through New Lincoln every month to see for themselves the miracles we were working with bright, creative, nontraditional students. We had a cadre of well-informed volunteer parents who manned the Visitors' Office and kept student and faculty distractions to a minimum while touring visitors through our school and answering their questions. They were quite professional and took pride in their work, more often than not generating hundreds of follow-up thank-you letters from professional educators, parents, research groups, and others.

On one occasion, after spending an entire day visiting classes and talking with students, parents, teachers, and administrators in the Lower School, the Middle School, and the High School, a delegation from the Virgin Islands notified the Visitors' Office that they could not leave without an audience with the headmaster, a most unusual request. Told I was busy, they pleaded and insisted, saying they lived so far away that it would be impossible for them to return at a more convenient time. Assuming they were black and knowing how far they had traveled, I relented and agreed to meet briefly with them in my office.

A tall, elegantly dressed, attractive black woman swept into my office, chatting animatedly at me before the rest of her delegation could enter or find seats—before I could ask her name or the names, schools, and responsibilities of the rest of her delegation, or introduce myself, or even welcome them to New Lincoln.

We had given life to the dream she had held for education in the Virgin Islands for years and years. She had read about New Lincoln but assumed our claims were empty public-relations rhetoric until she saw for herself. Would I give her a copy of the curriculum for every class taught in the school? Could she take them with her or would I airmail them to her before I left for the day? Did I have a teacher training manual that would explain what helped make our teachers so outstanding, so dedicated? How soon could I come to St.

Croix to conduct a teacher training seminar for her? If she paid my transportation, would I do it without a professional fee? How much, on the average, were we spending for supplementary materials for preschool students? Were they really ready to learn at age three? Did I hire preschool teachers from Bank Street College exclusively?

When she paused to catch her breath, I discovered that her name, aptly, was Ruth Beagles, that she was a dedicated but frustrated educator on St. Croix determined to revolutionize education for the benefit of the thousands of students who were voting against the public schools and their own futures by dropping out, walking out, and simply disappearing as soon as they were self-determined enough to do so and get away with it. Although the rest of her delegation were not as rapid-fire in their conversation as she, they shared her concerns and frustrations and pleaded for our assistance.

Several hours later, on my promise to mail curriculum guides, teacher training materials, parent training and development activities, and a full list of additional information, they left. I was exhausted —but flattered by their appreciation of what we had accomplished.

"There's a pushy little man who speaks funny on the line for you. He says he's calling for some kind of governor and must speak with you immediately. I told him you were in conference, but he won't go away. I'm sorry. He's on line one."

From her tone, I knew that Polly was irritated by the arrogance of this uncouth person on line 1. And even more annoyed that she hadn't been able to handle this call for me.

Polly Vann Zawadi had been my secretary at Xerox, where we had developed a close professional relationship that had extended over into a personal one. She was family, and when I left Xerox for New Lincoln, a non-negotiable condition was that Polly come with me.

"Harold Haizlip here," I said officiously.

"Good Dr. Haizlip. How nice to speak with you, sir. I'm Bruce Delemos, Confidential Administrative Officer for the Governor of the U.S. Virgin Islands. The governor has heard good things about your work from Ruth Beagles and told me to send you a ticket to come talk with him next Tuesday at 10:00 A.M. in Government House on St. Thomas. What address shall I send your ticket to? I just need to know that, for now. You know how confidential these matters are. I can't say more on the telephone because you never know who's listening. Ha, ha. What's your home address? I'll arrange for the governor's chauffeur to meet you at the St. Thomas Airport Monday afternoon, and of course the governor wants you to be his guest at our newly refurbished government Guest House during your stay with us. What's your home address, sir? And will you be staying through the weekend? Oh, and just in case, I need your home telephone number as well."

Delemos must be Beagles's brother, I thought.

"Exactly what, Mr. Delemos, does the governor want to talk with me about? And what's his name, again?"

"Evans. Dr. Melvin Evans. Honorable Governor of the U.S. Virgin Islands," he shouted. "His Excellency doesn't explain himself. He wants to talk with you in his office. Privately. Next Tuesday. At 10:00 A.M. sharp. I need your home address and telephone number so I can mail your ticket to you today."

"Does Mrs. Beagles know what the governor wants to talk about?"

"Good Doctor Haizlip," he sighed with exasperation. "I'm just doing my job. I have no idea what Mrs. Beagles knows. But I'll give you her telephone number if you give me your home address and telephone number first. Then we're finished. I'll be waiting for you next Tuesday morning at 9:55 to escort you into the governor's office at exactly 10:00 A.M. Okay? Now, what's your address?"

This was absurd, I thought, but I gave him my home address and telephone number, jotted down Ruth Beagles's number, hung up, and asked Polly to get Mrs. Beagles on the phone for me.

No question, it's beautiful here on St. Thomas, I thought, sitting in the rear of an oversized black car with flags on gold-topped poles fluttering in the wind on the front fenders. But I must be crazy coming all the way down here on my own time, without Shirlee, to talk to some damned governor who won't say what he wants to talk about. He hadn't told Ruth Beagles why he had summoned me to his office, but she was sure that it had something to do with his response to the report she had sent him on New Lincoln. I should have told Delemos to have the governor come to New York City, to New Lincoln, to my damned office, if he wanted to talk with me, and to bring his damned secrets with him. Who the hell does this government excellency think he is, anyway? And he's in for a real shock if he thinks a free round trip to St. Thomas will get me to do teacher training workshops down here for free.

A heavyset, middle-aged brown-skinned man with bright eyes, high cheekbones and a wide, sly smile that made him look like Amos of the Amos 'n' Andy team, the governor's chauffeur drove imperiously and impatiently. He approached any car ahead of us within inches of its rear bumper, turned on his amber flasher, and swerved around it headlong into oncoming traffic, grandly waving at drivers to pull off the road. After twisting hurriedly through the late-morning traffic on the waterfront, he whisked past a stately old lemon-yellow post office, roared up a steep hill banked on both sides with gracefully arching red, pink, and orange bougainvillea, and stopped in front of red carpeting that led from the street, up the center of ten or so wide, white marble stairs, and into the lobby.

"Welcome, sir, to Government House of the U.S. Virgin Islands. His Excellency, the Honorable Dr. Melvin H. Evans, Governor." A tall, slender security officer opened the car door briskly and stepped back in his crisp white shirt and black tie. His navy blue uniform was decorated with gold buttons in frogs, gold-fringed epaulets, and gold stripes on his sleeves, and he wore mirrored black shoes. I was hot, but he wasn't perspiring—probably because his brimmed hat was perforated around the sides to let his body heat escape. As soon as I stepped out and retrieved my briefcase, the governor's car sped off, flags flying wildly, for another imperial emergency, no doubt. According to my watch, it was 9:45. I was ten minutes early for the Confidential Assistant to His Excellency.

The foyer was a huge, high-ceilinged room with oversized frescoes of idealized island history on all walls. Tall white Grecian columns stretched floor to ceiling across one end and at the other, richly carpeted double staircases curved gracefully up to a landing across the rear length of the room, with four stairs leading somewhere at either end. Ahead of me, in the center below the landing, was an oversized mahogany oval table on which rested a large open book with gilded pages. An arrangement of fresh flowers graced one side; a brass pen rested in its brass holder on the other. On the white marble floor was a huge, thick round red rug embroidered with a large gold eagle perched on a globe in the center with its wings fully extended, surrounded by a black border with every single white fringe neatly in place.

"You're Dr. Haizlip from New York? To see Confidential Advisor Delemos?" Another security officer appeared from nowhere, his extended stomach about to pop his gold-buttoned frogs at any moment. "Please sign our guest book, including the time of your appointment with His Excellency, Honorable Governor Melvin H. Evans. Then I'll escort you to the Confidential Advisor's Office."

"Soooo nice to meet you in person, good Dr. Haizlip. Right this way. His Excellency will see you now." All business, Mr. Delemos beckoned me past several attractive secretaries at their desks, up a set of stairs covered with red oriental carpets, and into a private waiting room, where he pointed to an upholstered love seat and vanished behind two floor-to-ceiling mahogany doors with ornately sculpted brass handles that resembled fixtures on the main entrance doors of the Louvre.

"His Excellency will see you now." Delemos held one of the huge doors ajar for me to enter and closed it behind him as he left.

The huge color portrait of the governor facing what must have been a Virgin Islands flag dominated fully half of the wall space behind the massive, cluttered mahogany desk at which the governor sat busily signing documents captioned PROCLAMATION, in gold leaf. His Howard University Medical School degree was clustered on one side with large candids of the governor shaking hands with President Nixon, making a "victory" sign surrounded by people wearing boaters emblazoned with "MHE for GOV" on red, white, and blue bands, and the governor in hard hat with shovel, the governor cutting ribbons, the governor surrounded by gleaming schoolchildren in uniforms, the governor entering the White House, the governor everywhere else he'd been with his photographer in tow. On the other side were a large American flag and Virgin Islands flag, both topped by gold eagles with outstretched wings.

"I see you made it, Doctor," he began, not looking up from signing his official documents. "Have a seat."

"I'm not sure what you plan for us to discuss, but I certainly am enjoying your beautiful islands, Your Excellency." I was dissembling and beginning to feel insulted that after a four-hour flight to get here after his last-minute request, he was too busy to give me his undivided attention or even stand up and shake my hand in welcome. The thankless bastard. He continued signing, without looking up.

"Is there anything in particular that you want to discuss today, Your Excellency? It is, I believe, 10:05 on Tuesday morning, the time you insisted I be here in your office." My tone was purposely insistent, with a slight edge of impatience.

He slowly placed his pen aside and looked up at me, barely masking an uncertain response to the insistence of this uppity young Statesider who had traveled to St. Thomas on money provided by Virgin Islands taxpayers, at his invitation, seemingly without gratitude. A handsome man with sharp, chiseled features in his late forties, he had a lazy right eye. He raised his solid midriff from his chair and extended a well-manicured hand of welcome, smiling as if his photographer were behind me.

"I'm delighted and pleased," he began unctuously, "that you could take time from your busy schedule, good Doctor, to be my personal guest on St. Thomas, courtesy of the Government of the U.S. Virgin Islands." He was retaliating in kind (but nicely) to my earlier comment, I knew, smiling broadly as if I were his dentist.

He quickly got down to business, first summarizing in his own words the New Lincoln wonders Ruth Beagles had reported. After being appointed governor by President Nixon, he had recently been elected by an overwhelming majority of Virgin Islanders to a second term in which his priority was revamping and significantly improving the education system on St. Thomas, St. John, and St. Croix. After scouring the globe, he had concluded that only I was up to the job—under his able guidance and with his unwavering support. He wanted me to tour the islands, meet his education people, meet the leadership of the Virgin Islands Legislature, and then come back and talk turkey about what it would take for me to become a member of his cabinet and the next Commissioner of Education for the U.S. Virgin Islands. My tour was all arranged and would begin at noon. Advisor Delemos and his chauffeur had everything lined up. He looked forward to chatting with me later in the day. As if on cue, Delemos walked into the office.

Over dinner that evening, I told the governor that I was impressed by what had been accomplished during his first term but sensed that much, much more needed to be done in every area of both formal and informal education on the islands—for children and parents. He nearly leaped out of his seat upon hearing this confirmation of his own opinion. But, I added, I was deeply committed to a multiyear agenda at New Lincoln, under a multiyear contract, had children enrolled comfortably in private school, and a wife busily engaged in her own career and volunteer pursuits. I could not make any kind of decision on the spot. I needed to see more, get answers to many more questions both in New York and in the Virgin Islands, and discuss the possibility of relocation at length with my family. I could talk with him again within a couple of weeks. I was flattered by his interest in me for this position.

He understood, he said, urging me to be ever mindful of the once-in-a-lifetime opportunity he was offering me to put my training and talents to work for "your own people."

After a year of trips to the islands, conferences and meetings with the governor, the legislature, school administrators, private industry representatives, parents, and others—and intense meetings with my New Lincoln board, administrators, and faculty—I finally agreed to accept the offer we had by then negotiated.

While we were at the Taylors in New Haven to store furniture, furnishings, and winter clothes that we were not taking with us, uninvited visitors entered our West End Avenue apartment and made off with an antique eighteenth-century music box I had given Shirlee, the girls' piggy banks, and Shirlee's best costume jewelry. Returning home, we could barely open the apartment door, which was blocked by all of the blankets, clothes, linens, and our other belongings that had been pulled from our closets and thrown helter-skelter in piles on the floor. Shirlee's jewelry had been spread carefully over our bed and the best pieces removed. The girls' closets had been emptied, their mattresses thrown on the floor, and their toy bins upended. The apartment looked as if a whirlwind had blown through it.

None of the elevator operators or doormen had seen anyone in the building who did not live there, and access to our floor was possible only through the manned elevators. I was furious—and helpless. It seemed an ominous message that it was time for us to get out of New York City. We packed and planned our departure.

CHAPTER 9

American Paradise

𝒮HIRLEE: In the seventies, I would let go of my wigs, my girdles, and the "Mrs." before my first name, not necessarily in that order.

It began as an adventure. Despite two children, twenty-six suitcases, and our ragtag menagerie, the first part of the flight was uneventful. The airport at St. Thomas had not yet been enlarged to receive jumbo jets. In the cacophonous San Juan airport, we all made the necessary transfer to a smaller plane. For the hour-long hop between the two islands, the high-pitched bark of our dog in the hold below cut through the uneven drone of the engines.

I had no idea what to expect. Island pomp and circumstance for high-placed officials began for us in St. Thomas's World War II hangar, which had been designated the official terminal. The welcoming niceties competed with the serious heat slamming into me like a pod of angry linebackers.

Flashes. A darting figure. A wiry, dark photographer from the local newspaper kept clicking his lens. Tired after a six-hour journey and anxious because of the dog's distress, the girls, suddenly shy, clung to my skirt. Sweat dripped down my back. My stockings were soaked. The humidity attacked my hair and killed it. So much for cool elegance.

A handsome, small man with a sculpted face, natty in black pants, white shirt, and black tie, bowed almost imperceptibly. He was "Donovan," surname being a popular form of address, and announced that he was proud to be our driver. Following Donovan in an elegant government sedan, a small cavalcade of vehicles carried us and our belongings to our temporary residence, a guest house used by visiting dignitaries. We were at Estate Dorothea, one of the highest points of the island, on its misty and verdant north side.

The modest bungalow, part of St. Thomas's agricultural station, sat at the end of rows of dusty plants. Around the property, the ground was level for a few hundred yards then dropped off to the Atlantic in a precipitous cliff. Waves flounced onto much of the rocky shore below. Here and there, a house dotted the hillside.

Boppo, a gigantic, pleasant man who wore his dignity as gracefully as he carried his four hundred pounds, presided over the place and a small group of workers who were rarely in evidence. I could never figure out whether they worked there full-time or showed up as needed. My early interactions with Boppo taught me my first lesson in island culture. It takes a long time to get to know and be known by the natives, who possess a lovely kind of old-fashioned reserve.

Whenever I advanced, Boppo retreated. I was overzealous in my attempts to be friendly. Too many questions; too much presumption of familiarity. It didn't take me long to get it; I was being too forward. In the islands, you have to earn the trust of friendship. Eventually we would come to know Boppo as a font of information about this island's politics and personalities.

Around them the girls saw mostly brown people. Browns of all colors: tan, beige, pink, nutmeg, coffee, ebony, cinnamon, bark, coconut, mocha. Browns that have yet to be categorized. The local palette affirmed and reinforced the skin color of each girl, Dee Dee a tan, Melissa a chocolate. In that place their hues were as much a part of the natural order of things as were the colors of the hibiscuses or the shades of the bougainvillea. And constantly being in the sun made both their skins darker.

Once the charm and unfamiliarity of the guest house wore thin, the girls became restless and bored. Housebound, I was not too pumped up myself. Theoretically, Donovan was only supposed to drive my husband, unless I was traveling to an official function.

Theoretically. We had not yet enrolled the girls in school, wanting to wait until we had our official residence. Where we were staying was not a neighborhood, as such, and there was little to do in the immediate vicinity; encountering a chicken or a goat was a major event. Lack of sidewalks made walking hazardous along the winding, narrow road.

I knew no one, saw only the smiling Boppo and the reticent workers, and no one called on us. Except for official receptions at Government House, no invitations came our way. It's not that the islanders are unfriendly, but they must welcome thousands of visitors every day of the year. And until you lived on the island for several years, you were considered to be a visitor, passing through, someone not worth investing time in. I missed my family terribly.

Things brightened every weekend as we went to one of the island's many beautiful beaches. These trips were followed by a visit to downtown Charlotte Amalie. On the eastern end of the island, Lindquist, a private beach owned by a native family, quickly became our favorite because its vegetation was wild, unmanicured. Its waters were calm and shallow; its shoreline was rocky in some places, smooth in others. Best of all, no tourists. Generally Lindquist was deserted. Local lore had it that the Lindquist family was fighting to hold on to the beach, to keep it pristine, free of development. It was said they were waging a losing battle.

Often we went to Magen's Bay, one of the natives' favorite beaches, where cookout celebrations were a way of weekend life. The compelling aromas of curried goat, peas and rice, pick-up fish, and kallalou wafted through a sizable palm grove that filtered the sun. Those who know about these things call Magen's Bay one of the great beaches of the world. Its wide curve of sand forms a deep U-shaped configuration on the island's north side. The water, sometimes blue, sometimes aquamarine, is generally calm. The stand of tall, serene trees has the feeling of a holy place. When you walk through the grove, you take care not to make noise. Curiously enough, many of the natives did not swim or even venture into the water. I could never find out why. Perhaps taboos or fears rooted in their ancient history made the ocean a respected thing, neither friend nor foe.

The Virgin Islands was a place where necessities like water and fresh food were expensive, and luxuries like liquor and perfume were cheap.

Except for some French farmers on the north side, St. Thomas did not grow its own foodstuffs. Often we went to Market Square, the native market, for fish, north side vegetables, succulent homemade coconut squares, or delicious johnnie cake. An old open-air market with a central mud red overhang, Market Square served as a boundary for the commercial western end of Main Street. A welcoming jumble of color and noise, it was the perfect place for gossip and politics. There could be had avocados, mangoes, coconuts, passion fruit, lush orchids, peas and rice, and the latest bulletin on shenanigans in the legislature. The clipped accents from St. Thomas, Nevis, and St. Kitts stood out amid the Barbadian singsong or Tortollan whines. The girls picked up the local patois instantly. I could understand it but could not master its dropped consonants and double objectives, as in "give him the book, the ting."

When Monday came, it was back to reading children's books or watching the limited fare of St. Thomas television, which did not sign on until four o'clock in the afternoon, when the soap operas or "stories" began. National news on the station was a day old, having been taped and shipped down from Orlando, Florida. There was no CNN then, and the local papers, *The Virgin Islands Daily News*, and the *Post* carried scant national news. The cost of shipping made *The New York Times* an egregiously expensive way to get some sense of what was going on beyond the island's gorgeous horizon.

Planted by the governor's foes, pointed local newspaper articles appeared about the cost to the government of storing our furniture in a container languishing at dockside. Finding a house for us became of paramount importance; the search was not easy. Housing on the island was as expensive as that in New York.

One afternoon, Harold came home early and announced that he had found the perfect place in Estate Elizabeth, not too far away from the agricultural station. He took me and the girls down for a viewing. All I had to see was a foyer frescoed in blue clouds and Manet water lilies and the house was mine. The entrance embraced me, took hold and wouldn't let go. The house's marble-floored living room and whitestoned gallery hung over a terraced garden, several miles high above the harbor in Charlotte Amalie. A glance over the gleaming white balustrade told me how many cruise ships were in town. A jeep custompainted the same blue as the house's shutters came with the rental.

A banana tree forest was painted on one wall. In the bedrooms, impressionistic camellias camouflaged closet doors. A European library, a mansion-size kitchen, a cold storage vault for furs, and several gleaming bidets (surely anomalies in this land of scarce drinking water) added quirkiness to this stunning island house.

In the garden, a flamboyant tree, ablaze with red flowers, towered over rows of gardenias that filled our nostrils with splashy scents. Birds of paradise haughtily rimmed blue and gray stone pathways. Along one path, delicate orchids seemed to hover in midair, and everywhere, there was hibiscus of all colors. In a shadowy, fern-filled copse, a Buddha-like statue invited meditation or prayer. Could we really have this place?

A courtly island Frenchman, Albery Brin, who had helped build the house, continued to tend the place at the owner's expense, clicking his heels, bowing and touching his hat whenever he encountered me. The resident housekeeper, Sylvia, a gap-toothed Amazonian native of Anguilla who ordered her clothes from Frederick's of Hollywood, offered to remain.

What made Harold think we could afford this Eden? He had already arranged it. The owner had died; the house would probably be in probate for years, the island lawyer told us. The heir would like to keep it occupied, and the rent was not much more than our New York apartment. The government was off the hook. We moved in the next week and enrolled the girls in Sibilly, a small, integrated public school less than a mile down the hill.

We didn't know the house was haunted.

Everybody in my family believes in ghosts. My sharpest early memories were tales of my father's encounters with ghosts and spirits, including his mother's hand on his shoulder; my mother's vision of her dead mother; my sister who had been born with a caul over her face who "saw things" and did not like to go to sleep at night; the presences that had driven my family out of one of its first Connecticut homes. We accepted ghosts as easily as we breathed air.

It was the dead owner, Madame Eveque, née Dieudonné, who visited her mountain home. A benign spirit, she obviously was not ready to give up the you-know-what. A perfume heiress, she had died prematurely of cancer. Nonetheless, she wanted to continue the task at hand, decorating her spectacular house and developing her opulent garden. We saw her in the living room, elegant in gray cashmere pants and dark shoes. Her scent flooded the halls as her steps echoed on the marble floors. She was not pleased with the placement of one of our paintings. It jumped off a sturdy nail onto the marble floor, but its glass did not break. We moved it elsewhere and we didn't tell the children.

Once a picture fell out of a book in the library. The face was hers, Albery said. She looked like my mother.

Big-city gloss, small-town life. A man-friendly, woman-secondary place. That was St. Thomas in the seventies. People identified you by your family or your island of origin. Civility prevailed and "Good morning," "Good day," "Good night," accompanied all exchanges. Youngsters were expected to pay heed to all elders, whether known to them or not. Public school children wore uniforms and churches were full. Drugs had not yet made an inroad. In this small universe, Dee Dee and Missy would enter the middle years of their childhood in a place of comfort and friendly scrutiny. For them, the islands would always be home.

Some say all families are alike, yet for each one there is a different key to its dynamics. What are the forces that make a family meld, keep it distant, or destroy it? There was only one movie house, no malls, no arcades, no youth recreation centers, so island life promoted family activity. Parties, weddings, and most social events were intergenerational, encouraging attendance by children. The four of us went everywhere together, seldom needing a sitter. It was not considered uncool to be with your parents. This pattern would maintain itself for the next eight years. I am certain we came together in St. Thomas in ways that never could have happened in New York City.

Once, when we did not take Missy and Dee Dee with us to dinner, I found a note on my pillow that said, "To be opened only if your name is STH." Melissa voiced her complaints:

> This is a list of what I hate about Parents
> I Just HATE . . .
> 1. When they think you are a baby.
> 2. When you say something serious and they laugh.
> 3. When they embarrass you in front of guests.

4. When they don't listen when you keep up the same subject.

5. When they get mad at you easily and take it out on us

6. When we are hungry you don't believe us.

7. When sometimes they hit you for nothing.

8. When they love and believe the oldest kid in the family (ESPECIALLY AROUND THIS HOUSE (hint) (hint))

9. When they make you go to bed early.

10. Like if we say we don't want it, we *have* to eat it.

11. When I tell the truth and my sister tells a lie, you think she is right.

12. When My sister bosses me around

13. When my sister teases me

14. When my sister criticizes me with my spelling

15. When My sister says I'm vien.

16. When we are having an argument, you go on her side instead of mine

17. When my sister can stay up late

18. When I have to go to school even if I'm tired

19. When I have to be bossed around by my parents

20. When parents act like they are dog owners and we are the dogs.

21. When you don't understand me

22. When we get up if I'm cranky dad always has to tease

By your daughter, Missy

The next day, we talked through all of the points, being as empathetic as we knew how. A few days later we received a call around six-thirty in the morning. "We don't want to alarm you, but Melissa is with us," the caller said. Missy had left in the middle of the night with a small schoolbag on her back and walked a few miles until she became frightened and stopped at the house of a classmate. Harold went off to retrieve our runaway.

A barely patient slew of questions. "What were you thinking? What possessed you to leave? Don't you know you might have been kidnapped and killed, or worse? Do you know how we must feel? Don't you *ever* do that again." First round.

"What was so awful you couldn't tell us about it? Let's try to find out how to keep this from happening again."

For parents, no explanation of inexplicable behavior is ever satisfying. We thought we had been doing a good job, but there was always something we did not hear; something we did not see. The storm blew over as quickly and as inexplicably as it had arrived.

Each girl established her own passion for the islands, developing what would become lifelong interests there: Missy, dance and music; Dee Dee, horseback riding and design. Dee Dee had become an independent, hearty soul. Athletic and well formed, still with pinchable full cheeks and sandy brown hair, she struck me as a serious, no-nonsense child. Arrestingly pretty, her feelings flitted like elusive hummingbirds across her open, cherubic face. Frugal, she saved her allowance to order items from the States that she saw in comic books or children's magazines. She earned a place on the island's gymnastic team and several summers went to a horseback riding camp in Vermont, where she was annoyed that the other campers thought she was Puerto Rican or from Spain.

Early on, Missy was a romantic with intense feelings. Everything affected her: the weather, the news, the way someone looked, an iguana walking across the road. She was forever asking "why," pouring her feelings into poetry and pottery. Studying both ballet and piano during summers at Interlochen in Michigan, she agonized over the amount of time she should give to each. Small and delicately formed, her look was that of a fragile nymph. I knew she would be a great beauty someday.

When the girls finished Sibilly's last grade, they entered the world of parochial school. A traditional Episcopal coeducational school that had established an excellent academic reputation, All Saints attracted a healthy mixture of black and white, local and continental children. Green and blue plaid uniforms were required, imposing a sense of order. With their education including private, public, and parochial settings, the girls could not have been better armed for the vagaries of the outside world.

We made a conscious effort to understand and enjoy the culture we had chosen. There was a gender difference in how outsiders took to the island. Generally, men loved it, particularly the opportunities for golf, sailing, tennis, swimming, cheap liquor, accessible politics, a macho, posturing environment. For the very same reasons, I took longer to adjust.

We garbed ourselves in a new work ethic and an old colonial history, absorbing the proud attitude toward slavery and liberation, the proprietary relationship to the land and the water. After all, these were people who had been freed decades before American slaves. These were people who in some cases had driven their masters off the land, or jumped en masse from high cliffs to liberate themselves forever.

One of the best routes into island hearts is to participate in Carnival. For an entire week, the island stops its business and puts it heart, soul, feet, and mind into Carnival. There are two days of parades, finishing with an Adults' Parade. The first day, a Children's Parade features a large Indian troupe that all the children clamor to join. For several years, Dee Dee and Missy were Indians, with costume changes marking the various tribes. Once Dee Dee complained about one of the more creative costumes I contrived for her from a maroon and white vinyl tablecloth bearing patterns and designs that were vaguely Indian. "Mom, I've never seen an Indian wear anything like that," was all I heard for the whole week.

We joined the Gypsy Troupe, one of the island's oldest carnival organizations. At our clubhouse each week, each of us would work according to his or her special skill, fitting, cutting, pasting, sewing, sequining, feathering, and beading the costumes for the hundred or so in our group, all the while gossiping about the latest island scandal or political brouhaha. The Gypsies attracted young and old, white and black, Continental and native, teachers, politicians, ministers, priests, janitors, secretaries, lawyers, store owners. Once we marched as a pack of cards in silver and red; another year, señoritas, señoras, and bullfighters in ruffles and lace. Then came the time we were rain, clouds, thunder, and lightning, in silver and black lamé.

My favorite recollection of Carnival was the year we looked like extras from the Broadway musical *Kismet*. I wear sheer white harem pants over black briefs. A turquoise pear-shaped jewel glitters in my navel. A black and white lamé top with sheer sleeves and plunging neckline is topped by a large black minaret headdress that keeps falling to one side. Just before we leave the house, Harold looks at me and says, "Shirlee, are those your black panties you're wearing under your costume?"

"Now, Harold, would I dance down Main Street in my black panties? These were purchased for the costume." Of course they are my black panties. I fulfill my "I Dreamed I Wore My Maidenform Panties on Main Street in Carnival" dream.

We leave for the parade in the early morning, driving around the western end of the island to reach Western Cemetery, where the units casually organize themselves into formation. We had arranged for the girls to watch the parade with friends. By the time we park the car, the temperature is already eighty degrees. Greeting our troupe mates, we admire each other's costumes. The behemoth of a steel band leading our float is gearing up. Food and liquor are stored in the float and drinking and eating has already begun. It is not yet eleven o'clock, but the parade rarely starts on time.

The signal comes. We shuffle ahead, beginning to dance a rhythmic two-step in time with the music. Some people are cool in their dancing, taking small steps and saving their energy for the several-mile march. Others go all out, hopping and moving energetically from one side of the street to the other. By the time we get to Market Square, the temperature has jumped to ninety. Most of the troupe has donned their sunglasses. After Market Square, Main Street narrows and we snake along, squeezed in between onlookers six deep on either side of the street. A tourist jumps out in front of me, shakes his hips, and says, "Island girl, island girl, meet me at Bluebeard's after the parade." He flashes a business card. Harold gives him the eye and he moves on. We pass Palm Passage, a shopping alley, A.H. Riise, a department store. The sun is directly overhead. Sweat is pouring down from my minaret, and my harem pants stick to my panties. The glue in my navel melts, the jewel loosens. I'm beginning to wonder if I will make it past the reviewing stand.

Post Office Square comes into view. In the wider plaza, the sun is everywhere, flooding us like the brightest lights of the television cameras mounted on the balcony of the Grand Hotel straight ahead. Waving often, the governor holds forth in the reviewing stand. With renewed energy and a little less synchronism than the Rockettes, we perform our one number that we have practiced for weeks. Enthusiastic cheers and claps reward our routine.

Reluctantly, we give up our place to the troupe that follows. The street narrows again, and we head for Lionel Roberts Stadium.

"Are you going to make it? Your face is red. You look overheated," Harold says, somewhat anxiously.

"Yes, yes, I want to finish."

We turn at Norregade; the Stadium is in sight, gleaming like a beached white whale. A truck pulling a float breaks down ahead of us. The temperature is 98 and climbing, and some of us sit on the curb until the truck is pulled out of the line. I notice my belly jewel has fallen out, leaving a diamond-shaped patch of white glue in the middle of my stomach. Droopy now, my minaret is almost parallel to the roadway.

The march resumes. The whitewashed walls of the stadium burn, glistening in the heat. But just ahead is the first bit of shade. Cool at last. We enter the gates and the sun disappears for a few moments. Out into the brightness again. With one last burst of energy, we dance across the stadium floor and perform our number. We disband. For us, at least, the parade is over.

We head back over the western hills for home. While stumbling toward the bed, I take off my costume. The room is cool and quiet. We sleep until evening.

Paradise can be trying. Life as a beach is not necessarily fulfilling unless you are a marine biologist. With too much time on my hands, I turned to watercolors, watched a lot of television. I needed a job.

Harold's new post called for a significant amount of travel. Because I was not working, I could not afford to join him. I was restless and jealous. In early December of 1972, he took a dream trip to a meeting in Hawaii, without me. It was not enough for me to be on a beautiful island in a beautiful house with two beautiful daughters; I wanted to be with him on another beautiful island in a beautiful hotel.

In his Christmas letter to me he recognized that and my other concerns.

Christmas, 1972

Honey,
As you know I swore after the San Francisco trip that I'd take no more business trips without you unless there were compelling, insurmountable blockages. Hawaii was one of

those: no money. My trip was a personal disaster. I hated not being able to bring you with me; I hated having no money (you, of all people, know what that does to my self-image!) I hated being alone in a place where togetherness reigns; and as you know, I left home feeling many unresolved tensions. The trip was awful.

One afternoon, however, I decided to skip out on one of the business sessions because I'd had enough and because I felt generally upset with the circumstances of my world —i.e. you and me.

Quite by accident I fell into a store called Shell World. I knew you'd like the necklace made of the cut shell, so I bought it for you. Then I saw the black and white one and thought of your black and white skirt and your black top. I knew you'd like that one also, so I bought it for you.

Then I saw your Christmas gift. This one broke me, but I have never felt so pleased. Buying it for you seemed almost symbolic: There's nothing I have or am that I would not give up for you for your happiness with me. It caught my eye from the midst of hundreds of items and seemed, in its perfect symmetry, to be waiting for you. I *had* to get it for you. And I know what you will do with it—exactly—without asking. It's that much a part of our thing, of you and me.

We've had a good year, darling. Only one goal has gone unfulfilled: getting you the kind of job with the kind of salary that you want and richly deserve. This is my immediate goal for 1973—and I have already put more wheels in motion. I am confident that we will overcome this one too, and soon. I look forward to a ripe old age filled with you and memories of our life together.

Merry Christmas, darling.

Yours always, H.

The gift was a chambered nautilus shell.

We had been on the island for two years when my deliverance came in the form of the lieutenant governor, Addie Ottley. A genial, handsome man with a crew cut and broad shoulders, Addie had been a popular broadcaster, then a local senator. Summoned to his office, I listened as he told me he would be host of and needed help planning a conference for the lieutenant governors of the fifty states. Each of the three Virgin Islands would be utilized as sites for various activities. Of course, the constantly broke Virgin Islands government had no money for this kind of frill. Could I raise the funds for the affair, and could I direct it? No problem, I told him.

The islands' major corporations quickly jumped on the benefactors' bandwagon, the Senate approved the budget, and we were on our way. Talk about political correctness. In that land of factional fierceness, every group had to be recognized, consulted, and included in the conference's activities. Our strategies did not take into account an event that would forever alter the islands' tourism karma. A few days before the conference, several Cruzans, as the St. Croix natives are called, shot up a luxury golf course, not to mention a few luxury golfers, on a rolling green Rockefeller resort whose cliffs fell off into the Caribbean Sea. The golfers had the misfortune of being statesiders, and the news traveled faster than an atomic submarine to the mainland. "Race Wars," "Tourists Targeted," "Island Ill Will," "Militants' Mayhem" screamed the headlines. Should the conference be canceled? We caucused. Security was doubled, the meetings and social activities went as scheduled.

Despite all efforts, there was a big snafu. I felt as if a group of militants had burst into a hotel ballroom when twice as many gowned and guayaberraed guests as there were seats showed up for the dinner of the states on the last night. Prior to the event, the governor's office kept paying its dues by giving tickets of admission to the banquet, disregarding our diplomatic then frantic reminders of the capacity of the room.

But Houdini could not make more seats or a larger banquet room. No messiah could multiply the chicken and house salads. Years later, my most recurrent anxiety nightmare flashes back to that night when eight hundred elegant guests are trying to crush through the doors to claim four hundred seats. Glaring at me as her designer gown was being mashed in the crowd, the wife of the chief corporate benefactor said, "This is bad, Shirlee, this is bad." I still wake up in a sweat at that aspersion.

Those without seats were bussed to another hotel that had been commandeered at the last minute. Many huffily refused and walked off into the night. Angry callers besieged the governor's office. By then I had finished my assignment and collected my fees.

Using my new connections with the island business community and with Ellis and public television, in 1974 I talked myself into a position with WBNB, the CBS affiliate of the Virgin Islands. As a production assistant at a nonunion station, I learned everything I could under the tutelage of the curmudgeonly station owner/manager, Bob Moss, whose own reliance on his chief engineer, Sam James, a handsome, courtly British Virgin Islander who worked for years to get his green card, was complete. Habitually brushing a long strand of oily hair back from his eyes, a slightly bent-over Moss shuffled when he walked and muffled when he talked. Squinting already small eyes, he rarely smiled. He fashioned himself an architect of the island's destiny, seizing every opportunity to editorialize about and chastise the various government departments. But by the time I got to the station, Moss had tired of running the place and was ready to sell, to retire, to pontificate from some sunny gallery overlooking the blue sea.

A group of statesiders subsequently purchased WBNB, becoming the first black owners of an American television station. One of the group, Ted Ledbetter, the son of a minister friend of my father's from Connecticut, became my new boss. We were contemporaries and had been friends as preachers' kids in New Haven.

The new owners wanted a general manager who would get out into the community, would go to the beach, would join a Carnival troupe. Ted was not social. Strains developed. Washington spoke. The owners promoted me to general manager and Ted left the island. I felt bad for him but happy for me. At that time I was the first and only female general manager among all of CBS's affiliates. I was also their only black. A bona fide, genuine two-fer.

I inherited the management of a business that was fodder for a situation comedy. The undistinguished offices and studio were on the second floor of a bank building abutting one corner of Market Square. The old structure dated from colonial times. Seedy if not dilapidated, the warren of rooms included an audio studio, a sound stage, and a control room that you reached by climbing a narrow spiral iron staircase. A significant inventory of mostly B movies from the thirties, forties, and fifties in dusty gray canisters occupied another room.

The station's small staff might have come from Central Casting. Sam continued to be the heart of the station, keeping it on the air throughout the week. Two island French girls performed administrative duties. Dave, a handsome gray-blond Continental tennis player, always dressed in the tennis whites he wore as the Hilton's pro, where he gave daily lessons, relieved Sam on the weekends. Ruben, a St. Thomian, was also a weekend cohort. Stockily built and dark brown, Ruben was a literal thinker. A postal worker during the week, he loved his television job and had a deeply proprietary feeling about *his* station. It conferred a special status on him among his postal colleagues.

An enormously attractive and savvy local woman, Leona Bryant, had been the station's local programming doyenne for years. Her position undoubtedly helped her navigate the political waters in which she loved to swim. Especially beloved was Joe Potter, a black Continental sportscaster who had been on the island for many years and had developed a loyal coterie of fans. Susan Sikora, a lively, brown-haired Continental charmer who worked for Harold as an English teacher and for me as a newscaster, enchanted us with stories of her priest-turned-hotelier husband, Skip. Another Continental, Jody Owen, a Bahai sportscaster, endeared himself to the locals by developing a local children's program. Amid much grumbling about accents and breadth of experience, I hired Isidro Gomez, the first native-born newscaster. It took a while for him to feel comfortable.

Soon after, Ruth Jones, the wife of the former Harlemite and Tammany politician known as the Silver Fox, J. Raymond Jones, became the president. Wearing comfortable muumuus, the stocky owner created a raft of systems for keeping track of her new kingdom, vigilantly overseeing me and everything else. Ruth had been a U.S. Customs official and her demeanor suggested she was always looking inside every box, every package, every letter for a hidden agenda. Cutting through her dourness, every morning Jody would come into Ruth's office, drop to his knees, and sing "Me and Mrs. Jones."

Week after week, month after month we managed to send our programming from a transmitter atop the island's highest point, Mountain Top. The signal went out for hundreds of miles, reaching Puerto Rico, some of the British Virgin Islands, and pods of whales.

The English-speaking people of Puerto Rico formed a major contingent of our overall audience.

Virgin Islanders hungered for positive images of themselves. What they mostly saw was standard network prime-time fare. What we added were documentaries of local interest—a portrait of local artist Albert Daniel, a look at problems at the airport, a snapshot of the island's first high school graduating class.

For me, the most satisfying of those was my work with Albert Daniel. Albert had been born on the island in 1897, a quieter and more pastoral time. One of the first Virgin Islanders to devote his entire life to painting and sculpture, he taught himself, freely admitting to the influence of another painter who had lived on the island, in fact in the same downtown house where Albert had lived for a while, Camille Pissaro. Albert's subjects were the working people of the island, the farmers, fishermen, market women. Bright colors, strong images, and religious symbolism characterized his style. His paintings had been snapped up by visiting tourists and various museums.

I met Albert when he was in his late seventies. A small, handsome man with silver hair and a face that looked as if it had been carved from rose-colored granite, Albert loved to quote poetry and be in the company of beautiful women. A childless widower, he lived alone in a little house on a scruffy hill known as Agnes' Fancy. Albert was frail and I worried about his health, often inviting him to dinner to make sure that he would eat. He'd arrive dressed neatly in a pale gray suit with a yellow tie and a white shirt. While Harold was cooking dinner in the kitchen, Albert would recite poetry to me outside on the gallery. He told Harold that if I had not been spoken for, he surely would have me.

Sometimes he'd call in the middle of the night and tell us that his roof was leaking. Could we come and fix it? We went. I held Albert's hand, listening to more poetry while Harold placed pots and plastic under the leaks.

My show about Albert spanned his life and his art. We played it in prime time on a Sunday night, after *60 Minutes*. The station was bombarded by calls from people who wanted to help him fulfill a wish he had made known during the program: to see the great works of the European masters. Enough money was raised to send him and a companion to Washington and then to France, Italy, and England. When he returned, he was a hero in his own time.

I loved what I did. Although I had liked all my other jobs while I was doing them, this one filled my soul. To be in charge, to create, to initiate meaningful dialogue was all deeply satisfying. More than that, though, was the knowledge that under my direction, the station was celebrating the community and reflecting the vividness of its life, much as Ellis's *SOUL!* had done. In this highly macho culture where women were generally dismissed, I had a seat at the table. I was a player. And I had become Shirlee Taylor Haizlip. The locals called me "Shelly Taylor Haizlip."

Polyester made its way to the islands, as did bell-bottom pants and platform shoes. Weeks after they popped up on screens in America we saw *Saturday Night Fever*, *Star Wars*, and *Jaws*. After *Jaws*, none of us felt like swimming much. And with apologies to Nat King Cole and Johnny Mathis, we enshrined Roberta Flack, Marvin Gaye, Lionel Richie, and Barry White into our personal pantheon of the world's greatest singers.

Despite television, despite the one movie theater, despite a constant stream of off-island visitors, we experienced American culture of the seventies, long distance and diluted, as if through a scrim. Special events traveled through the ether by way of satellites beamed at Puerto Rico. The Watergate hearings kept us enthralled. We watched Nixon flash his resignation "V" and disappear into a helicopter. Although compelling television, it all seemed irrelevant to the immediacy of life in the islands. Our concerns had little to do with the machinations of Washington or New York.

During the eight years we lived in St. Thomas, many things of lesser consequence never reached the islands. Now whenever someone refers to a play, a movie, or an event I've not heard of, I always ask, "Did it happen in the seventies?" Usually the answer is affirmative. This vacuum of information has made a difference in what we can claim as collective memories. We are deficient and still trying to catch up.

Does anyone lead a perfect or near-perfect life? I wonder. For a while, ours was as near perfect as one could get. Although we were not making a lot of money by mainland standards, both of us had jobs we loved, our children were healthy and doing well in school, we had a great house, two great dogs. We traveled a lot and made a host of new friends. Life was still full of celebrations.

In June of 1974, Harold wrote:

My darling,

Verbose as I am, there nevertheless are certain occasions on which I find myself speechless. The 27th of June in 1974 is one such occasion, for it is our fifteenth wedding anniversary.

I know of no way that I can tell you adequately how much I have enjoyed our years together, and how much I look forward to a minimum of 50 more years. Oh, how much I remain consumed by you—willingly and gladly.

If we had choices to make yet again, I would not hesitate for one second to ask you to marry me. And should you say yes, my joy would again be as unbounded as it is today.

To commemorate this occasion, I have chosen a ring with three hearts, one for each of our five years together. The last one is centered with a diamond, which for me represents the eternal fountain of our love. It will glow forever.

Happy Anniversary, Darling. I love you and I will until I die; and I will love you even thereafter,

Yours,
H.

*H*AROLD: During the year-long courtship before I accepted appointment as Commissioner of Education, Governor Evans and I had talked frequently by telephone and in person about a wide range of topics that he felt I needed to understand. What he really meant was that I needed to understand his politics and priorities and get on board with them before I set foot on the islands as Commissioner.

Of prime importance to him was that in his first election campaign, improving public education had been one of the central planks, and he wanted to deliver visible, dramatic results quickly. A Cruzan and a lifelong Democrat, he was a native son who returned home after completing Howard Medical School and established on St. Croix a highly successful general practice before being tapped by President

Nixon for appointment as governor, provided he switched political parties and became a registered Republican.

The vast majority of the islands' registered voters were Democrats. A small, vociferous, and growing number of disaffected Democrats had recently left the fold and formed a new, more aggressive social action party, the Independent Citizens Movement (ICM). The Republican party enrolled the smallest number of registered voters by far. A majority of the Democrats and ICMs were African American, while white Americans and Europeans were strongly represented among the Republicans. The governor, of course, was black.

The Legislature of the Virgin Islands was a unicameral body consisting only of the Senate. In 1971, the majority of elected members were Democrats or ICMs. One was Republican—and white.

It was important to the governor that I understand this political scenario and its implications for him and for me. He viewed his successful campaign as an endorsement of him personally more than of the minority Republican party. His Democratic opponent had been a strong, well-qualified candidate who waged a vigorous, well-heeled campaign, which, toward the end, became vicious and personal, in the governor's opinion. The governor had nevertheless won, but it was apparent that his campaign scars were deep and raw, his anger and hurt still palpable. In his own quiet way, he was determined to even the score with those on his enemies list, one way or another, sooner or later.

An intelligent, articulate, and proud man, he was quite kind and sensitive beneath his public, political bravado and bravura. I began to suspect that behind closed doors, he might possibly have quite a temper. His ego was certainly obvious. But I forgave him that because I believed all politicians were ego driven. The challenge for the electorate was to decipher and decide which candidate's ego needs were likely to serve the people best—always a tough call.

After New York City's noisy buses and honking taxis, jammed subways, congested traffic, the grinding trash trucks, and millions of people, I anticipated the serenity, peacefulness, and slower, more humane pace and lifestyle on the islands, the seemingly kinder and more gentle, more caring people. It would be paradise for us. And, most of all, in that place where I live privately with my conscience, I eagerly anticipated freedom for the first time from the emotional, physical, intellectual, and social shackles of racism. As I thought about the extraordinary challenges of my new job, I took comfort in telling myself, "However bad the mess may be, it's our black mess, and we blacks will deal with it as we see fit." And I expected that I would learn much from Virgin Islanders about my new sense of freedom because they had freed themselves long, long before my arrival.

Early in the morning on the day after we arrived on St. Thomas, Shirlee and I were admiring the foliage outside our windows and the waves crashing against the shoreline far below when the Government Guest House telephone shattered our reverie. I answered, unable to imagine who would be calling us so soon, so early.

"Best of the morning to you, good Doctor. At the request of His Excellency, Honorable Governor Melvin H. Evans, I have arranged for Mr. Dennis Donovan to pick you up in half an hour for an urgent meeting with the governor. Mr. Donovan is very busy today, so please do not delay him. He has many other assignments to complete before his day ends."

"Might you be the good Mr. Delemos, Confidential Advisor to His Excellency, Honorable Governor Melvin H. Evans?" I asked, attempting the same formal tone and presumptuousness that Delemos assumed with me.

"By all means, good Doctor. Delemos here. I hope you and your family are rested and refreshed on this wonderful Virgin Islands morning."

"Actually, we're neither," I said. I paused for his response, but he kept silent. "Mrs. Haizlip and I did not rest well because we were overtired. We've had neither coffee nor breakfast this morning, our clothes are still packed, and your call just now awakened the children. There's no way I can be ready for Mr. Donovan in half an hour. Please apologize to the governor and let me know what time will be convenient for him after 1:00 P.M. today. I'll be expecting your call."

"Good Doctor. That's not the way it works here. You see, the governor is a very busy man with the entire Virgin Islands government reporting to him, not just Education. Your appointment is in one hour, and I'm squeezing you in then only because he said he must talk with you today. No other time will be possible this week. Wear a tie and he'll excuse the rest. I'll have coffee waiting for you when you arrive, although it would be better if you had tea with the governor because he doesn't drink coffee, ever. He says it's bad for you. He's the doctor, and he should know."

"Mr. Delemos, good Mr. Delemos," I began. "I cannot be ready in half an hour because your notice is too short. Please do what you can to squeeze me in after 1:00. I appreciate your kindness and will be awaiting your call to reschedule. Best of the morning to you." I hung up, thinking both the Governor and Delemos needed a new attitude.

Precisely at 1:00 Delemos whisked me into the governor's office and suggested I make myself comfortable until the governor returned from a photo session with visiting dignitaries.

"Dr. Haizlip, let's get right to it," the governor said, perspiring heavily as he barreled toward his padded chair with one arm half out of his jacket. "You'll be meeting with the V.I. Board of Education at 3:30 today so they can ask you a few questions and vote 'Yes' on your qualifications to be Commissioner. It's just a formality. I've already spoken with each one individually, so it won't take long. But be nice to them and don't say anything controversial. Understand? You just got here, so all you can really talk about is your background, your training, and that school in New York."

"Well, Governor . . . ," I began.

"I want you to keep it short, sweet, and simple. No issues, no opinions. Understand? There'll be ample time for opinions later."

"I'll certainly do my best to avoid controversy, if that's what you're concerned about, Your Excellency. But if anyone asks me anything substantive, I'll answer—briefly. We don't want them to think you've chosen an airhead for Commissioner of Education. Right?"

"The briefer, the better. *Comprendes?* Am I clear? Keep it short. Trust me. I know those folks all too well, and they'd love to start some kind of melee. Just to get at me."

"Melee?"

"Melee. A whole lot of noise about nothing, to get their names and pictures on the front page of the *Daily News.* Listen, I don't have time to repeat everything over and over for your benefit, Commissioner. Let me get to my next point."

"Just trying to understand as quickly as I can, Your Excellency. What's next?"

"You don't have a minute of time to waste before tackling your job. And I want you to get rolling ASAP. I've scheduled your confirmation hearing before the legislature for Friday at 10:00 A.M."

"What kind of confirmation? I thought I was meeting with the Board of Education for approval this afternoon. What's the legislature got to do with my getting to work?"

"It's just another technicality. Don't worry. When I finish revising the Virgin Islands constitution, these old procedural vestiges will be history. Until then, it's a technicality. By the old laws, I have to give them an opportunity to vote on my senior executives—the commissioners of my departments."

"Will this be a private session?"

"I haven't heard what they're planning to do. But I wouldn't be surprised if they put on a real show. For the media, of course. Education is a hot topic, so I'm sure they're going to try to milk your hearing for all they can get out of it. For themselves, of course."

"How long should I expect to be questioned, and about what? I just got here last night. Remember? What will I know after three days?"

"Don't worry. I've taken care of that. You'll spend most of tomorrow with my lieutenant governor and two of my closest advisors who know what the real deal is and all the players. If you listen to what they say and handle yourself the way they tell you, you'll be fine. Remember: just another technicality to give them a chance to say that in their independent opinion, they support my choice for this critical job."

"I'm not too comfortable with this plan, Your Excellency. You see, my preference would be to . . ."

"Just a second. This is my show, Commissioner. I'm the governor. I call the shots. Your preference? It will be the same as mine by the time you sit in that chair at the legislature Friday."

"I see. And will you be there to introduce me?"

"Me? Introduce you? Doctor, you don't seem to get it. I am the g-o-v-e-r-n-o-r. The governor of the U.S. Virgin Islands. The only time I go to the Legislature is to deliver my annual State of the Islands Message. Otherwise, they come to me. *Comprendes?* You got it yet? Mr. Delemos will arrange for my aide to escort you. I'm having your resume hand-delivered to each senator, personally, this afternoon. That's all the introduction they need. They'll be waiting for you Friday like starving lions in a den."

"They're all Democrats, right? Is this a setup?"

The governor became a study in absolute stillness, except for the "lazy" eye still rolling around trying to focus on me. When it locked in place, he rose slowly from his chair, walked around to the front of his desk, and glared stonily at me, in silence. He was angry.

"Let's get this straight, once and for all," he said. He had come within six inches of my nose, his eyes squinted almost closed, and he dropped his voice to a low whisper, tightly clenching his teeth behind barely moving lips. "Education is at the top of my agenda this term, and I'm depending on you to deliver what I promised: excellence everywhere, in every school. I'm investing my credibility in you, mister. There are not now, nor will there ever be, any setups. *Comprendes? Verstehen zie?* Got it? Let there be no misunderstanding: I do not set up my own people. Never have. Never will. Yes, they're nearly all Democrats. But we need to keep politics out of education. I said that over and over during the campaign, and I intend to stick by it and make sure they do the same. Good grief. I'm behind schedule. We'll touch base Friday morning before your hearing. On your way out, tell Mr. Delemos I need him on the double. Follow my advice and you'll be just fine."

His anger was subsiding.

"My pleasure, I'm sure, Your Excellency. *Comprendes?*"

He stopped struggling to get his jacket on, his arms caught midway in both sleeves behind him, and stared intently at me until his rolling eye found its niche, no doubt trying to decipher whether my use of *"comprendes"* was smart-assed or complimentary. Uncertain, he smiled thinly, his eyes narrowed. "Just make goddamned sure you *comprendes* me, Mr. Commissioner." His lips barely moved. "Now get Delemos in here, pronto."

With fender flags snapping briskly in the wind, the chauffeur snaked the governor's car up the center of a narrow, winding hill, forced all oncoming cars into the open gutters, and stopped in front of an old, unpainted house. Four well-worn steps bridged the gutter up to a small porch that framed two huge screenless windows on either side, their shutters folded open.

"Welcome, Dr. Haizlip. I'm Dr. Roy Anduze, chairman of the Virgin Islands Board of Education. Let me introduce our members. We're expecting two more from St. Croix at any moment, but I understand The Goose is behind schedule today. The center seat at the far end of the table is for you." The Goose was the name given to the island's seaplane commuter service.

A motley collection of chairs, stools, and benches filled the converted living room on all sides of the recycled school lunchroom table in the center. I thought I could hear from the open-raftered ceiling echoes of angry shouting matches.

Elegantly dressed and slightly built, Dr. Anduze was cheerful and classy as he summarized the backgrounds of the members present, emphasizing which island they represented. Glancing frequently at my resume, they asked about my growing up in D.C. and made sure I knew that nearly all were Howard graduates. Inquiring about challenges and accomplishments in my previous jobs, they asked why I had left a good job in New York City to come to the islands, "where everything is quite different." They probed my feelings about race problems in the United States and intimated that they were quite different in Paradise.

I thought the meeting was positive and that they would endorse my appointment more because of our exchanges than because of their political allegiances, which I assumed were Democratic. I sensed that what they really wanted to know—but were too genteel to ask—was whether I was an outspoken man of my own convictions or another mouthpiece for the governor. Pleased with their reading of me, they seemed almost cheerful at the prospect of fireworks.

This is a goddamned circus, I thought, as I followed the governor's aide through the crowded entrance and scanned the sea of brown heads jammed into every seat, two and three people perched high on ladders around the periphery, and, outside, five or six rows of faces clamoring for a peek through every window. What the hell's going on in here today?

In a semicircle at the far rear of the room, twelve sour-looking men, most in three-piece suits, sat behind large, oversized desks, each with a microphone arching within inches of his mouth, chatting with the aides filling water glasses and distributing documents—probably including my resume. On a raised, carpeted platform in the center was one vacant chair—the hot seat, I assumed—with a glass of water on a nearby table. Large ceiling fans whirled resolutely overhead.

The president of the Senate, Earle Ottley, a short, owlish-looking man in oversized eyeglasses, followed the governor's aide to the entrance where I was waiting and extended his hand. As I introduced myself, blinding television lights ignited the room, flashbulbs exploded, and we were surrounded by reporters jockeying over and around each other, thrusting microphones topped with their call letters toward us. For on-the-spot commentary, several reporters walked backward ahead of me, commenting on the live action for their viewers. They followed as I approached each senator's desk and shook hands, before settling myself in the hot seat.

From the moment the president gaveled the body to order, the confirmation hearing was a free-for-all. Upon being recognized, one senator after another summarized his life's resume at length and praised retired or deceased teachers and administrators. Each addressed the overall problems of the education system, as well as the unique problems on each island, at each school, in different communities. Many criticized as wholly inadequate the leadership of the current administration and the acting leadership of the Education Department.

Periodically, they interrupted themselves and asked how and how soon I planned to solve these problems, especially working for a governor who "talked the talk" but hadn't "walked the walk." If my replies were not specific enough, several used the occasion to ask pointed follow-up questions directly challenging my professional training and/or understanding of the issues, or indirectly criticizing Governor Evans for seeking confirmation of an unqualified candidate. On such occasions, my own temperature rising, I snappily interrupted or begged to differ with the inference of a senator's comment and took equal time to reframe the issues needing to be addressed by confident, trained leadership in the Department of Education— which I planned to provide. Politely and firmly, I made clear that I welcomed their opinions but considered myself, not them and not the governor, the professional educator and planned to run the department accordingly. I urged them to share their concerns with me and judge my results, rather than prescribe what I should do, since their responsibility was for policy, not operations.

When I reached the driveway at the Government Guest House, Shirlee rushed into the yard and gave me a big hug and long kiss. "You were fabulous," she said. "Great job. Did you know you've been on radio all day long? They broadcast your hearing from start to finish. All day long. You were really great. I know the tongues are wagging all over the islands tonight."

"What a melee," I said. "I'm exhausted. Did you hear that bastard insult me after lunch, asking if I really had graduated from Harvard and announcing his intention to telephone the university for verification since they'd previously had problems with fake degrees?"

"I did, and I prayed you'd keep your cool. You handled it well, but I knew you were furious; I know he'll never ask you another insulting question like that again. You gave him what he deserved."

"He shook my hand and apologized after the hearing and said he had done that to give me an opportunity to dispel rumors in his community. I wanted to rearrange his fucking teeth. I'm really whipped. How about a dinner date tonight at a nice restaurant on the beach with my three best girlfriends?"

Approaching the house, we heard Dee Dee calling, "Telephone for you, Daddy. Mr. Delay the Most, or something."

"Hello?"

"Delemos here. The governor wants to have a word with you. Just a moment, please."

"Commissioner. I just received notice from the legislature that the vote was unanimous on your confirmation. Congratulations and welcome aboard, officially."

"What wonderful news, Governor, and thank you for telling me personally. I'm very pleased, although I had my doubts about how a couple of senators would vote after our somewhat heated exchanges."

"I told you there'd be a lot of noise, but I had the votes. You'll learn to trust what I tell you, without question."

"Thanks, again, Governor. I plan to begin first thing Monday morning. Would you like to stop by and introduce me?"

"I'm tied up, but I'm sure you'll handle it just fine. By the way, make an appointment to see me Monday afternoon for a few minutes. I want to make sure I understand exactly what you meant by the statement that you are the professional educator and you will run the Education Department, not the senators and not the governor."

The *Daily News* carried a front-page photo of me gesturing and talking pointedly to a senator, under a bold headline, the lead story capturing the "He, Not They and Not Gov., Runs Department" flavor. An editorial welcomed a strong, outspoken leader for the embattled Education Department. Throughout the weekend, people introduced themselves and shook my hand enthusiastically at the supermarket, walking along Main Street, during lunch with Shirlee, at the beach, and even while we were selecting new shoes for the girls. In traffic, people honked their horns, raised clutched fists out of their car windows, and shouted "Commisshonnah. Weh t' go, mon." Everywhere I went, I heard, "Commisshonnah Hezzz-lip. Wilcom to de i-lands, dem. An yoo, too, Mizzuz Hezzz-lip."

The full staff, from department directors to secretaries to maintenance workers, turned my first day into an extraordinarily warm welcome. They obviously had watched every second of the hearing, because throughout the day, I heard my words, phrases, and whole statements spoken back to me—with great pride and affirmation.

After assessing my office for the first time and noting my direct telephone number, I tried to telephone Ma in Washington to tell her what had happened so far. Several times I dialed her number direct but could not reach her. In frustration I dialed the long-distance operator and told her about my difficulties.

"Is this the new Commisshonnah, Dr. Hezzz-lip, speaking?" the operator inquired pleasantly.

"Yes, it is. And I will appreciate your help reaching my mom."

"Commisshonnah," she began plaintively, "can you help me? My son is having a problem with his English class at Charlotte Amalie High School. His new Continental teacher doesn't understand our ways and says my son will not graduate in June because he doesn't write English good enough. I spoke to Ruth Thomas, the principal, who promised to look into it, but nothing's happened. Can you help? He's already been admitted to college in the States next year, with a scholarship."

"Certainly. If you'll give me your son's name and your name and telephone number, I'll speak with Ruth Thomas and get back to you as soon as I can."

"Oh, t'anks a million, Commisshonnah. I watched you giving the business to those senators on television Friday. You're a good, a strong man, and I'm praying for you because you'll need a lot of prayers to deal with their constant melee. I'm sorry, Commisshonnah, did you want to make a long-distance call? What was that number again?"

Touring schools on St. Croix with Superintendent Gloria Canegata, I discovered that she and Ruth Beagles were lifelong best friends, that both were active political supporters of Governor Evans, and that Dr. Anduze, chairman of the Virgin Islands Board of Education, met regularly with them to discuss education on St. Croix and throughout the islands. In meetings with St. Thomas and St. John school administrators, I discovered that many were related by blood or marriage to each other, to the governor, and/or to members of the legislature. Everybody in my department appeared to be related in one way or another. By the end of my first week on the job, I had begun to recognize that despite the thousands of tourists daily, we really had moved to a small, closely interconnected community, far, far from the anonymity of New York City.

As St. Patrick's Day approached, I learned that St. Johnians and St. Thomians customarily went to St. Croix for a parade, which was followed by parties all over the island: an interisland mixer, of sorts. Since there weren't too many people of Irish descent in the islands, I wondered why this parade was such a big event. We went to see for ourselves.

Along the parade route nearly everyone was black, and I thought this was a wonderful statement of racial harmony. The Irish, I assumed, were decked out in their shamrocks and would soon march down the parade route. I thought I was experiencing a sunstroke or that my eyesight was failing when I saw the parade marshal approaching. He was a man I knew. Black. A very dark-skinned, handsome black man. His last name was O'Bryant. Why the hell is he leading the parade? The term "black Irish" took on new meaning for me. It was a long parade, and nearly all of the marchers were black, outfitted in green everything. As we made the round of parties that evening, whenever I saw someone I knew well enough, I tried to find a way to ask questions without being insensitive or offensive. Their answers solved the mystery. The paraders were Irish. Blacks with Irish surnames. Some knew their heritage and the specifics of mixed marriages or liaisons in their family history that made them who they were. Others didn't worry about the details but vigorously celebrated their Irish heritage.

This turned out to be an especially important insight for us, the beginning of our upward learning curve toward understanding and appreciating race awareness among Virgin Islanders. They understand American racism toward blacks and empathize with those bearing its weight, but they shed it much earlier and have been free of direct domination for a longer period of time.

Virgin Islanders place great emphasis upon, and take great pride in, being born in the U.S. Virgin Islands. Whites living there but born in Europe are "Europeans," identified by their country of birth. Blacks born in the British Virgin Islands (Tortolla, St. Kitts, Nevis, Anguilla, etc.) are labeled "aliens" or "noncitizens." In rank order of status in the islands, native Virgin Islanders are first; Europeans, second; white Continentals, third; black Continentals, fourth; and aliens or noncitizens, fifth and last, the "niggers" of the caste system.

In the mid-fifties, the Virgin Islands government made a conscious decision to pursue tourism as the mainstay of its economy. Local lore is that native Virgin Islanders would not agree to become "slaves" to white tourists—would not drive taxis, become hotel bartenders, maids, handymen, or the like. The natives staked claim to priority rights on lifetime government jobs, regardless of required qualifications. To supply the manpower needed to support a tourist economy, aliens and noncitizens from the British Virgin Islands would be allowed to immigrate and work in the islands' tourist economy.

In the early seventies, much to my horror and surprise, the children of aliens and noncitizens legally residing and working in the Virgin Islands were not allowed by law to attend public schools. Instead they attended a number of substandard church-sponsored schools or no schools at all. In addition to the provisions of immigration laws at the time, arguments to support the denial of access to public education focused on the fact that most aliens lived cheaply and sent the bulk of their earnings to family members in the British Virgin Islands, thus milking the U.S. Virgin Islands economy by not recycling their dollars where they had been earned. The cost of educating alien children was said to be so high as to be unthinkable, especially in view of the high, unmet cost of improving public education for native and Continental children.

Virgin Islanders did not see this as blacks discriminating against blacks. It was, for them, a purely economic (and possibly class) matter. I understood and agreed with the cost implications but could not ignore what I nevertheless considered discrimination. The difference between them and me on this issue was obviously cultural.

A group of alien parents and children, however, filed a class-action lawsuit against the government of the U.S. Virgin Islands in general, and the Virgin Islands Department of Education in particular, challenging the denial of access to free public education to alien children. Like most native Virgin Islanders, Governor Evans was furious and fought the case vehemently on appeal before the Third Circuit Court of Appeals in Philadelphia. The Appellate Court ruled in favor of the aliens' petition and ordered that all alien children be provided access to free public education in the U.S. Virgin Islands forthwith. Time frames were set—with severe financial penalties for failure to comply. No resources to assist the islands in complying with this order were provided by the court. Hysteria, anger, and outrage filled the air and airwaves.

Within thirty days, the Department of Education had certified thousands of alien children—some arriving by boats, planes, inner tubes, and any other means from the British Virgin Islands—for enrollment in public schools. To accommodate this growth in the near-zero time allowed by the court, we commandeered and refurbished temporary facilities on all three islands, placed schools on staggered and double sessions, recruited novice teachers across the United States on an emergency basis, floated school construction bonds, and ultimately built seven new schools in record, fast-track time. Our budget was completely out of whack.

Public dissatisfaction was palpable. Native vs. alien hostilities reached an all-time high and were potentially explosive. But the tourist economy could not function without unskilled alien labor, labor that generated 90 percent of the revenues of the islands' government, the very government on which a majority of native Virgin Islanders depended for their survival.

The first two years were the most difficult period of my life in the islands.

After a rocky start, Governor Evans and I developed a mutually respectful and positive working relationship. Both strong-willed and determined, at the outset we clashed often over whose views would prevail. I came to realize that in demanding space to run the department, I was denying him his desperate need to see himself as expert in all areas, including education, because he was the governor. After ideological or strategic boxing matches that often left him so angry with me that he could barely speak, I found ways to reconnoiter and devise new plans that could lead to a rapprochement between us. This worked for both of us. He was reinforced by my appearing to back down and accord him his due as governor. But I never did back down. I learned how to avoid his hot buttons.

All the while, I admired him greatly. He had an extraordinary capacity to store and retrieve information on demand; was highly verbal and quick on his feet; and had a sixth sense for politics. I loved working with and for him. I even loved sparring with him. I just didn't want him telling me what to do, even if I agreed with him.

Toward the end of his second term, Governor Evans decided to run for a third but felt that the accomplishments and benefits of his administration were so positive, so well known to the voters and so appreciated by them, that it would not be necessary for him to campaign aggressively for reelection. I disagreed with him on this position and argued vehemently against it. His political advisors convinced him that he was a shoo-in. To cap his reelection bid, however, he decided to macadam nearly every mile of road on each island, completing the job one week before the election so that voters could not/would not forget.

His opponent, Senator Cyril King, was also bright, articulate, cunning, hard-nosed, and determined. Shrewdly, because education touches so many voters directly through their children, King made education a major plank in his campaign. With drama and flair, but with less than full or accurate information, he often took to the air-waves to describe problems in education. The governor's political ploy was not to dignify these charges by responding. My response was to contradict or correct them head-on by holding a news conference or appearing on radio and television programs. At some level, I clearly was defending myself and my reputation from these attacks. The problem was that I was not the candidate for governor.

This was heavy-duty stuff because, secretly, King and I enjoyed and respected each other's intellect and ability to command attention and shape public opinion. Our scrapping was partly the product of an intense rivalry that only true friends could sustain without killing each other. In private, he often reassured me, "It's not you I'm after. It's the prize. The governorship. You're a vehicle for me to get what I intend to have. Don't take it personally."

As election day drew near, the governor was fixated on his roads improvement project to reassure his reelection victory. Unfortu-nately, four days before election day, stormy weather set upon the islands, and it began raining heavily around the clock. The downpour did not let up for three consecutive days, and by the fourth, there was catastrophe: the roadbeds became saturated, flood conditions devel-oped, and runoff pouring down the mountainsides began loosening and ripping up the newly poured macadam all over the islands. Roads became impassable, as huge chunks were whipped loose and washed down the mountainsides by tons and tons of water running out to sea. By election day, macadam was everywhere but on the roads—even at the edge of the harbor, fully visible to every voter headed to the polls. Disaster. Pure disaster.

Governor Evans lost his bid for a third term. By Virgin Islands law, the resignations of Governor Evans's commissioners were mandatory, effective January 1, the day Governor-elect King would take the Oath of Office.

Mandatory resignation from a job I was so deeply committed to was difficult to accept, especially when there were strongly expressed beliefs among political leaders, parents, media, students, teachers, and colleagues that I had done a great job and should be allowed to continue serving the Education Department, the students, and the parents. Because I knew of no comparable slots outside the Virgin

Islands government, I made halfhearted inquiries stateside about positions available but received halfhearted responses to my candidacy, which was fine with me because I did not really want to leave.

Shortly before Christmas, Governor-elect King asked if I would remain as his commissioner for three or four months until he could complete a national search for my replacement. This was a ruse, because I knew that the the Board of Education, school administrators, the teachers' union, groups of parents, and a number of political leaders had strongly advised him to retain me. I told him I needed a week to think over his request. I decided to accept—both for him and for me.

During this period of great uncertainty, Shirlee was offered a promotion from program manager to general manager of the CBS television station, a wonderful recognition of her accomplishments. It was an extraordinary opportunity for her—in the same way that accepting appointment as Commissioner of Education in the Virgin Islands had been an extraordinary opportunity for me. I told her that just as she had rallied behind me despite the unknowns, I now rallied behind her, prepared to cope. Between equals, it was a role reversal. For the short run (I hoped), it would be my turn to become the housekeeper, cook, shopper, and chauffeur for the girls' many activities around the island.

I decided not to orchestrate any effort to pressure Governor King to continue my appointment. I knew and he knew that we had fought so openly and directly throughout my tenure that he would only lose credibility by retaining me. I also predicted that if he had retained me, my life would have become hell because he would have been more determined than Governor Evans to silence and/or control me. He could not allow the solid support I had achieved throughout the islands to compete with his image as a take-charge governor.

My last day was most difficult, not only because I was leaving but also because I was going nowhere. I was transitioning out.

Sheilah Newton, my secretary, and Evelyn Sprauve, my office manager, moved around the office as if preparing for a funeral, quietly and somberly packing my personal files, effects, and mementos, including my award from the American Institute of Architects for the Best Design of a U.S. Elementary School in 1974. Principals and teachers stopped in for bear hugs and best wishes, vowing to keep in close touch, asking about my plans, and urging me not to leave the islands.

It was hardest, in some ways, to say goodbye to Dennis Donovan, my driver, because he had become a trusted friend and companion to my entire family. Mr. Donovan (as we always addressed him) kept pace with everything going on in my life and often was a surprising source of keen political insight. He kept my government car spotless and shiny and memorized my schedule every morning to make sure his actions would support it. When he dropped me at home for the last time, he helped me unload my boxes into the garage, where we shook hands for a long time and finally gave each other hugs.

"You're a good man, Commissshonnah," he said, his eyes filling with tears. "It's been an honor working with you. Thanks for everything. I'll go upstairs to say goodbye to Mrs. Hezzz-lip, Dee Dee, and Missy. Then I have to get back to the office."

My first couple of weeks of unemployment were like playacting. After getting the girls to school and Shirlee to work, I tackled my days as if I were on a long-overdue vacation, planning and shopping for elaborate meals; lazing on Lindquist Beach alone with a good book; repairing my old Volkswagen station wagon, which had become one of my neglected hobbies; and catching up on various projects around the house: repotting the large aloe plants flanking our entryway; repainting our porch furniture and having the cushions reupholstered; and painting the girls' rooms in the new colors they wanted.

The knowledge that we were spending more money than was coming in each month focused my attention on reality: I was not on vacation, I had no job prospects on the island, and we could not maintain our current lifestyle on Shirlee's income alone. I had to find work. Soon.

An anxiety I had not previously experienced moved in with me, deep down. In education, there were no jobs comparable to the commissionership anywhere in the islands. I had two choices: a lesser education job, or anything else I could find that was interesting, doable, and with decent pay. I knew Governor King would never approve a job for me in public education, so I was limited to nonpublic education opportunities at considerably less than I had previously earned.

I thought I might have to reinvent myself as having general management skills beyond those I applied at the Education Department. I did not want to do this: I loved being an educator and did not want to forsake this love simply to get a job. But I had to get a job, and this change might have to be the personal price I would have to pay. I was not happy.

The church came to my rescue—on the beach, of all places. A casual conversation at a Magen's Bay party resulted in an invitation to meet with the bishop of the Diocese of the Virgin Islands, our next-door neighbor, and with the parish leadership to discuss the headmaster position at Sts. Peter and Paul School, a well-established kindergarten through grade twelve parochial school around the corner from Shirlee's office, near Market Square. The major hurdle, I thought, was that I was not Catholic.

The parish priest was Father James Freeman, a handsome, gregarious, silver-haired man with intense blue eyes, who, at the lectern, looked like Christ in African-inspired regalia. Father Freeman and I quickly concluded that my passion for education and for at-risk kids was my personal priesthood, not far removed from a spiritual mission blessed by God, he said. That I had not worshiped as a Catholic was less relevant and important than my having a solid spiritual core that could embrace and respect any organized religion. The bishop, Father Freeman, and I concluded that I should become the next headmaster at Sts. Peter and Paul School until the Sisters of Charity, the order to which the nuns at the school belonged, could identify, appoint, and relocate to the islands a highly qualified nun from one of their communities across the United States. This would likely take two years.

I felt at home again—back to my roots in schools, close to teachers and kids and parents in the daily transactions of creating futures for young people on a minute-by-minute basis, child by child. As the days went by, I began to realize how greatly I had cheated the parochial schools as commissioner, remaining aloof from their enterprise and authorizing routine minimal assistance through public funds as provided under the strictures separating church and state.

Most important for me, however, was that Sts. Peter and Paul School connected me to the community of those faithful sisters and brothers who had chosen, studied, and sacrificed everything to become a nun or a priest. Father Freeman and the male staff belonged to the Redemptorist Order. I relearned daily from them and the nuns the quality of mercy, the rewards of goodness without price, the joy of giving, the beauty of belief—all of which my mother had first instilled in me. Less obvious or nonexistent were the personal agendas, the competition, the self-promotion typical among staff in any school or other human enterprise. Sts. Peter and Paul School was the closest I had ever come to my dream of serving the needs of children—selflessly.

After two years, the church found a nun to lead Sts. Peter and Paul. We decided it was time to return to the States.

During our life on the islands, I felt a greater sense of personal freedom than ever before or ever since. Because a majority of the island population has been black for hundreds of years, blacks and the prerogatives of blackness pervade all areas of life, in the same way that whites and the prerogatives of whiteness pervade life in America, where an ever-decreasing majority of the population is white. Being a member of the majority is empowering in all ways imaginable, I found. And as one who suffered from the oppression of whiteness in America, becoming a member of the majority on the islands empowered me.

Racism and ethnocentrism, however, are worldwide and therefore inescapable, even for African Americans living among people of Caribbean and African descent. To many of the thousands of white Americans and Europeans disgorging gleefully from cruise ships for a day of sun, shopping, and fun, the native-born islanders and the aliens alike are an undistinguished lot of freed slaves at the beck and call of tourist dollars. Their haughtiness and disdain are barely disguised by their curiosity at the natives' ability to speak English and their desire to hear renditions of "Yellow Bird." They become "ugly" American tourists without being aware of their messages, attitudes, and actions.

Continuously exposed to such tourists, most native Virgin Islanders not working in the tourist industry simply avoid interacting personally with them. Aliens working in the industry ignore negative tourist attitudes and focus instead on the money to be earned from them.

The challenge for each of us, black or white, is to learn to see, understand, and accept others beyond the prisons and prisms of our own race-based ethnocentricity.

CHAPTER 10

❧

Coming to in America

𝒮HIRLEE: In 1977, in an island-wide election, I was chosen a delegate to the first national women's conference in Houston. The year had been designated International Women's Year, with the theme "American Women on the Move." With wide eyes and an overflowing heart, I sat with Gloria Steinem, Coretta King, Betty Friedan, Shirley Chisholm, and Bella Abzug. Sitting among this powerful sisterhood, I knew then, I was the woman I wanted to be.

Our lives changed when Harold's situation changed. We both knew and accepted with resignation that there was no available place for him in the foreseeable future on the island. I had no desire or interest in separating my life from his. There was no future there for me, either. We had no alternative but to go back to the States. With no savings, a few months' severance pay, a houseful of furniture and pets, we moved to stay with my parents until we could find housing and jobs. Our furniture went into storage. When would I see our things again?

It was a hard move. The girls were leaving the home and friends they best remembered. There was no predicting our future; I was frightened, but excited, glad to be going home.

We arrived in time to plan a Christmas wedding for Pattee and Jim Brown. Once again a family ritual lifted our spirits and propelled us through another doorway. My parents' living room, full of holly and candles, framed a radiant Pattee, romantically clad in her ivory Mexican wedding dress. Again my father married her, this time to a tall, handsome man who would bring her the constant joy that had eluded her for so long.

While we were in the Virgin Islands, two things happened in the late seventies. First, America went into a deep recession, which financial types privately called a depression. Second, black people and their needs were no longer causes, no longer fashionable, no longer chic. Employment for blacks dried up. The two things were not unconnected. Nineteen-eighty (and Ronald Reagan) was just around the corner.

New Haven at its best is a pleasant large town. Manageable. There's something comforting in the way the old elm trees create languid green bridges over most of the city's streets. Yale and its facilities provide the cultural focus, while the Shubert Theater carries on the tradition of the Great White Way. The park known as the Green in the center of the city remains the intersection of town and gown, where the truce between the two is not always easy.

At its worst New Haven suffers the ills of larger, neglected places. By the eighties much of the city's old housing stock had become blighted and the welfare rolls had swollen out of control. The inflammable mix of gangs, drugs, and guns was building up. The public schools were on a downward spiral.

Various coalitions of town, gown, labor, and management struggled to keep New Haven vibrant. Macy's opened a store on the Green as development of the waterfront began. The library was refurbished and the Shubert spruced itself up. New Haven's pulse regained its steady beat.

The year we lived with my parents, both of the girls were restless. They wanted to be in "their own house" again. It was not an easy time for any of us. I had turned forty-two. Luckily my parents had moved to an even larger, Tudor-style house with seventeen rooms, so each girl could still have a space of her own. Dee Dee and Harold began to clash at least once a week as she said something flip to her father and ran up the steps to her bedroom. The scenario was usually the same, Harold chasing her, demanding an apology, followed by both dogs barking, nipping at their heels. Her cat led the pack, running between her legs. Doors slammed. "As long as you live in this house you will go by my rules," came drifting down the stairs. Quiet. Harold sprang back down, wiping his forehead and puffing furiously on a cigarette. Missy was more compliant. Her time would come.

The last summer Dee Dee went to Camp Interlochen was after she had had minor surgery on her earlobes. She was sixteen. She wrote a letter that captured her girlhood concerns:

July 23, 1980

Dear Mom and Dad,

I went to Dr. Tobin today, and everything went well. He said that my ears looked very good. The injections didn't hurt at all. Either I'm getting older and feeling less pain, or the doctors are getting better. Dr. Tobin is very pleasant. He's young, too. I noticed that he got all his certifications in 1969. The visit only took ten minutes, but I waited around to be taken back to camp. It's good I'm not home-sick. I could have run away soo easily.

When are you and Mom going to move into the house? Before we get home? I hope so.

Guess what I did? Aunt Pattee sent me some money, and I received her letter on the afternoon that we go to the grocery and drug stores. Since I was loaded down with extra spending cash, I decided to splurge. One of my cabin mates, Jocelyn Gertel, and I bought two Sarah Lee cheese-cakes. One with strawberries and one without. We divided each cake into sections and both ate half. They were great! Of course I gave Missy a piece. The cake without the straw-berries tasted better than the one with. It was so nice not to have to save any. Yum!

Are you going to get my senior pictures? You can wait if you want, but it would be nice if I could have them.

Why did you suggest that we buy tickets to all these blasted concerts? My bank account is dwindling. I spent eleven dollars on two rotten seat tickets. Last Saturday night I was bored to death by Stephen DeGroote in the Van

Cliburn benefit program. He did four encores. Piano concerts are soo boring.

Well, I have to go to drawing and design.

Bye,

Love,

Dee Dee

To the delight of my parents, Harold did all of the shopping, cooking, and house and lawn maintenance. He even made washing his car
and my father's car a regular routine. Because my father insisted on
having his meals between four and five in the afternoon, we had two
sittings, which worked out well. Sometimes, when they had things to
do in the evening, the girls ate early with their grandparents. I was
pleased that the girls could be with their grandparents on a daily basis.
I suppose I was living out my own fantasy of being in the company of
grandparents I had never known. My father, ailing with a severe case
of emphysema and on the verge of being forced to retire by Macedonia because of his health, was less sanguine about our being in the
house than my mother. Although he never once said anything, I suspected he could not understand how the careers of his "successful"
daughter and son-in-law had come to a crashing halt.

Unlike during my early years, we did not attend church every Sunday, but we did take the girls from time to time. Seeing their grandfather, "Poppa," in the pulpit and meeting the people who had known
me all my life and had been to their christenings made a deep impres-
sion on them.

I hoped that our daughters' high school years would be as happy as
mine had been. Life for me at Ansonia High School had been a *Happy
Days* forerunner, a small-town extravaganza. Several years earlier,
Missy had told us she wanted to be called "Melissa" henceforth. Dee
Dee would wait until college to claim her given name.

Given our belief in public schools, we were genuinely pleased
when Dee Dee and then Melissa enrolled in Wilbur Cross, an old
urban public school. I remembered Cross as a pretty good school. By
the time our girls entered there, it had a mixed reputation. Some of
its top students still went to "good" colleges. But many others were
left to wither on the vine, probably because it had undergone a

change of complexion. The majority of its students were black children from working-class or welfare families. The few white students who did stick it out were mostly children of liberal Yale professors.

For Dee Dee and Melissa, who had been in private or small public schools with some degree of privilege, in some ways Cross was a major lesson in the scenarios of the real world. But in other ways, they would remain apart. Designated as "gifted and talented," they were exposed to the fullest resources, the best classes and teachers, including courses at Yale. They would graduate near the top of their classes, with honors. Yale admitted both girls with scholarships based on merit.

Still out of work, our main occupation continued to be looking for new jobs, which did not come knocking at the door. But being back on the mainland and connecting once again with family and friends and seeing the expanded social, cultural, and academic opportunities for the girls made me certain we had made the right decision to leave the island. Of course, we missed its beauty, its weather, the friends we had made there. We missed its easygoing life and being at the top of the heap. And I worried a lot about Harold's ego. I knew he would get a job, but I brooded about the toll the search and the wait was taking on him and me. It was no easy feat to stay optimistic *and* idealistic.

After we had been in New Haven for almost a year and on a day that I received a "thanks, but no thanks" letter to one of my dozens of job queries, I received a call from a man with a cheery voice that I did not recognize. "Jay Iselin," he said. "Come chat with me about what we do here. You might hear something that interests you." Someone had given him my name, he said, because they thought I would be an asset to his operation. It was the most roundabout invitation to a job interview that I had ever received. Because I was not in the loop of the New York literati, I had no idea who John Jay Iselin was. Turns out he was a direct descendent of John Jay, America's first Chief Justice and very much a cog in the WASP social wheel of the East Coast. He had a reputation for brilliance, charm, and idiosyncrasy.

His brilliance and connections landed him a job as a *Newsweek* editor; he then became the president of WNET, the flagship station of the Public Broadcasting System. We met. We clicked. Living up to his reputation, Jay convinced me there was no better place to work than WNET in the whole of the New York metropolitan area. He offered me a job for which he created a new title, "special assistant to the president." I loved its vagueness. Jay assured me I would get a "feel" for the entire station from his viewpoint.

New positions for Harold and me allowed us to settle into an exquisite blue Victorian house owned by Yale two blocks away from my parents' home. It was a lovely place of light and air, nestled in the middle of an acre of land. On one side there was another large Victorian house and on the other, the Georgian architecture of the Yale Divinity School.

For the next six years Harold and I would commute by train to New York every day. Each morning I prepared myself for an explosion of speed, holding my breath as we tore out the driveway, zoomed down Prospect Street, and, ten minutes later, rocketed to a stop in front of the train station. I jumped out, ran to the 7:55, claimed a seat, and waited for Harold, who parked the car. Often, the conductors held the train for a few seconds when they saw him dashing to get it. A few times he tried their patience and missed the train, taking too long to get a cup of coffee and *The New York Times.*

The express train started in New Haven and stopped at Bridgeport, Stamford, and Grand Central Station. After a while, the faces that boarded the train each morning became familiar, and sometimes, comfortable. People nodded at each other, exchanging pleasantries and newspapers. Sometimes Harold would go off to play card games with a group of other smokers and coffee drinkers he had met before I began commuting. Everything was as quiet and orderly as the pretty little towns we passed on our way.

In a black person's head there are always two levels of consciousness. One has to do with being part of the broader community; the other, with being black. Depending on what is happening, the two levels operate in a large sea, like atomic submarines. Then a movement, a current, a flash activates the sonar of the black psyche. Things change. The submarine goes on alert.

Every once in a while the thought flitted through my mind that we were among the meager number of black people on the train. I often wondered about this awareness with our fellow white travelers. Did they think about it as much as we did? Did they talk about it with each other? "Hey, there's that black couple again. What's their story?" Pity is, I'll never know. My white friends tell me they don't talk about black people nearly as much as we talk about them.

And when we got off with other bodies, bobbing and weaving in the leaving-the-train dance, we moved toward the throngs emerging from nearby trains. Harold, tall, slender, and dark, especially stood out. How brave I thought he was to swim in that pale sea. How smart and how strong he had to be to withstand the onslaught that at any moment might become unfriendly.

Our commuting time kept us close. We sat together without the distraction of the telephone, the doorbell, or others' conversation. Uninterrupted, we shared thoughts and feelings at the beginning and end of every day. I cherished that time with him.

This time around, we were in New York but not of it. I'm not sure what it was, but we stayed in touch with just a small core of our former friends. Twenty years change things. We were different people, sobered, hurt, and matured by job loss and unemployment. No longer the parents of toddlers, we had two teenagers. The discoes were gone. Dance clubs and different drugs had taken their place. We couldn't hang out until three and four anymore. Frivolity was out. We had grown up.

Although our life was oriented toward New Haven, sometimes we stayed in New York for special events. We loved those evenings; they were like mini-honeymoons. Once we met an African king, Otumfuo Opoku Ware II, the Asantehene of Ghana. Known for the gold that his country mined and the ceremonial gold that he wore, the Asantehene was a legend in Ghana. After parading through Central Park West, borne on a golden litter, he welcomed a bevy of New York's elite at a dinner at the Museum of Natural History.

In honor of the occasion, I wore all the gold chains I owned—paltry, I knew, in comparison to his. Except for my wedding band, I had not owned any gold until I lived in the Virgin Islands. There, it was unthinkable to acquire costume jewelry. Gold jewelry signified that you were not a peasant; that you were indeed a person of substance. I had no trouble buying into that cultural expectation.

Mostly white people, dressed in silk, satin, and black tie, formed a long line to greet and gape at the exotic visitor as if he were part of a diorama in the museum. As we approached His Highness, sitting under a golden umbrella, we saw an obese, dark, cheery-looking man. Gold rings hung from his nose and ears. Gold rings squeezed his chubby toes. Gold bangles surrounded his ankles and wrists. Gold chains, large as link fences, hung from his broad chest, dripping over his pendulous breasts.

So this was an African king. His teeth and eyes glowed brightly against his ebony-colored skin. A broad smile stayed on his face as he graciously greeted every guest with a nod or a twinkle. He's like Santa Claus, I thought. "I like your gold," I said inanely. Looking at my gold glistening across my cleavage, he said with unmistakable meaning, "I like yours, too."

It was nice to live in the same town with one of my sisters again. Pattee and I had a chance to know each other in new ways. After we'd closed the boutique, Pattee had taken a job in a social agency, which had so motivated her that she wanted to go back to school. I was so proud of the way she had managed to get an advanced degree while mothering three boys. She lucked out when she married Jim the Christmas we returned home from the Virgin Islands. The four of us went out frequently.

Pattee and I shopped—too much—together, went to the hairdresser together, dyed our hair too blond together, drooled at Marvin Gaye in one of his last concerts, danced in the aisles at a Temptations and O'Jays concert, and generally cavorted as only sisters can.

She had become a stunning woman. Her new career as a school social worker, combined with an adoring husband, was a constant tonic. Pattee and Jim had big plans for their future. Pattee got another bonus in her new husband. He liked to dance and to play his music loud, and he cut a mean figure in the kitchen. Whenever the four of us got together, Harold and Jim cooked, as they did for all family gatherings and holidays. Such a time they had in the kitchen, laughing and drinking, crashing around with the pots and the pans. The results were always spectacular. Harold had found a kitchen mate at last. I was glad he was in the family and married to my sister.

Jim, handsome in a charismatic way, had a charming, gap-toothed smile. A former star basketball player in local and state circles, he was well over six feet tall, with a massive physique. His was an imposing figure whose size belied his gentleness and humor. He loved being silly and laughing at himself. A born storyteller, he entertained everyone from the moment he came into a room. And he adored Pattee.

Jim was an instant fit and an instant hit in our family. It was if we had known and loved him all our lives.

I remember all of his stories verbatim. This is one of my favorites.

Imagine, if you will, a grinning Jim leaning over the kitchen table, a rum and Coke in his hand:

> A man came into a crowded bar on a cold night. He was seedy looking and seemed down on his luck. He asked the bartender for a drink but said he couldn't pay in cash. "What can you offer instead?" the barkeep said.
>
> "I will show you something, the likes of which you have never seen before and will never see again. I have it right here in my jacket pocket."
>
> "Take it out and let me see it before I give you a drink."
>
> The man proceeded to pull from his pocket a miniature sleek grand piano, a tiny matching bench, and a mouse in white tie and tails, which he sits on the bench.
>
> The barkeep started to pour the drink.
>
> "That's not all, man. Wait a minute," the seedy one says. From the same pocket he pulls out a canary dressed in a red sequined gown and two-inch red pumps, with bright red lipstick on her beak. The mouse begins to beat at the piano. The canary starts to sing—like Ella Fitzgerald, scat and all. The bar goes deathly quiet.
>
> A well-dressed man at the bar pulls out his wallet and says, "I'll give you five thousand dollars for that duo."
>
> The bartender says, "Man, don't sell. Don't sell."
>
> "I'll make it one hundred thousand dollars, but I'll have to write you a check and get it certified."
>
> "Don't sell, don't sell," the bartender implores.
>
> "Look man, this is my final offer. A million dollars."
>
> "Sold," the owner says. "You go and get the check and I'll wait here."
>
> Playing and singing, the mouse and canary keep the crowd spellbound as they wait for the buyer to come back. When he does, he hands over the certified check, claims the mouse, the canary, the piano, and the bench and rushes out the door.
>
> "Man, I don't know why you didn't hold out for more,' the barkeep says.

"It's O.K., man, really, I made out fabulously. What that rich guy doesn't know is that the canary doesn't really sing. It's the mouse. The mouse is a ventriloquist."

My six-year relationship with WNET television found me in a special place inhabited by an extraordinarily talented group of producers and writers. How lucky you are when you love to go to work every day, afraid you'll miss something if you don't. It was a brilliant, quirky world of ideas—ideas about art, music, science, health, politics, community. Brilliant, quirky people as well. I hired Polly Zawadi, Harold's former secretary, to be my assistant. When she was promoted, I hired Sharifah Jamal to replace her. Both excelled at what they did and, in doing so, enhanced my performance.

Part of my job was a pass-through role: proposals on their way to and from the station president or various department heads landed on my desk for review and comment. I knew that I was not a "green lighter," a player in terms of what projects got made, but I was comfortable in my role as an ancillary pundit and critic.

My years at WNET coincided with the development of such series as *The Brain, Brideshead Revisited, The MacNeil/Lehrer NewsHour, Civilization and the Jews, Great Performances, American Playhouse,* and *Dance in America.* And WNET sent me to the White House at least six times.

Before a WNET "In Performance at the White House" event, Harold and I went through the receiving line, shaking hands with the Reagans. As much as I was tempted, I did not let politics stand in my way. I wanted to see the president's house. I wanted to experience the Blue Room, the East Wing, the visitors' bathrooms, with their elegant white hand towels embossed with the presidential seal. As a livery driver around the turn of the century, a cousin of my mother's had delivered passengers to the White House in a horse and buggy, but he never got in. That night, I crossed the residential threshold for him and everyone else in my family. Later, from the pulpit, I would tell the members of my father's church about the visit, letting them know that I had brought their spirits to the White House as well. Their hearty "amen"s affirmed their pleasure.

My family took to heart the notion that life should be celebrated. We put on a party for every occasion. The morning of Melissa's six-

teenth birthday party, I had taken time to get my hair done. Then I saun-
tered over to a florist on Whalley Avenue, across from Yale's campus. A
hand clasped my shoulder as I picked up some yellow stock. The urgency
in Harold's voice touched off an inner alarm I never wanted to hear. "We
need to get to the hospital. Poppa's there. We need to get there now."

"I'm almost finished, I'll be right there," I said.

"No, you've got to come now." He led me away as the helpful saleslady said she would finish the order and have the flowers
delivered.

The next few hours became the dream sequences that shock cre-
ates. I remember waiting in a private area near the room where they
were delivering electric shocks to my father's heart. I can only recall
it in the present tense: Pattee and my mother are there. Pattee's face
is drawn into rigid lines. Only my mother's eyes betray her feelings.
They are as large and flat as buttons.

I move toward the door to see. It's important to see. Harold puts
himself between me and the door. "You don't want to see your father
like this," he insists. I do want to see but I back away. Time drifts. We
are led to an even more private room. A doctor comes in and speaks
to my mother while looking at all of us. I don't remember his words.

After that, I make the calls. I only start to cry when I ask Bishop
Williams, my father's lifelong friend, to come to the hospital.

Harold and I told those at home that we would prefer to tell
Deirdre and Melissa about Poppa's death. They had guessed, of course,
because my parents' home was filling up with people. It became the
girls' job to call all of Melissa's friends, postponing her party. I suspect
the act of repeating the story to almost one hundred party guests
helped the immediate reality of their grandfather's death sink in.

We planned two family events at once, a party and a funeral.
Scores of out-of-town relatives and friends who gathered for the
goodbye joined us in bringing in Melissa's sixteenth year. Since there
were many from the "old school" tradition, we braced ourselves for
some potent criticism for going ahead with the party. We heard nothing. Perhaps it was out there, but we just did not hear it.

It is an odd experience to have a major party as you are marshal-
ing pallbearers, eulogies, and coffins. Teenagers danced frenetically
under a tent. Older folks huddled in corners quietly talking. Harold

and I accepted condolences for my father and congratulations for my daughter.

This was the girls' first immersion in death and grief. Unschooled and curious, they questioned every formality. Their grandfather had been a looming presence in their life, indulging them with toys and other treats. They had watched him in the pulpit with awe, although they did not have the same kind of bonds with the congregation that I had had. Now the man who took them to the market, who banged on the ceiling of the dining room with his cane when they ran through the upstairs halls, who came to their school assemblies was gone.

Absenting herself for a while, Melissa wrote a poem:

QUIETUS

A shadowy inanition
Ignoring all resistance of our will,
Darker than gloom;
Hovering,
waiting,
What are you? You come and
Yet I did not call.
It is not I whom you seek, though
Your chilling presence has nipped
My bones:
a warning . . .
I am young, *I* can escape your
Inevitable grasp,
Or so they say . . .
But no,
I must acquiesce, yet
I will leave a new born rose
Behind me.

As funerals go, my father's was impressive. At least a thousand crowded a New Haven church: relatives, friends, church members, politicians, people he had helped along the way. Dozens of ministers in the pulpit, each wanting to outspeak the next. Sentinels from the

Masons and Elks somberly guarded the coffin; missionary women dressed in white tended the grieving.

My mother bore her grief well. She did not hide her tears, but she did not get hysterical. Pattee and Jewelle followed her example. Brother cried a lot. My father's two daughters from Washington, my half sisters, wept quietly.

We had planned as short a funeral as we thought we could get away with; the ministers had other things in mind. They said this was "Julian's day." They would praise him as long as they had a mind to. They got no argument from us.

When my father died in 1981, I was forty-four. It was my first adult experience with the death of a close family member. I had always felt my father's life was tenuous, because he had several heart attacks and other close calls as I was growing up. I imagined that I might see him drop like a stone in the pulpit after some particularly strenuous sermon or a squabble with the deacons. I never dreamed he would die after falling out of his bed on the Saturday morning of his granddaughter's birthday.

For a while I was in a daze. I kept Harold at a distance, my wounded soul riddled with tiny pits of sadness. I cried at random, when I heard one of my father's songs, saw a snappily dressed black man. But I did not have the long, hard grief I expected. After a while, the sharp, clean lines of life came into focus again. The eighties would not end without death blurring those lines several times more.

Having grown up in the New Haven area, it never occurred to me that I might have a daughter attend Yale. It was our hometown school, for men only. On a sunny September afternoon, Harold, my mother, Pattee, Jim, Melissa, and I found ourselves on the old campus moving Dee Dee in. We were certain my proud father's ghost was standing there with us. Whiffenpoofs were singing, leaves were falling, and parents were thinking about tuition bills ahead. I resigned myself to the fact that I might as well endorse all of my paychecks directly to Yale for the next four years. It was what I knew I had to do. My father sent me and my sisters to school as a matter of course. I was carrying on a family tradition.

Dee Dee was trying to be cool and attached at the same time. After we moved her into her room, we were airily dismissed, but she kept checking in on us.

Even though we lived next to part of the campus, Deirdre enjoyed her life fully as a residential student, rarely coming home. She allowed us to wave at her wildly when she was a Yale cheerleader. Otherwise, we had to be cool.

Two years later, Melissa followed the same blue brick road to Yale. A skilled pianist, a budding dancer, and an honor student, she turned down other acceptances. Yale's pull was too strong. This second Ivy Leaguer extended my paychecks to the university.

Another two years passed. In 1985 we sat on the old campus, watching Deirdre receive her B.A. degree. A number of Harold's relatives had come up from Washington and North Carolina, as had many of mine, because we combined two celebrations, Harold's fiftieth birthday and Deirdre's graduation. Noticeably missing were my father and my brother.

"Brother has lung cancer. A lump in his chest they say is inoperable," my mother told us, her black eyes welling up. After years of traveling up one road and down another, Brother had finished college. That B.A. degree meant more to him than any of the jobs he had held, nurse, mortician, trucker. I imagined he unrolled it for St. Peter at the Pearly Gates.

When I was a little girl, Brother was the love of my life. For the most part, he tolerated me. Two years younger, I followed him everywhere. I was standing near him behind a batter playing softball when a bat connected with my forehead and the corner of my eye. Both of us screaming, he hurried me home, holding his hand over my eye to keep it from falling out. The eye stayed in and healed.

Sometime when he was around ten or eleven, Brother began having trouble. Little things, cutting up in school, sneaking into the movie house. A residential school for boys was recommended. It didn't work. Away he went to my half sister's house in Washington. He ran away. Back to Connecticut, where he stayed with an undertaker and his wife, fascinated by and learning mortuary skills. Maybe the military would straighten him up. Enlistment in the air force. Wrong move. Teenage marriage to his first wife. Two babies quickly followed.

A series of moves between Connecticut and Massachusetts. Once he lived with Harold and me in Cambridge. A good tenant and faithful babysitter. Marriage to a Boston Irish girl brought two more children. Managing a mortuary business bought for him and owned by our father in Hartford. The dying did not make his life successful.

Brother was a handsome man, a light-skinned version of my father. Quirky, fast-talking, and fun-loving, he parlayed a keen intelligence into a series of confabulated experiences. Why his life was not more conventional is a mystery to me. Because he was a minister's son, people had great expectations for him. He just found it easier not to live up to them. Being a light-skinned black man may have been a factor, although numerous sociological studies tell us that American society favors light skin over dark. Being sandwiched between two aggressive sisters who achieved academic stardom may have had something to do with it. None of us will ever really know.

The cancer claimed him when he was forty-nine. He died before his children could get to know him.

I mourned my brother for what might have been. I was glad that we had come together before he died. Self-righteously, I had distanced myself from him for some time, not wanting his life, his problems to tarnish mine. I was in my forties, married with children. But I hadn't fully grown up. More than anything else, his death marked the end of childhood for me.

The rain poured down, dripping through the tent and onto the rainbow-colored tables. Gray curtains of water had been blowing all day. Denying the weather, I made my last preparations for this outdoor twenty-fifth wedding celebration. My carefully straightened hair reverted to my grandmother's woolly pompadour. The swing band of senior citizens had called to say the rain was slowing up their bus from New York. An hour before the party, Harold was shinnying up the branches of a large tree, trying to create a makeshift cover for the buffet table.

I slipped into the antique lace dress Harold had designed for me. I should have had on a wet suit and flippers instead. The evening was ruined, ruined, ruined.

My dead father spoke to God. Just a few minutes before eight o'clock, as the first guests arrived, the downpour abruptly stopped. Stars blinked. Clouds scudded away, revealing a surprised moon. The rest of the June night was soft and sweet smelling. *The New York Times* did a major feature on the party, celebrating the fact that a black couple and their family could make it that far unbloodied and unbowed.

We found it hard to believe we had reached this milestone. Where had the years gone? Did we look that old? Was it all downhill from here? What lay ahead? The Monday after the party, we boarded our usual train car. Someone came by and dropped an anonymous note in our laps. "Congratulations, friends, on your anniversary and party. Read about it in the *Times*. Hope the next twenty-five go as splendidly." That random act of kindness buoyed our spirits.

"Mom and Dad, I need to go to New York. I can't do what I want to do at Yale," Melissa kept telling us during her sophomore year. Panic lurked at the edge of our discussions. Not finish college in our family? Unthinkable. How do you deal with a young adult about a life-changing move? Gingerly. Arguments about degrees, qualifications, the educated person flooded the endless conversations like a midwestern river during spring thaw. There was no denying her talent. Everyone who had seen her perform said she captured the stage and captivated the audience.

Harold argued. I cried. A heavy pendulum swung between. Sometimes we agreed she could leave. A few minutes later, no way. What about all the young black people who would die for this opportunity? What about all the old black people who *did* die for this opportunity? What about uplifting the race? Maintaining family standards? Supporting herself if she lived alone? What about Jodie Foster, who was there at the time, finishing her degree?

I have to give it to her, she held her ground. Gracefully. She was strong. No amount of pressure, subtle or otherwise, would deter our younger child. We made clear our preferences but let her know we would support her decision and her life for the next two years. She left Yale the same year Deirdre graduated.

At twenty, Melissa relocated to New York to try her luck in the world of theater and dance, moving into her first home, the large East Side apartment of an aging diva who rented her a room. Dancing since she was five, she had been attracted to the world of classical ballet. Never had I seen her so upset when, as a high schooler, she had been turned down at an audition for the ballet school of the American Ballet Theater. A furious Harold literally took her in hand and demanded to see the head of the school and the head dance teacher. He also demanded a second audition.

Several school officials watched the second tryout. Yes, Melissa was quite good; had good technique, they said. But she could never be a dancer because her feet were black feet, not quite structured right for classical ballet. We knew, of course, that they were hiding prejudice behind alleged anatomical differences.

Welcome came from the Dance Theater of Harlem School, where Melissa won a scholarship. Soon after, modern dance played its siren call and caught Melissa in its whirls and twirls. She made the switch. Ecstasy is a happy dancer. "Mom, I'm learning all of Alvin Ailey's repertoire," she reported excitedly. Parts in Off-Broadway, Broadway, television, and movie productions followed. The year she was to graduate, she danced with Baryshnikov. Duets with Ben Vereen, Gregory Hines, and Savion Glover would follow. The New York Post critic Jerry Tallmer gave a full-page rave review to her leading role portrayal of Josephine Baker at La Mama Theater. But a life in the theater is no crystal stair. She also faced months of unemployment, grueling schedules, and perennial job uncertainty. We have always wondered whether we did the right thing in not being more insistent that she stay in school. She says she'll go back someday. I believe her.

Ellis was still at WNET when I arrived, fantasizing about new funding sources while living on the last of the grants for his program "Watch Your Mouth." A decision had been made. More money would not be made available for black programming.

Ellis's office was in the arts and performance area, five floors away from mine. We talked almost every day and went out to lunch when we could. I sensed that his star was waning at WNET, as part of the general dimming of things black. I could talk the talk, but I had no power to change things. That power lay in the hands of the barons and earls of the station. Their goal was to protect and enlarge their fiefdoms. They disenfranchised him. Ellis became a nobleman without a kingdom.

But we did not talk of those things. Instead he told me about the latest poet, singer, or actor he had discovered. The latest play he had seen off-off-Broadway. In 1981, because of budget cuts, without fanfare he left the place where single-handedly he had given voice to the decade's most important black talent. Leaving WNET was the beginning of his end. But his video legacy remains to this day.

Five years later, amid secret meetings and closed doors, I, too, began to sense that I was sitting on the wrong side of the executive corridor. The decision had been made to unseat WNET's long-standing, charmingly autocratic president, Jay. It's funny how those actions become known. There's a lot of indirection, a host of coded words, much talk about "moving on to do other things." All to save face, to disguise the "F" word. "Fired."

As the president's chief aide, I was slain in the palace revolt. "Budget cuts" had now become "downsizing." It was my first taste of corporate and personal politics. The news that I would be severed shook me to my core. Ironically, both Polly and Sharifah would stay on. I went into an emotional decline, feeling dreadfully sorry for myself. I had an overwhelming anger toward the dragon I could not slay, the executive vice-president who recommended I be terminated.

"I want you to meet Graham," my mother said coyly. It had been five years since my father died, and my mother was being courted. She had sold the Tudor house and had moved in with Pattee and Jim in their new home in North Haven. A stocky, handsome butterscotch-colored man, Graham had been eyeing my mother once a week at church. He got bolder. He sat in the pew with her and they shared a hymnal. He started taking her to lunch. Next he was at our house.

Plain-spoken and an outdoor man who had grown up on a family farm in Virginia, Graham was far different from my urbane father. What they had in common was their gentlemanly ways. He made my mother happy, holding her hand and calling her "Angel." He wanted her to live with him in his cute little bungalow. That was enough for us.

We made plans for a June wedding. Daughters and granddaughters as attendants in old-fashioned sailor dresses of pink and lavender; sons-in-law and grandsons in blue blazers and white pants as ushers. In my garden, lavender and pink bows fluttered in the trees. A gazebo covered in African daisies. Mother in her lavender confection of tulle and chiffon. Graham looking somewhat uncomfortable in a tuxedo. Those who had helped to bury my father were on hand to resurrect my mother's new life. We had a father and grandfather again.

I was grateful to have another event to plan. For a time it pushed aside the shock, the anger, the hurt of losing my job. Harold was at a loss to console me. He gave me a book about passages and acceptable losses. It went unread.

A desire for revenge, to send a box of tarantulas to the man who fired me, filled my days. More than an injustice, this was my first failure in life. My first D on a report card. I was also scared. My pension plan was zapped. I would be fifty in a few months. Who would hire me? Being forty-nine, unemployed, female, and black was no picnic in 1986.

I was ashamed, embarrassed to tell my family. They were so proud of the job I held at WNET. I, too, had been proud. At WNET I had learned how institutions are run. As the corporate secretary to the board of trustees, I saw the strengths and weaknesses of the guardians of the arts. I was privy to and had input into many of the programs whose names became household words. Whenever I could, I gave black artists and producers access to the president and the station's program chiefs. I learned the fine art of soliciting wealthy patrons: never ask them for money.

In sum, I measured my success by the broad scope of what I was doing: by good relationships with the board members; by bringing in major gifts to the station; by ensuring a constant stream of favorable publicity, and by championing black programming. I thought my work mattered. So much for real insight.

Soon after, Harold lost his job. So here we were, married twenty-seven years and both out of work again. At first we subsisted on our severance packages. But after six months, we stood in the unemployment line. Waiting there with so many other people did not bother me. I was there through no fault of my own. I had paid taxes, so I felt entitled to whatever benefits the government had.

During this period the system changed in Connecticut, and you did not have to go to the unemployment office every two weeks. I did feel badly for Harold, though. Although we did not talk about it, I sensed his pride was battered by this second unemployment waltz.

I threw myself into community activities and tried free-lancing in writing and public relations. Depressed New Haven offered few opportunities. As volunteers, Harold and I worked against gang violence, and rallied the black community to help defeat the nomination of Robert H. Bork for Supreme Court Justice. We rode our bikes all over town to collect money to buy a full-page ad in the *New Haven Register*. The effort attracted press attention. Pretty soon, people were coming by our house with donations.

I was named to the board of trustees of the Shubert Theater, Harold to the library board. I wrote guest columns for the *New Haven Register*. Harold volunteered for Head Start administration. To the public, we were still the glamorous couple that *The New York Times* and the *New Haven Register* had profiled after our twenty-fifth anniversary. But the mailman kidded us about picking up the mail in our bathrobes. It was the faith and support of our family that pulled us through.

Only our children and some of our immediate family knew how hard-pressed we were. Our car was constantly in the shop, draining whatever resources we had. There was no extra money for vacations, shows, the little extras one has when there are two salary earners in the family.

Psychologists rank the most stressful things in life as the death of a parent, death of a spouse, loss of a job, moving. In the eighties, we became Job's siblings and experienced all of those traumas except spousal death. In some ways, though, I believe a little of us died as the certainty of our lives frayed and partially unraveled.

In 1987 word reached us that Ellis was ill. Thirty people and one relative showed up at the hospital for the family conference. "I should have held this meeting in the amphitheater," the doctor muttered grumpily. The diagnosis was sketchy. At first it was thought to be a stroke, then a heart attack. Unintelligible mufflings slurred Ellis's precise speech; bands of cotton blurred his vision.

X rays showed a lump on his chest. They removed it. Some weeks later, another lump addled his brain. In 1988 he began a slow recovery at a friend's home on a lake in Guilford, Connecticut, two hours away from the city. All that summer, scores of his colleagues, artists, and protégés made the trek to Guilford, as if to see a prophet. Grandly, Ellis received his guests in a long white caftan and a colorful kofi. He seemed to be on the mend. At the beginning of 1989, he planned a celebratory funeral for our friend Alvin Ailey. African drums, balloons, and Ailey dancers sent Alvin home in style.

Yale needed their Victorian house for a professor. Moving day found me a member of the walking dead. Pattee and Jim helped us transfer our belongings to a modern town house not far from New Haven's historic Worcester Square. The area was home to the core of New Haven's large Italian community and was most noted for its Italian festival parades and world-famous pizza. Cherry trees lined our street on both sides. In spring, delicate pink and white flowers created sensuous walls of blossoms and made a carpet of the sidewalk and street. The trees and the proximity to downtown were the best things about living there.

I missed my blue house terribly. I had lost my real home. Sometimes I had to catch myself because I blamed Harold for the turn our lives had taken. This is where being a modern woman comes in. I knew that I was as much responsible for the choices we had made as he was. When we went to the Virgin Islands it was to further his career. We remained there to further mine. We returned to the States for the sake of the entire family.

The high hopes we had on returning home were dashed, resurrected, then dashed again. We who had been golden children, golden young adults, golden professionals could not get used to the idea that underneath all that gold lay iron, ready to corrode.

Our cultural history tells us that many people got rich during the eighties. I knew some who did: Henry Kravis and Ivan Boesky. Kravis came on the WNET board of trustees, for which I was the corporate secretary. Boesky was all set to fund the station's *Civilization and the Jews* when the news broke about his illegal financial dealings. Kravis got richer. It was reported that Boesky retained many of his holdings, despite a prison sentence.

We got poorer, due in part to the move home without any jobs, the double Yale tuitions, and the loss of our jobs. We had no golden parachutes. Ours were wash-and-wear, and they had worn out.

*H*AROLD: Landing at JFK Airport with Shirlee, two daughters on the cusp of adolescence, an independent but protective Kerry blue terrier, a frightened, snarling Lhasa apso, and fifteen to twenty suitcases, I had a sense of déjà vu: eight years before, we had departed from this same airport—for a life unknown, full of excitement and promise in the Virgin Islands. And here we were, passing through the same airport, older, enriched, more experienced, and personally closer than when we left, facing, this time, a future unknown. The one constant: Shirlee and I were still together, still lovers and best friends, still enthusiastic about our girls, and confident that we would successfully build another good phase of our lives together. What, when, and how were the questions that had kept me awake many nights on St. Thomas after I had carefully organized our antiques, large and small, and the stuff of four busy people's lives for the three days that the moving company's best packers would spend artfully wrapping and taping. Specially crafted boxes and crates would slide easily into a huge sealed container on an ocean freight liner bound for New Jersey—along with my beloved beige Mercedes 300 SEL.

Reverend and Mrs. Taylor welcomed us into their sprawling home as much for the lively "entertainment" and excitement of two adults, two granddaughters, and two dogs in a house so large that they, themselves, had been "lost," as for the company that Shirlee would be for her mother and I would be for Reverend Taylor on a day-to-day basis. Shirlee and I staked out the third floor, while Dee Dee and Missy settled on the second, down a long hallway from the off-limits suite to which Reverend and Mrs. Taylor retreated at day's end. Hannibal and Ginger, the dogs, had the run of the house during the day, and slept at the foot of our bed at night.

I soon found myself once again driving Reverend Taylor to Ansonia for his circuitous business stops all over town: at the Chrysler dealer, three different banks, various apartment buildings he owned, the Elks Club, the brass factory, the mayor's office, the NAACP office, a fellow minister's home, a gas station for REV T's free gas, and wherever else, depending on which tattered slips of paper and envelopes scribbled with notes he pulled from his bulging address book. Because I liked to cook, Mrs. Taylor and I jointly planned and prepared the meals, unless there was a special dish that only she could prepare to Reverend Taylor's satisfaction. I soon remastered the ditto machine in his office so that I could prepare the programs for his Sunday services at Macedonia to his exact specifications. The lawn mower, rakes, hedge clippers, and other garden tools magically seemed to have been imprinted with my name, for my personal use—at my discretion, of course.

For a while, the girls were quite happy with all of the attention focused on them. But they soon became anxious to be surrounded by their own special things that were on the high seas heading home. Dee Dee was especially concerned. She seemed to need a permanent base, an anchor, from which she could safely deal with all the changes she was experiencing in herself and in her life, and to which she could safely retreat when fed up, uncertain, or challenged. Remembering my dad and Vira, I tried to remain understanding and supportive of her quick mood shifts and her search to identify herself, succeeding most of the time with help and advice from Shirlee.

I never anticipated the wall I encountered searching for a job from New Haven. No one knew or cared to learn about the enormous challenges I had successfully overcome as Commissioner of Education in the Virgin Islands. I was shocked, distressed, and depressed to discover that many high-ranking professional school leaders and industry executives with whom I talked job opportunities had no idea where the islands were or what language islanders spoke. They could not comprehend, and weren't interested in, the challenges of hiring young, inexperienced, mostly white teachers from urban centers and hamlets across the United States and preparing them to teach successfully in 100 percent black elementary and secondary schools in which the students considered themselves superior to white Continentals and spoke in a dialect teachers could not comprehend. They had no idea of the intricate problems to be overcome in order to build seven AIA Award–winning new schools at offshore locations where nothing was manufactured and all heavy-duty construction equipment, supplies, and skilled manpower had to be imported from the mainland or Europe. No one saw transferability in the skills used to quadruple income from federal entitlement programs because of demonstrated need rather than the number of people in the base population. And politics in the Virgin Islands were assumed to be unsophisticated at best, hardly relevant to skills needed to maneuver successfully through stateside political scenarios.

I felt caught in a conundrum. To fill the void of ignorance about the Virgin Islands and the skills necessary for what I'd achieved there, I had to talk a great deal and in the process risked being perceived as self-promotional, if not arrogant—and certainly boring to anyone not interested in the Virgin Islands in the first place, and not willing to learn enough about the context to appreciate the universality of its challenges and issues. On the other hand, without accounting for the Virgin Islands experience, my resume had a huge, gaping hole, suggesting I'd dropped off the face of the earth for seven years.

I nevertheless mailed resumes every day, made endless telephone calls, attended professional meetings, conventions, and seminars, and tried to rebuild my recognition, reputation, availability, and leadership experience as broadly as possible in the education community. To relieve some of my unremitting stress, I ate sugarcoated spice drops all day for three months and gained thirty-five pounds. I ended up weighing more than I had ever weighed in my entire life.

I struck gold when I reconnected by accident with an old friend from Harvard who had recently been appointed president of Manhattan Community College, one of the community colleges in the City University of New York system. Although he, too, knew little about my assignment in the Virgin Islands, he was aware of my track record and accomplishments prior to that time and the high regard I had enjoyed in the education community at large. He was building a new team to lead Manhattan Community College and recruited me to administer a substantial, across-the-board federal grant to improve the faculty, staff, and support services for 5,600 students.

Serving mostly minority young men and women who were high school graduates or had GED degrees, who ranged in age from eighteen to thirty, who worked full- or part-time, who on the average had one young child, and who often were the first in their families to attend college, Manhattan Community College was effectively the stepchild among CUNY community colleges, occupying second- and third-floor rental space at and around Broadway and Fiftieth Street. A priority for the new president and his team was to build a new, state-of-the-art campus in Manhattan within a few years.

In all college communities, there are off-campus spots that have become a part of the legend and lore of student and faculty life. Around Yale there are pizza shops, a Brooks Brothers clothing store, live music and beer joints. My choice was Clark's Dairy, a cozy, unpretentious restaurant specializing in the best bacon and egg combos, hot dogs, hamburgers, grilled cheese, tuna salad sandwiches, and homemade soups. Its ice cream and frappés were legendary. Clark's was for gownies and townies, catering to Yale students, faculty, and staff and long-term New Haven residents. While looking for a job, it was my favorite place for a morning coffee, a cigarette, and *The New York Times*. It was also the favorite stop-off for A. Bartlett Giammati, Yale's president. Bart and I developed a regular schedule of meeting at Clark's Dairy several mornings every week to resolve the problems of Yale and the world over coffee and cigarettes.

During one of our conversations he asked if my family and I might be interested in a beautiful old home he himself loved that was soon becoming available. He described the house and gave me the telephone number of a colleague to call on his recommendation to see it. The house was three blocks from the Taylors', on the same street. It was all that Bart had described and much more: several acres of land with stately trees; a three-story Victorian; double living room, large dining room, a master bedroom, and two guest rooms and baths on the second floor, and two bedrooms, a bath, and huge storage space on the third, for the girls. We loved it and made arrangements to move in as soon as our ocean liner of furniture and furnishings reached New Haven. The girls were thrilled that they could have their own rooms again and walk only a few blocks to school, to the Yale campus, or to the Taylors'.

My average workday at Manhattan Community College consumed twelve or more hours of my life, including the round-trip commute from New Haven to Grand Central Station. Considering the alternative I had lived with since returning from the Virgin Islands, I gladly paid this price. Not without being aware, however, that it was a high cost in personal terms. I had very little time for myself—for reflection, for hobbies, for Shirlee, for the girls, for projects around the house, for anything. From 6:00 A.M. until dinner at or after 8:00 P.M., from Monday through Friday, my entire life was driven by commuting and work. I seemed to live on the train and at work. I slept at home.

The familiarity and friendship of fellow commuters eased this burden somewhat. Over time, strangers who come together regularly for the same experience begin to connect, chat, and share information. I developed a small circle of white friends who boarded the train in New Haven, Milford, Bridgeport, Fairfield, Stamford, and Greenwich, looking for seats I'd saved from New Haven so that we could share coffee, *The New York Times*, family and work issues, and rousing, intensely competitive games of Hearts. In the evenings, by pre-arrangement we met in the bar car of the express train for beers and recaps of the day's developments. On one of her trips to New York City, Shirlee accompanied me and was surprised that I had developed so many new friends among regular commuters. She promptly dubbed me the Ambassador of Metro-North. This was before she began working in the city and joined me on the train, basically curtailing my social hours.

After my uncles in my youth, in my adulthood Reverend Taylor became my father-in-law, my surrogate father, and my close friend— roles and relationships that I believe were as important to him as to me. He knew that I admired and respected him greatly as a man and as a black man; that I appreciated his accomplishments, his style, his elocution, his faith, his public persona, and his steady commitment to Mrs. Taylor. And he knew that I was ever grateful to him for Shirlee.

As perceived agents of God on a divine earthly mission, ministers enjoy privileged status among their faithful congregants, in the community, and at home. Reverend Taylor totally internalized his mission and gave himself fully to Macedonia Baptist Church, to the town of Ansonia, and to the problems affecting the lives of the members of his congregation and community. He officiated at their weddings; he got them jobs; he counseled their children; he loaned them money; he co-signed mortgages and automobile loans; he prayed for the sick and arranged health care; he arbitrated family disputes; he arranged bail; he harnessed free legal counsel; he baptized them and buried them; he celebrated their achievements; and he provided whatever they needed but couldn't obtain on their own. He established an NAACP chapter. He organized political action groups. He negotiated labor disputes. He worked tirelessly. For these reasons, they loved him. They respected him. They were grateful to him. So was I.

In their youth, his children lived in reflections of the spotlight always on their father. As they grew older, the three girls sought to carry his torch forward by excelling in school and finding ways to do something special for society with their lives. Brother moved out of the spotlight and got lost in the dark, to his father's sorrow. But he always supported his son.

When I trailed Shirlee into his life and reached out to him to satisfy my own needs, we meshed in ways that gave him a son to boast about, another son from Harvard, no less. He responded warmly to my interest in his sermons, even when I criticized them or suggested that he used overblown elocutionary tactics. He appreciated my readiness to help him serve his congregation in any way I could, at any time. He appreciated my knowledge of the Classics and interest in language. And, always careful with his money, he welcomed my handyman skills because they spared him the cost of plumbers, electricians, carpenters, gardeners, and others. He knew nothing about such mundane things and hated having to pay others who did. To our personal friendship, each brought something valued by the other. When he died, I grieved deeply. I silently thanked him for loving me unconditionally for so many years.

At Chambers Street and the Westside Highway in lower Manhattan was an abandoned construction site stretching several blocks north along the highway and one block east. Huge steel beams rusted helter-skelter in the mud, testimony to dreams deferred and subsequently abandoned. Neighbors in the mixed-income housing development facing the site from the east were thankful that the abandoned construction project would leave their view of the river unobstructed, thus enhancing the value of their property.

This had once been the site of the new home of Manhattan Community College, projected to open in 1977. But New York's 1975 fiscal crisis halted construction, laid off faculty, and reduced services to students. Scandal forced the removal of the president, and political forces supporting aggressive civil rights action began to dissipate. It was assumed that the college would never occupy its new home.

Our new leadership team set out to renew consensus among students and faculty, the CUNY board of directors, Manhattan residents, the leadership at City Hall, the New York State Dormitory Authority, and the New York State Legislature on the need to fund and construct the new, permanent campus of Manhattan Community College. The escalating inadequacies and limitations of college classes conducted in abandoned midtown offices, coupled with the inappropriateness of Broadway as an environment for an educational institution, reinforced our determination. Our work was focused, intensive, and exhilarating.

After years of planning and monitoring construction activity, we jubilantly occupied the new seven-story $127.3 million campus in January 1983 with citywide, state, and regional celebrations. Ours was a true Cinderella story as thousands of students marched down Broadway to Battery Park City, leaving behind substandard, crowded, inadequate facilities for a new 4.5-acre campus offering new classrooms, lecture halls, laboratories, study carrels, a media center, theaters, dance studios, a gymnasium, and a swimming pool. Thereafter, our enrollment grew steadily to more than 13,500 students preparing to transfer to four-year colleges or enter the workforce.

I became vice-president and assumed responsibility for external affairs, including resource development, the Performance Arts Center, public and community relations, and student government, building a broad base of private-sector support and attracting a steady stream of income to enable further improvements in the college's capacity to meet student needs.

It hardly seemed possible that Shirlee and I had been married for twenty-five years. The time had passed so quickly. And I thought I was still holding my own against the vicissitudes of gravity and aging, still looking fairly youthful, still feeling vigorous, still aggressive, and still "giving back" in ways important to me. We decided to celebrate.

First, as an anniversary gift for Shirlee, I arranged for a young black designer I had met at the Fashion Institute of Technology in New York, whose original wedding dresses were being featured in the windows at Bergdorf Goodman, to create a special occasion dress just for her. After several fittings and adjustments, Shirlee was thrilled, and in the dress she was drop-dead gorgeous.

Close family and friends began arriving days in advance for the tented spectacular on our huge lawn. Ever the event planner, Shirlee commandeered a volunteer army to help execute her plan for decorating the tents and tables with color-coded feathers, balloons, flowers, sequined dust, candles, and mirrors. Caterers set up their serving tables. The party-rental people stacked crates of stemmed glasses, flatware, and china in the garage, unfolded a dance floor in the largest tent, and set up a platform for the senior citizen orchestra I hired from New York City. Electricians attached power lines from the house to the tents.

On the day of the event, heavy clouds gathered early in the afternoon and released a torrent of nonstop rain. Because I had no rain contingency plan even remotely in mind, I prayed that the rain would stop soon but began focusing on the what-ifs, borrowing tarps from Yale, lining up backyard tents, checking the flow of water around the big tent. The rain was relentless.

I was high in a tree above the serving tables, attaching a tarp through the branches to deflect the rain, as the guests began arriving in black tie and gowns. Shirlee was frantic because I had not shaved, showered, or begun to get dressed.

Eventually the rain stopped. The clouds rolled away. I dashed toward my bathroom.

Family and friends from far and near were on hand. Ma, Vira, Allen, Jr., and Elnora were there, along with Aunt Minnie and Dot from North Carolina, Uncle John, friends I grew up with in Deanwood, and a majority of the bridesmaids and groomsmen, and the flower girl from our wedding, all grown up. Ellis and Shirlee's cousin, Billy Taylor, co-hosted, and the elegant, gray-haired Black Senior Citizen Band from New York City was a hit. A contingent of the friends we loved from Ellis's entourage embraced us with gifts of their talents.

A few months later, the president of Manhattan Community College abruptly resigned without notice to accept a position in California. The entire college community was stunned. The president had invested so many years of time and energy into building the new campus that no one remotely suspected he would leave so soon after it opened. The job in California, he told everyone, was an unexpected, once-in-a-lifetime opportunity that he could not let pass. He left within a couple of weeks.

Without consulting with—or considering—the BMCC staff, the CUNY board of trustees immediately appointed an acting president from outside, who brought in a handpicked team of associates and promptly displaced all remaining members of the old team.

I was unemployed. Again. Without warning. Without cause.

The stress I experienced was enormous. Both Dee Dee and Missy were at Yale on minimal scholarship aid, necessitating substantial monthly tuition payments in addition to our regular expenditures. I had felt secure in my job and had invested hard work and long hours to succeed. Yet suddenly my house of cards had collapsed without warning. At a time I could least afford to be unemployed. There was injustice here. Something wrong with the order of things in my universe. I could not understand why this had happened to me for no reason. Where was my recourse? What had I done wrong? How had I failed to secure my future? Where was the fairness I believed in?

I knew that the answers would have to come from within, fashioned, rationalized, and accepted by me. This is the unanticipated price I must pay for serving at the pleasure of the president—without security, tenure, or any other implicit or explicit obligation from him, the college, the university, anyone. This was the deal I had accepted. I assumed but did not negotiate in writing continued employment and job security for a job well done, whether he remained as president or not. I assumed that others shared my sense of obligation to team members. I assumed wrongly and faced a terrifying lesson.

This downside of the agreement was now my problem, alone. No one else really cared about the havoc the president's personal decision created in my life, my wife's life, my children's life. What difference would nitpicking the issues of my employment agreement make now? There's no going back. Only forward—where I need a job. I must pick up the pieces of my life, handle my obligations as best I can. Start over. Work smarter. Avoid previous mistakes. Find a job. Again.

I updated my resume and started the outreach, searching for a new job in high gear—suppressing the terror that kept me awake nights, plotting alternatives to keep my life together until I succeeded, and trying to see a bright side, some potential for a good outcome of this tragedy that would enable me to assuage, if not release, my hurt, disappointment, rage, and anger. I feared that if I didn't get a handle on my inner self, my out-of-control emotions could trigger a massive heart attack at any time and send me to an early grave. My fiftieth birthday was less than a year away.

To fill some of the downtime while looking and waiting for a job, I accepted the mayor's appointment to the board of directors of the New Haven Cultural Affairs Commission, worked with a committee to hire a new executive director, joined efforts to support refurbishment of the New Haven Public Library, and planned the summer Concert on the Green season, which attracted thousands of picnickers on balmy summer nights for free concerts by leading jazz artists. Because of my long-standing commitment to Head Start, a national replication of the demonstration preschool project I had birthed for the Ford Foundation at A.B.C.D. in Boston, I signed on as a consultant to train staff at various Head Start sites around the city. I attended evening meetings and volunteered to help the NAACP address some of its issues more effectively, especially problems affecting the education of African American children in area public schools.

This was basically busywork, distractions, therapy I knowingly applied to myself to help stabilize me until my next breakthrough, until I found relief from the terror slowly but surely gripping me, strangling me.

We measured two major milestones in our lives during the same late May weekend in 1985: Dee Dee's graduation from Yale and my fiftieth. Our now famous (in the neighborhood) tents again covered the lawn, the party rental people were back. Chairs and tables rolled into place. Volunteers set china and decorated the tables, and a friend from Hawaii, Mabel Trujillo, made gorgeous floral centerpieces for each table at my basement workbench.

At the height of the party, Shirlee floored me before our guests and well-wishers, announcing her gift: a three-week trip for two, to London, Paris, Rome, and Florence. In front of the crowd, I was speechless for once. As soon as I could speak with her privately, I wanted her to tell me, for sure, whether the tickets were in fact paid for. They were.

My pride was boundless as Dee Dee marched across the stage to receive her degree in the courtyard of Morse College at Yale. As I watched, I had flashbacks of the squiggly little thing jabbing her legs into the air from that bassinet in Boston, surrounded by yards and yards of pink tulle. I recalled how eagerly she had left us to join the fray of her preschool class at Calhoun School in New York. I saw her wearing platform shoes and bell-bottomed pants, with big puffs of hair above either ear, going to her first disco party in St. Thomas. My baby of yesterday was now a Yale graduate. Imagine.

That same summer, when Missy insisted on going to New York to try her luck on the boards, I tried to practice what I had preached to so many parents during my career: make space in your psychological lives as parents for the emerging independence and self-determination of your children. Shirlee and I talked over our personal fears and concerns for days. Once we'd granted our approval, she moved to New York City within two weeks.

One day, nearly two years after Shirlee's termination, when I answered the telephone, a cheerful Jay Iselin began chatting amiably as if to catch up with me. The gall, I thought, masking my rising anger. He wanted to speak with Shirlee.

Ever gracious—sometimes more gracious than I—Shirlee spoke at length with Jay and gave him no hint of the trauma escalating daily in our lives. When Shirlee finally got off the phone, I waited angrily to know what Jay wanted, why he had telephoned her, pretending there was no history between us.

When I learned that he had called about a job he had recommended her for in California, I began to feel a little better. It sounded like a splendid position, and I encouraged her to pursue it. I didn't give a thought to the reality of relocating to California, where neither of us knew a soul.

Within a few weeks, after interviews in Washington and California, Shirlee had an excellent employment package. I agreed to relocate and take my chances, as she had done so many times before for me. In California, of all places.

CHAPTER 11

❦

California Dreamers

 $\mathscr{S}$ HIRLEE: After being deposed from WNET, Jay Iselin had landed on his feet as president of one of the country's most highly endowed colleges, Cooper Union in New York. The ease with which Jay, a son of privilege and the same age as Harold but with one less graduate degree from the same institution, could move with a hop, skip, and a jump from the top of one institution to the next did not escape me. Many would see nothing unusual in that.

In an act of characteristic generosity, Jay recommended me to a friend of his at the National Endowment for the Arts. Jay's friend was looking for a person to go to California to take over a post I didn't know was troubled. All it needed, he said, was a special person to pull it into shape. Big life lesson for me: if a job has been difficult to fill, run, don't walk away from it.

Los Angeles, 1989. Moviemaking was returning to the city and I was taking a job in "the business." Director of the nation's film preservation program with offices at Kennedy Center and at the American Film Institute. Hot stuff. Harold encouraged me to take it.

But there was no job waiting for him in the city of the angels. That troubled me, and it became an issue in my accepting the position. The film business of Los Angeles is built on a maze of relationships. Those who recruited me assured me they would do everything they could; they would use their networks, their relationships to help get Harold a job. None of that panned out.

They say you shouldn't move fine furniture around too much. Every time you move it, it gets nicked or broken. I wonder if that applies to people, too. This time, we transported one dog, a cat, and no children from East Coast to West. A distance farther than the islands were from New York.

The move was far more traumatic. Leaving New Haven was leaving the home that the girls had known from high school through college. We offered them cherished items from their rooms, children's books, Beatrix Potter china figurines, jewelry they had worn as teenagers, cheerleader outfits. With tears and sighs they took some. Other things they wanted to leave with us, "at home."

My antennae must have been folded up, because I had no idea the move would impact them so. After all, they were grownups in their twenties with lives of their own. All of a sudden I felt like a witless mother abandoning her brood. I think they felt it, too. To make matters worse, we lost "the dirty angel." She was a one-inch bit of wood, feather, and cardboard. Her round bald head had a smudged cheek, her wings were tattered, but every year, she was the last ornament to go on the tree. She would not make it to the land of her sisters.

I knew Jewelle, living on the Stanford campus, would be pleased to have one sister nearer. After moving to California from Minnesota, her career had taken off. Receiving her Ph.D. in clinical psychology, she had a practice and taught at Berkeley. Included among her specialties were suicide, black adolescent males, and children of color. She wrote a groundbreaking book, *Young, Black, and Male in America: An Endangered Species,* which made her in demand as a speaker. As a full professor, she was honored with an endowed chair. Jim, too, had flourished, authoring a book, becoming a Stanford dean, and also being honored with an endowed chair, in anthropology. Their sons both completed college, one Cornell, the other Harvard, and the older one also received a law degree from the University of California's law school at Berkeley. Jewelle's family enjoyed a comfortable, privileged life.

But for years she had complained of feeling left out because she was the only family member on the West Coast. Although we would be some eight hundred miles apart, we saw that as a pleasant day's drive or an hour's quick flight.

I was not ready for the numbing sense of displacement.

Easterners can be quite snobbish about the West Coast. Some of our friends were horrified when we told them we were moving. "Even the best-seller list is different," they averred.

We left for Los Angeles with open minds. I was fifty-two, didn't have a driver's license, and a car came with my job. My first car. Previously, I had had no desire to drive. Maybe it's because I lived in a small town and walked everywhere, or my father drove me wherever I needed to go, or because I went to a residential college where student cars were not allowed. Or maybe it's because I simply liked to be driven; I had the illusion that I was born with a chauffeur pushing my carriage.

In Connecticut on the last of the dreary November days, I learned to drive, six weeks before moving to Los Angeles. Harold peeked out the window each time I pulled away from the curb, repeating more than once that it was odd to see me at the wheel.

The lessons took place on small, two-lane roads in and around New Haven. The day I got my license, I felt as if a Ph.D. in astrophysics had been conferred on me. The tester told me I had done a good job for "a woman my age." "Usually," he said, "people your age are more nervous than younger folks."

"What age? What a nerve," I said, as I walked away with the photo ID in my hand. Professionally made up, I made sure this long-awaited photograph would be a memorable portrait.

In recognition of the license, old friends sent me balloons, champagne, flowers, and cards. My daughters, both of whom had had their licenses for many years, told me that I had finally become a modern woman. My family was relieved. No longer would they have to say, "Suppose Harold gets sick and you have to drive him to the hospital. What will you do?" "Call a taxi," I would say. Now I was the taxi. Until we got to Los Angeles.

The job put us up at a hotel in Beverly Hills, forty-five minutes away from the American Film Institute in Hollywood. For two weeks. I rented a car and with Harold guiding me, drove white-knuckled from west to east in the height of rush-hour traffic. Harold tried to act cool, but I knew he was nervous. I paid him no mind as he jammed his foot into the floor, cringed, covered his rolling eyes, or breathed heavily.

After finding a temporary apartment, Harold went back to Connecticut to supervise the move. I returned the rental car the day I bought the new car, and I asked a salesman to drive me home. He laughed. "Why?" he said. "Because it's a new car and I'm new to the city. I don't want to get lost, get nervous, and bang up the car." Whether or not it made sense to him, he drove me home.

On my second day of car ownership, I was filled with dread about driving to work. The previous night, I couldn't sleep and had visions of accidents. The institute was only ten blocks away and I could have walked, something nobody seemed to do in Los Angeles.

The car waited for me in the parking lot behind our apartment. Returning the favor, I waited for the car until the rush-hour traffic tapered off. Mysterious knobs and buttons winked at me as I surveyed the dashboard. Overnight, someone had added a score of them. I managed to turn on the ignition as sweat formed at the edge of my hairline. What brilliance. I had to back up and do a three-point turn to get out of the driveway. What skill. Most of the other cars in the parking lot had left. The sweat started to roll.

I rolled, too, down the driveway to the edge of Los Feliz Boulevard, one of the busiest streets in Los Angeles. Cars jetted by breezily, expertly, casually as I sat there rigidly facing six lanes of traffic.

If all of those folks can do it, so can I, I said to myself, venturing out into the right lane. The slow lane. I could hear something thumping in my ear. My heart. Two blocks rolled by; I breathed heavily, nervous but pleased with myself. I was driving, alone.

A trash truck picking up garbage drove out in front of me, challenging my confidence. Frantic signals came from the sanitation worker to go around the truck. I refused to do his bidding. He stopped. I stopped. He scratched his cap in puzzlement. I reached my destination, my one right-hand turn coming up. With casual aplomb I drove up the curving driveway. Everybody seemed to be in. Two parking spaces, side by side, remained vacant. Just my luck; they were on the horizontal. I angled lopsidedly into them, taking up both spaces, turning off the ignition, wiping my sweaty forehead, and muttering, "Thank you, Jesus."

All that day, I sweated out my drive home. Waiting until dusk to leave. It took me about twenty minutes to find the button for the headlights. Nearing our apartment, making a three-lane left-hand turn would be the challenge for the evening. In jockeying for space with a city bus, I lost and got into the wrong lane, forestalling my turn into my driveway. Heading for Glendale, where I had never been, I panicked. "I'm going to get lost, run out of gas, be mugged in a seedy neighborhood, or set upon by the Ku Klux Klan members who live in Glendale." The litany cruised through my head as I cruised through unfamiliar territory.

"Calm down, calm down. Just take your first right turn and make your way back," my driving angel said. I followed her instructions and found myself back on Los Feliz Boulevard.

The ordeal was not over yet. I arrived at my driveway to find it partially blocked by a police car. A telephone pole bordered the other side. Making my peace with the pole, I barely skimmed it. In the parking lot, I let out a deep breath, turning off the lights and the ignition. For the next hour I lay on the sofa, hyperventilating. I called Jewelle and told her the tale. She laughed hysterically. It went that way for two weeks until Harold returned. I have not driven in Los Angeles since.

I do envision myself driving again on some quiet lane, passing an occasional car. I suppose that will have to be in Vermont.

The organization I headed was designed to be an umbrella for more than a hundred film and television archives, each with its own history, needs, and agendas. Archives large and small politely competed with each other for films, funds, and funders.

I loved being a boss, a leader. What an opportunity to be compassionate: to teach, to learn, to inspire. I wanted everyone to do well, to feel valued, to understand and utilize their special talents. I got that old cheerleader feeling of running with the team as they crossed the goal. In my soul, there was great disdain for and hostility to the old-fashioned kind of patriarchal, authoritarian manager.

My job was to advocate for film preservation and look for a mother lode of money. Seeking support, I went everywhere. I was incredulous that the moguls of the film industry and their studios had to be practically bludgeoned to put up a pittance to preserve their professional and artistic history. Their reasoning: they had their own studio archives to maintain.

One of my fundraising jaunts fulfilled two long-held fantasies. When I was prepubescent, I dreamed of meeting Alan Ladd, Joseph Cotton, Gregory Peck, and Tyrone Power. Why them? There was a personal connection. Ladd reminded me of a neighborhood crush, Georgie Spader, the Polish boy with whom I'd played softball and cowboys and Indians. Cotton had crimpy hair and full lips. I imagined he was passing. Peck's dark good looks reminded me of fair-skinned black men I had known in Washington.

In my thirties my taste shifted and focused on just two actors, Omar Sharif and Peter O'Toole. For me, Sharif had a black look. My attraction to O'Toole was a mystery. I think it was his charm, though, which my father would have called "devilish." At the elegant English embassy in Washington, I met the men of my latter-day dreams.

A screening for the restored version of *Lawrence of Arabia* attracted starstruck Washington types. Everyone said Sharif and O'Toole would be there, but I didn't believe it. After I had dutifully forewarned him of my possible starburst, Harold and I arrived early at the imposing Washington mansion. As we coolly scanned the few faces in the room, a butler took our coats. Through no will of my own, my eyes turned into surveillance lasers beaming directly at Them, standing side by side, chatting and smiling, still handsome, still hypnotic.

Someone introduced me to the British ambassador, who wore a dark gray pin-striped suit. Though he was quite attractive, I hardly looked at him. The idols had locked in my attention to the spot where they stood. I couldn't move. They saw my fixed stare. I imagined they said, "Let's give this woman a thrill." With a wide smile, Sharif came toward me. A dark suit deepened the dark of his eyes, the black of his hair. Looking at my name tag, he said, "Well, hello, Preservation Lady. Thank you for restoring our film." He kissed my hand. I have no idea what he or I said after that.

A yellow silk handkerchief spilled artfully out of the breast pocket of O'Toole's light-colored English suit. With deep-knee action, he moved silkily, like a large cat. Was it my imagination, or did he loom over me? When he kissed my cheek, I went into shock. Memory evaporated. Harold receded, soft focus, into the distance. After a while, a short interval, I think, he came into focus again, chuckling. "Well, I guess you've had enough star power for life," he said. I had.

At least until I went to the black Oscar nominees' dinner. Black Hollywood turns out the week of the Oscars to honor past and present black nominees. The number of honorees is minuscule compared to the group that turns out. Every black actor who is alive and can walk attends and is charmingly accessible. So now I have a Hollywood album of pictures of myself with Spike Lee, Denzel Washington, Morgan Freeman, Sidney Poitier, and a host of others, snapped by Harold. The only place I've shown the album was at my father's church. I knew they would love it, and by association they elevated me to star status.

After a few months, we moved from the temporary apartment to a comfortable small house in Hancock Park, a historic central Los Angeles neighborhood of large old houses and small lawns. Nat King Cole had been the first black to move into Hancock Park. When he did, someone burned a cross on his lawn. No such warm greetings welcomed us. There was no welcome, period.

After we had been in the house about a year, we learned that our landlady of the blond ringlets was a well-known porno star. Until we checked out some of her titles from a video store, we did not believe she did what she did. Each time we saw her we found it hard to reconcile her sweet nature and her hard-edged life. We wondered how many other porno stars were walking around in Hancock Park.

The porno star wanted to sell her house. We moved again, selecting a place close to where I worked. Where we live now, I can't see the Hollywood sign from any of our windows. If I go outside and walk south one block to the end of my street, where it intersects Hollywood Boulevard, I can spot the landmark easily. Its location helps me find my way around town. The sign and some of the mountains are north; the ocean is west and south; the county hospital and Dodger Stadium are east.

We live in one of the least fashionable parts of Los Angeles, on the eastern edge of Hollywood. Around us, undistinguished buildings, mostly long, three-story affairs, house immigrants from Armenia, Mexico, Central and South America, the elderly, people on government subsidies, and old-timers from the film industry. Our building stands out "like Camelot shining on the hill." Tall, white, newly refurbished after the 1994 Northridge earthquake, the Trianon, as the building is called, is a seventy-seven-year-old historic landmark, ancient by Hollywood standards. After its completion by Mary Pickford, Douglas Fairbanks, and a host of imported European artisans, it housed the Fairbankses, Charlie Chaplin, Fatty Arbuckle, and Lily Pons.

The story goes that Mary Pickford went to Europe for the first time on her honeymoon with Douglas Fairbanks. She told him she wanted a house that looked like the castles she saw. Thus the Trianon. We occupy the castle itself where Mary and Doug lived. A balconied, two-story living room, a turret alcove, and a lavender tiled bathroom are souvenirs from the Pickford occupancy. I am reminded of the Nikki Giovanni line, "If these walls could talk, I wonder what they would say."

In the daytime, the neighborhood is lively with vendors. They call and signal to their clients, mostly women, with distinctive horn beeps, blares, and whistles. Emerging from their vans, they bellow in Armenian toward the open windows. Clothing, pastry, fruits and vegetables, ice cream, and whatever else happens to be available on a particular day materialize in boxes or on racks. Although I never buy, I love the vendors. Something about them reminds me of the islands. Harold thinks they are a nuisance, noise polluters. I tell him he's a curmudgeon.

Our guest room is seldom empty. For a variety of reasons, a succession of family and friends have taken up residence. Leaving a New York career in theatrical production, Rick, the son of my foster sister Althea, stayed with us for six months, landing a job in casting at the Disney Studios. Hospitalized and near death after a serious illness, Rick asked his mother to come. Althea arrived, stayed with us for four months, willed Rick back to life, and took him home to Connecticut.

After working as my assistant at the Preservation Center, Mariah, a brilliant, talented actress and writer, came to live with us for what she called her "Artist in Residence" stay. We saw in Mariah a young black talent who had transcended a difficult childhood; life in the St. Louis projects, a single mother, a mentally handicapped brother. She stayed with us for six months and had other young hopefuls call us about the possibility of a similar "grant." Mariah is now studying at Smith College for her master's degree in playwriting. Although we both have mentored many young people over the years, here is a more deeply personal way for us to reach out, to push up, to encourage, and to foster.

For someone grounded in the geography and culture of the East Coast, Los Angeles is a different world, with its own form of apartheid. This was a disappointment to me. I believed what I read about the great multicultural conglomeration that peopled Los Angeles. It was a partial truth. All the multis live on the East Side.

You gravitate toward people like yourself. There are the racial, class things, I suppose. In Los Angeles, few blacks and whites make efforts to be with each other. That's probably true everywhere now, but in California with all of its brown, tan, and yellow faces, it is especially odd.

Part of it is geography, Los Angeles being a mammoth place. But the Thomas Guide maps obscure the boundaries of the two largest foreign countries within the city limits: South Central and the East Side. I have met many people and been told of others who do not venture beyond Los Angeles's West Side, for anything.

Having lived and worked there, I know that in New York, people do go all over the city, to the galleries on the lower East Side, the Village on the West Side, lower Manhattan and SoHo, and Harlem. That's part of the excitement and stimulation of New York. This ease of crossing boundaries does not exist in Los Angeles.

We had been in Los Angeles for five years when the civil disturbances erupted. Then the Simpson case consumed us. While we were visiting on the island of St. John, we watched Simpson's flight in the Bronco.

Despite all the talk, all the hurt, all the rage, little has changed. We still find ourselves the only blacks at gatherings. We are still questioned as if we are space creatures, as if people with brown skin could not possibly lead a normal life, go to college, meet on a blind date, have children who went to Yale.

For the first time in our lives, we found it difficult to make friends. Was it because it's harder to make connections as we get older? Were we more critical? Less interested in the uninteresting? Had our social antennae dulled? Did we talk about the wrong things?

Life continues to intervene in unexpected ways. "Mom, Mom, how's your weight these days?" Deirdre inquired unsubtly. "You need to get it down for a photo shoot; you're going to be in *Glamour* magazine."

Her one-page "Best Mom" essay reported, "Since the beginning, life with Shirlee has been an adventure. Mom kept me and my younger sister entertained and enraptured by detailed stories about fascinating characters in interesting situations. She artfully used those stories to guide our behavior in the direction of her choice. . . . my mother (with much help from my dad) has helped me become the woman that I am today. . . . for Miss Bauble, as I call her, my sister and I are her most precious gems."

The *Glamour* photographer captured us as we cavorted around the edge of the fountain in the center of our courtyard. The shape of our faces and the arcs of our smiles left no doubt about our genetic connection. I didn't look too bad. A bell-shaped jacket provided a lovely disguise for my less than supermodel figure.

In 1991, word reached us that Ellis had died. A committee had been formed to plan his funeral celebration. Harold and Melissa were asked to take part in the ceremonies, in Ellis's home church in Washington and his new church, the long-unfinished St. John the Divine in New York.

A soul would not stay long in that place. That February day, the vaulted space was cold, damp, and somber. At even intervals, slanted rays of sunlight worked at warming up the huge chamber. They did not succeed. ·

The crowd had already put itself in the best seats, knowing they were in for an experience. A sizable group waited quietly behind the pillars. They were family, close friends, honorary pallbearers.

Amiri Baraka, whom Ellis had once presented as Leroi Jones,

looked down at his notes. Maya Angelou greeted admirers. Judith Jamison made arching motions with her famous neck, as if to relieve some sorrowful inner tension. The elegant Arthur Mitchell talked quietly with choreographer George Faison. Roberta Flack, wild-haired, stood beside Richie Havens, who pulled his cape closed for warmth. Melba Moore scanned the crowd for friends. Nick Ashford looked down at his tiny wife, Valerie Simpson, as she checked some lyrics.

George Page, host of WNET's *Nature* series and longtime Ellis boss, stared absently into the middle distance. *Essence* editor Susan Taylor and her husband, Kephra Burns, were a unit unto themselves. In a gorgeous dark gray coat, David Dinkins, mayor of New York City, walked briskly to the front of the line. Just in time.

Offstage, the African drummer Olatunji began a steady beat. Dressed in white from his kofi to his sandals, he mounted the steps, striking an instrument that sounded like a chime, then a bell. Another drummer in a cimarron yellow suit assumed an honor guard position. The procession began.

In the chancel, the focus was a miniature catafalque on which rested a small casque draped in red. Beside the scarlet cover sat a solitary dark brown leather kofi with a bit of Kente cloth on its rim. A billboard-size portrait of Ellis looked out at the audience with bemused satisfaction. His dramatically lit face and hands emerged from a background of total blackness. Heavy, dark-framed glasses outlined his eyes. A thick mustache concealed his upper lip. The angle of the portrait captured only one of his large, protuberant ears.

Priests swinging incense, acolytes holding tall candles, a choir robed in white and red led in African dancers who whirled their way to the stage in filmy flashes of pink, green, orange, yellow, red, white, and blue.

Mayor Dinkins opened the proceedings, Ashford and Simpson closed them. Speaker after speaker told how Ellis, like a brown pied piper, led them over the mountains and through the valleys of arts, letters, entertainment, politics. Along the way, Roberta Flack sang and Aimiri Baraka read, saying that Ellis was really a soul man now. Phoebe Snow brought down the house with her deeply soulful rendition of "Amazing Grace." Adding a special Ellis touch, a choir of reformed alcoholics and drug addicts swayed to and fro.

When I was a young twenty-something, Ellis had opened a new world for me. He pushed me into the center of the black arts movement. He made me think about the world Malcolm X wanted as well as the world of Martin Luther King. He nourished my acceptance of people whose sexual orientation was not the norm. He urged me to stay in touch with my roots and to help young people who might have no other resource except what I could provide. He encouraged me to live my life boldly, unafraid, and with flair. As my guru, my confessor, my dearly beloved brother, Ellis prodded me toward adulthood. Aside from my parents and Harold, he was the most influential person in my life. There is not a week that goes by without some reminder of him.

Congress made drastic funding cuts in the National Endowment for the Arts, one of film preservation's key grantors. After that the money picture was grim. I had been in the job for three years. Tired of the Faustian politics within the field and the struggle to raise money in an industry of fabled wealth, I decided it was time for me to move on.

Then it was unemployment lines again. Los Angeles's had a different spin than New Haven's. Lots of unemployed actors.

I had no heart for working for anyone anymore. Too many imponderables, too many variables, too many things beyond my control. I needed to be in charge of my own life. There had to be another way. Harold never suggested I go out and look for another job. Instead, he supported my vocational uncertainty. Officially, I was "between opportunities."

$\mathscr{H}$AROLD: Shirlee and I are the "Nature" referred to in the phrase, "Nature abhors a vacuum." Since our honeymoon, we have been collecting stuff that we happened upon and liked at roadside stands, antique shops, yard sales, auctions, moving sales. Much of this stuff I carted home and gave new life to, refinishing elegant old tables; replacing mirrors and regilding elaborately carved frames; reupholstering chaise longues, grand old sofas, and Louis XIVth chairs. Lots more stuff traveled with us as works in progress that I had not yet paid attention to: chandeliers, floor lamps, large frames, wall sconces; sets of chairs, paintings and posters, vases, candelabra, rococo valances, and sculptures with missing arms, feet, or other body parts. In labeled boxes, we stored hundreds of 45 rpm and 33-⅓ LP records; specialty books; honeymoon clothes; unused wedding, birthday, anniversary and Christmas gifts; christening dresses; first baby shoes; college term papers; slides, photographs, and scrapbooks; Selectric typewriters, and God knows what else.

From these bulging reserves, we created eye-catchingly interesting environments everywhere we lived, appropriate to the architecture and bones of the structure. None of it matched, but we always had an eye to make it work well together. When we left the blue house for the town house for the first time as a couple *sans* resident children, we decided it was time to pare down, to shed some of the baggage we'd carted around the world. For our yard sale, we lined the driveway with racks and racks of children's, women's, and men's clothes for all seasons; a washer and dryer; several bicycles; folding chairs; garden umbrellas; boxes and boxes of books; chairs, sofas, and tables; brass flatware; iron pots and frying pans; fireplace screens and andirons; toys; lawn hoses and mowers; garden tools. Also on sale and the first thing to go, my beige vintage Mercedes from the Virgin Islands was the star attraction. The sale was a whopping success.

Only then did I realize how much we abhorred vacuums and how prepared we were to fill any we encountered. In fact, as I surveyed the full expanse of the "few" things we felt we could do without, I surmised that we could have furnished a second, multistory home with stuff from the yard sale alone. And inside our house were the furniture, clothes, artwork, and furnishings we had not begun to pack for the move.

And as we neared the end of packing, we realized that we had to impose on Jim and Pattee to store a great deal in their garage. We simply didn't have room for everything; we needed a larger vacuum than the town house for the essentials we didn't have space for but couldn't/wouldn't dispose of.

Shirlee has been her "own" person since I met her, and loving her the way she is, and not wanting her to change from the woman I've loved since we first met, I've spoiled her rotten. The most blatant anachronism which most people found amusing but I found charming was that she never learned to drive an automobile and, thanks to me, I suppose, never felt a need to do so. When the girls were babies and even after both became licensed drivers, I drove Shirlee wherever she wanted to go and brought her home if I could. Otherwise, she was quite comfortable taking taxis, busses, and subways on her own.

Preparing to relocate to California where a new car of her choice would become available, she decided to learn to drive. I declined to teach her because I anticipated the necessity of occasional sharp warnings or caveats while she was behind the wheel and knew that she would be more concerned (hurt?) with my voice and tone than with any imminent danger we faced. We both could be killed, I thought, if she began crying from something I said, rather than taking swift, corrective action.

She confirmed for me that she was a real trooper—even at age fifty-two—as she gamely white-knuckled the driver ed car slowly into traffic under the watchful tutelage of her instructor. And passing her road test on the first try really pleased her (and me) no end. The photo on her Connecticut license clearly reveals her joy and pride at joining the ranks of registered vehicle operators.

Moving to Los Angeles offered a new beginning for Shirlee and much greater employment potential than the New Haven area for me, in Virgin Islands–like weather that we both had loved. I had great pangs about being so far from Deirdre and Melissa in New York, from our closely knit family and friends in New Haven, and from Ma, aging under Vira's watchful eye in Washington, D.C., since I knew there would be fewer in-person visits for which telephone conversations were not adequate substitutes. On the other hand, Jewelle and Jim were only an hour's flight away in Palo Alto, and Allen and Elnora just an hour by car north of Los Angeles. With Shirlee's guaranteed income and my affable, extrovertish determination, I was willing to try a new start—being realistic, I hoped, about the challenges of connecting into networks and systems where I would be a total outsider.

Standing in the street in front of our now-vacant town house, watching the movers roll our last packing box onto the eighteen-wheeler that would find us in L.A. in about six days, I heard Ma's voice reassuring me with unshakable faith, "God may not come when you call Him, but He's always on time." I thought about Shirlee and me being so far from the safety net of family, surrounded by strangeness and strangers everywhere, alone and on our own, with my angst about finding rewarding work as quickly as possible. I wondered how and where to start my job search. I worried about how we'd cope if one of us became ill or died. There were so many unknowns that I was reluctant to call upon God. I did pray, however, that in His infinite wisdom, He would be on time.

From our small furnished efficiency near Shirlee's new office in Los Feliz, with my unfailing *Thomas Guide* I began exploring different parts of this huge city in search of neighborhoods where we might like to live. Within one day I found Hancock Park and loved its stately old New England–like homes with lots of space and history, fronted with rolling green lawns and brightly blooming flowers. Old, fully grown trees arched the broad, quiet streets, giving the entire neighborhood an aura of serene permanence, constancy against change. I had lucked out. This was for us.

At the sidewalks in front of several homes in the neighborhood were discreet, quiet "For Sale" or "For Lease" signs with an agent's name and telephone number. I jotted down the information for several sale and lease properties and returned to our efficiency and the telephone.

"Are you serious?" I asked in stunned disbelief.

"And it's an absolute steal at that price, sir. Would you like to see it today or tomorrow?"

"Let me make sure I understand. The house is a 'steal' at $2.1 million?"

"Oh, absolutely. For Hancock Park, it's a very nice but not extraordinary property. Can I show you something a little nicer? For comparison purposes?"

"Not today, thank you. I'll talk with my wife and let you know if we'd like to see any of your listings. Thank you."

Later in the day, I drove by these properties again to make sure I had not taken down the wrong address or telephone number.

I checked job openings with all of the two- and four-year colleges and universities, with the Los Angeles and surrounding school districts, and with foundations and corporations. I registered with nonprofit placement groups and attended education job fairs, conferences, seminars, and professional meetings. I attended meetings of the Harvard and Amherst southern California alumni organizations. I checked the classifieds every day. I checked federal job listings for education positions in southern California. I was meeting people but getting nowhere.

One weekday morning, I received a telephone call from the president of the Los Angeles Museum of Natural History inviting me to lunch in his office. Also an Amherst alumnus, in the Class Reports section of the current *Amherst Alumni Magazine* he had read Tom Herzog's report on my relocation to Los Angeles to pursue work with and for at-risk youth and wanted to tell me about a collaborative project that the museum and several other institutions wanted to initiate.

Our luncheon conversation led to a meeting with senior staff from the Office of the Mayor, the Pacific Bell Telephone Company Foundation, the Museum of Science and Industry, the University of Southern California, Mount St. Mary's College, Hebrew Union College, the Southern Christian Leadership Conference of L.A., and several principals from public and parochial elementary schools in the vicinity of Science Park and the University of Southern California, on the periphery of South Central L.A.

After meeting for several months, this group had decided to form a consortium through which they could share their institutional resources in programs to improve the school success of Latino and African American students attending public and parochial schools in South Central. They had received a modest six-month grant and general commitments from each participating institution, including an office, desk, and telephone at USC. They offered me the executive director's position for six months. My success in designing collaborative programs and raising funds to support both program and overhead costs would determine the future in the seventh month and beyond. I accepted the job as a challenge, an opportunity to explore education networks in Los Angeles, and a source of income.

Within two months we had our first breakthrough: a $23,000

grant from United Way for after-school science enrichment programs in several elementary schools. With help from teachers and principals in other schools, we then developed proposals for after-school programs in reading, math, art, and English as a Second Language and sought funding from several major foundations.

Months later, not one was funded, and I was stressed. Really stressed.

In my follow-up meetings to find out why, the foundation officers praised the quality, uniqueness, and promise of our proposals but declined to fund them because every college, university, and cultural institution in the consortium had contributed only unutilized in-kinds to support their own proposals (office space for me and limited use of facilities)—and not one single dollar in cash. They interpreted this as an indirect indication of the consortium's lack of commitment to its own organization and the activities we were asking others to support. Additionally, because of declining resources and many more organizations seeking money for worthwhile causes, most foundations had established a policy of funding direct services to children, not the overhead or administrative costs (including salary for me) of the sponsoring agencies.

I had anticipated this problem and unsuccessfully sought cash commitments for each proposal from consortium members. In the wake of the Rodney King incident and the civil disorders that set Los Angeles ablaze, however, L.A. colleges and universities (and especially those located near South Central, where the conflagration was greatest and where the consortium focused its efforts) experienced a drop in applications for admission, a rise in transfers, a sharp decline in enrollment and tuition income, and, concomitantly, a serious budget shortfall. To scale back operating costs, academic departments consolidated, class sizes increased, and the number of adjunct faculty was reduced. There were no extra dollars for any purpose, however important and compelling—including the consortium. Any faculty and staff time the consortium needed for its programs had to be borne by consortium grants.

Despite continuing requests for assistance and redoubled efforts to attract money from the business community, after six months the consortium was broke and prospects were grim. The board decided to reduce consortium activities to a monthly newsletter until its financial picture improved. I turned elsewhere for employment.

I was invited to join a task force created by the mayor, school officials, the Department of Justice, and a host of community and youth service agencies to devise strategies, programs, and services that would heal the city and prevent the recurrence of future disturbances. With L.A. school officials focused on the needs of children, we crafted a community service prevention/healing plan for students and parents in riot areas.

I subsequently founded a nonprofit organization, The Children's Art Collaborative, and successfully competed for foundation and federal funds to use visual art as therapy for inner-city children who were brutalized by the unrest. I hired established and emerging African American, Asian, and Latino artists and developed a series of workshops. For months and months I spent most days in elementary schools surrounded by kids whose resilience, creativity, and love were simply overwhelming. On many occasions, I felt as if I were an overgrown kid myself, reliving my days at Carver Elementary—where teachers truly respected, loved, and worked hard to teach their young charges.

Working directly with young children in riot-area schools and communities revealed to me how deeply the Rodney King incident and the subsequent uprisings scarred them. The image of police officers severely, repeatedly beating and kicking King was seared in their memory and they talked about it angrily, sometimes volunteering casual asides about the police brutality their families, friends, and neighbors had experienced. When I tried to get them to discuss the King incident in the context of learning how to manage anger, hands waved in the air as they shouted what King should have done and boasted broadly what they would have done had they been King. They talked about defending themselves against the police with knives, guns, and other weapons. Some said they expected to be killed by gunfire before their sixteenth birthday and wanted to take out a police officer before being wiped out themselves. Many had participated in the upheavals and looting or knew others who had. They saw little wrong with the disturbances and only wished more police officers had gotten their due.

It was frightening to anticipate the future of these children. In their art and conversation, their anger and hopelessness were dramatically apparent. Only a revolution, not programmatic tinkering on the periphery of their realities, would in any way alter the course they were on. I was distressed to learn how "old" they were.

When Ellis became ill, the love he enjoyed became evident from one end of the country to the other. Friends telephoned friends who telephoned other friends in the middle of the night to share urgent information about the status, the diagnosis, the treatment, the prognosis, the whereabouts, and the caretakers of Ellis. On the mid–East Coast, we could always rely on Diana Edmonds for up-to-date information; on the West Coast, Anna Horsford; in Boston, Florence Ladd Harris; in New York, Novella Nelson; in Washington, D.C., his sister, Doris Sanders. When word reached us that Ellis had died, I felt that I had crossed over a one-way bridge; that I had lost a brother—and best friend to myself, my wife, and both of my children.

At his funeral at the Church of God in Washington, I tried to share the importance of Ellis in the lives of everyone privileged to know his talents and free spirit. At his funeral at St. John the Divine, Melissa, whose future he predicted and nurtured, spoke for his theater family. In Washington and New York, there was standing room only.

California is like a suit that for unknown reasons simply doesn't fit right. Although we have met lots of people, we have few friends. We like the weather, but we're seriously frightened of earthquakes. We've been here almost eight years yet feel like newcomers. We're in crowds, but we're alone. We talk about leaving, but we're still here. In many ways, this disappointment is a blessing: Shirlee and I still find each other the most interesting persons we've met and look forward to our time alone together.

Some folks have said that it takes ten years to know California. We have two years to get there.

CHAPTER 12

❧

Mutual Forbearance

*S*HIRLEE: There was time again. I spent a lot of it thinking about my history and what had brought us to California. More and more my thoughts turned toward solving the mystery of my mother's family. Since girlhood, I had been curious about the story of my mother's life. With the approach of her eightieth birthday, I wanted to give her a special present, a kind of "this is your life" personal document, solving some of the puzzles that had obscured her origins. The mysteries had to do with race, color, and racial transformation—that is, "passing." Something most of the people in her family had done. I had no idea what or who I would find.

The computer piece took on a life of its own. I began writing for hours on end. I told my friend Faith Childs, a literary agent whom I had met through Ellis, about the project. She read the material and said I had a book. She sent the material to a number of publishers and secured an advance. I said goodbye to my friends on the unemployment lines and spent the next two years writing my first book, *The Sweeter the Juice*.

Archives, libraries, historical societies became my new haunts. Stripping away layers of my mother's memory, I traveled to some of the places in her sad history. In my father's safe, I found a cache of his diaries spanning the years from 1933 to 1981. From them I gleaned a sense of my parents' constancy, their sacrifices for each other and their children, and the breadth and depth of their lives.

Harold was with me every step of the way, keeping the household going while I was traveling or at the computer. Sitting by my side, he researched in the archives, read and critiqued my manuscript.

The summer of 1992. A season of illness and death. Another funeral would bring us back east. Jewelle and Jim, on leave from Stanford and Berkeley, had been spending the year in the nation's capital while Jim served as a research associate at the Smithsonian Institution and Jewelle as a Distinguished Scholar at the Joint Center for Political and Economic Studies. While in D.C., Jewelle's husband of thirty-five years was diagnosed with prostate cancer. When I arrived, Jim was in the hospital, recuperating from surgery the doctors claimed was successful.

Jewelle was a mess. Dark rings circled her dark eyes. "Jim is not getting well as quickly as he should. I don't know what they are doing to him in that hospital." Jim was in Bethesda's highly regarded Suburban Hospital.

Spending her days at Jim's bedside, Jewelle took every opportunity to talk to a doctor or nurse about Jim's progress. Their reports left her unsatisfied; something, the medicine, the anesthesia, the trauma of the operation, was keeping Jim in a distracted, irrational state. While he talked of rocketships and journeys to the stars, Jewelle talked of new regimens and medications.

I went to the hospital as much as I could. The place was quiet, manicured. It even had its own gourmet restaurant. No one would dare die in a place like this, I thought. Besides, Jim was too young to die and Jewelle wouldn't let him.

Death was for elderly people like my uncle Percy, my father's brother, who died unexpectedly in New York while Jim was at Suburban. Harlem Hospital, where Percy breathed his last, was a far cry from Jim's hospital. Dirt, nonfunctioning elevators, confusion about patients' rooms greeted me.

Percy had no children, no relatives closer than his nieces and nephews. On a break from a research visit in New York, I had taken him to lunch in midtown Manhattan to retrieve some family photos from the twenties and thirties. I walked him to the bus stop, and, grinning his gap-toothed smile, he waved goodbye, boarded the bus, went up to Harlem. At his local butcher shop, he bragged about his fancy lunch with me and ordered some pork chops. While he was waiting, a heart attack pounded him like a meat softener, and in the doorway of the shop, he dropped like a side of beef. Like my mother, who had been his childhood friend, he was eighty. We thought it best not to tell Jim.

At Suburban, Jim seemed delighted to see me. In his sweet, earnest manner, he tried to tell me a story I couldn't quite grasp. He moaned a lot, not in pain but in some kind of altered ecstatic state. I remembered what a crush I had on him the year he and Jewelle got engaged when he was a resident tutor at Adams House at Harvard and I was a freshman at Wellesley.

I had not yet met Harold, and Jewelle was working at her first job for the federal government in Washington. All that academic year I hoped I would be lucky enough to meet a man as special as my sister's fiancé. Now here he was, perhaps at death's door.

Jim's illness made me think a lot about Harold, about his mortality. I gave no thought to my own. Nothing was guaranteed, I understood.

Finally, Jim got better; the cancer was caught in time. I left to celebrate my mother's eightieth birthday in Connecticut.

Jim, Percy, Graham, three key men in our family, all ill at the same time. Only Jim survived. On a lovely, warm afternoon in a hospice in Branford, a few days after my mother's celebration, Graham died of his prostate cancer. Mother had been married to him for just six years. She moved in with Pattee and Jim in North Haven. In this new summer of old sorrow, she bore up well. Again.

Amid a vortex of emotions, coming out of all that illness and death, I met my aunt Grace, my mother's only living sibling, at last. A fantasy fulfilled; a dream, a wish, an obsession resolved. It was as if she had been waiting for me all of her life. Instead of an ogre, a demon whose head turned in a 360-degree circle, I found a sweet, soft-spoken old lady who looked like my mother.

It was a time of answered prayers and unanswered questions. I did not want to overwhelm her, to frighten her, to hit her in the head with a baseball bat from the past. With a directness I had not expected, Grace answered many questions about the missing family. I came to understand that for some questions, there would never be any answers.

My mother came west to meet her sister. Race had separated them for seventy-six years, Grace living as a white woman, my mother as black. Each had a daughter named Patricia and a grandson named Geoffrey. The difference in their color was that between eggnog and vanilla ice cream.

Years of sorrow left my mother's soul. She had found her sister and reclaimed her family. Her birthday present was complete.

While we were away on a book tour, word reached us that a major tremor, the Northridge Quake, had struck Los Angeles. We called home, where our housesitter was playing host to a number of neighbors whose apartments had been heavily damaged in the quake. Our place suffered some damage and our cat would not come out of the closet.

Harold arrived home a day earlier than I, to assess the problems and clear away the crystal and dishes that had shattered. When Harold called, the cat emerged. One of our neighbors, Helen, stayed with us for four months after the earthquake.

Helen is an octogenarian actress between opportunities. A contract player at Universal Studios in the forties, she can recall chapter and verse the glory days of the star system. She came to Los Angeles from a small town in Missouri. Her ancestors were Irish, Scottish, and English. Then she was a flaming redhead with pale skin and a pinup girl's figure. Her career started when she won a Miss Missouri contest. For a long time, she was married to a radio director who also wrote for magazines. Silver-haired and widowed now, Helen is a living historian, attracting young and old alike who want to know what Hollywood was like in her time.

Helen is my mother's age, and we interact like mother and daughter. In the afternoon sun, we sit in the garden talking about books, movies, plays, the current crop of stars. Often, Harold and I invite her to join us for a new movie or a restaurant meal. At Christmas, we took her to see the lights of Beverly Hills. Every night, we share our dinner with her.

Sometimes, people mistake Helen for my aunt Grace.

At first, she was startled and embarrassed. Now she seems to enjoy the mistaken identity. She gets upset if people don't think she's related to me. When my mother comes to visit, she and Helen create a world of their own, a sisterly world. The years fall away as they chatter and laugh about the things they did when they were young.

In 1994, I developed vitiligo, a skin disorder in which the melanocytes, those cells that form the pigment melanin, run amok. Although people of any racial type can suffer from this condition, it presents itself most dramatically in people of color. Vitiligo can be a cruel affliction. There is no certainty yet as to what causes it, but some specialists suggest virus and stress as factors.

Many who have vitiligo look as if they have been splashed with bleach, resulting in the development of large patches of lighter skin, often on their faces, their necks, and their hands. Were the gods playing dirty tricks on me for messing with their natural order of things? In my book, I had revealed that all those Americans with white skins may not indeed be white.

By 1995, a five-inch oblong on my upper thigh faded to a lifeless noncolor, much like the circle around a white rat's eye. And it was spreading. In despair, I went to a dermatologist who assured me that, through the wonders of modern medicine, vitiligo could be treated by a variety of means.

My regimen required a special ointment, followed by sunning my thigh twenty minutes or so daily. I was to apply a cream at night. The doctor assured me my color would return after an indefinite period.

This vigil became a daily, in-my-face reminder of the mystery, the complexity, the divisiveness of skin color in my family in particular and in America in general. We had experienced our personal pigmentocracy.

As far as I know, none of the relatives on my mother's side had vitiligo. The light shade of their skin, the neighborhoods they lived in, the jobs they worked at, and the schools they attended confirmed to

other white Americans that my relatives were indeed white. My kin-
folk did not refute their racial assignment.

Their secret divided my family. For three generations we lived
apart. For three generations, those of us who lived as black wondered
why we had been abandoned. Those who lived as white wondered why
their family was so small. For three generations, we had ill will in our
hearts for the family that was not our family. For three generations we
thought about the day when we would meet. And that day had finally
come for my mother in Anaheim, California. Now both sides reach
across the abyss. We keep in touch by mail, telephone. We attend family special events, engagement parties, birthday parties, and funerals.
And we meet each other's friends. We are determined to be a family.

Secrets cut many ways. All of them, and us as well, were denied the
splendor of knowing the full range of America that resided within us.

In a sense, my family has lived the American Dream, the American
Nightmare, and the American Reality. For some, the dream is to be
free, white, and twenty-one. For others, the nightmare is to wake up
one day and find out one is black. This has happened numerous times
recently, as many Americans are coming out of the racial closet.
Books and newspaper articles now appear frequently about people
who are discovering their black ancestry. Dozens of letters have come
my way with similar stories. For many Americans, the reality is that
their backgrounds reflect the creolization of America: the walk, the
stroll, the glide across those evanescent boundaries we call race.

I continue to oversee my melanocytes in their march around,
across, and through the borders of my depigmentation zones. Recon-
necting the brown edges, the epidermal soldiers decenter and gently
cover up skin that is so pale it is beyond white, turning it from a
lighter to a darker hue once again.

For all of 1994 and most of 1995, I traveled a lot, speaking about
identity, race, culture, and family. On my way back from a reading in
Martha's Vineyard, I stopped in North Haven for a few days before
July Fourth to see Pattee, Jim, and my mother. Pattee had just been
named a school principal. Jim was supervising the final baseball activities of the Special Olympics, which had been hosted by the city of
New Haven for the first time. Jim had also involved himself deeply in

the Masons and their lore. He loved the fellowship and good times of the group he had joined a few years earlier.

The night before I left for Los Angeles, Jim fixed me supper. Pattee was out at a school meeting. In the kitchen, he studied his Masonic material while he kept an eye on the dinner he was warming in the microwave. Jim had lost more than ten pounds on an Herbalife regimen. That night, he kept hitching up his pants, which no longer fit his thinning frame.

"It was hotter than hell on those fields, Shirlee," Jim offered. "But the heat helped me lose some weight." He grinned. "Speaking of heat, did I ever tell you the story about the devil and the colored people?" We laughed and laughed and laughed. It was still hot outside. Idly, I thought how I would welcome my return to Los Angeles's cool weather as Jim served me dinner.

"Sorry I can't stay to eat with you. I have to meet my Masonic brothers tonight. See you when you come next time." He hurried out of the kitchen, holding his book in one hand and his pants in the other. I left the next morning.

It always takes me several days to unpack after a long trip. My suitcases were still on the floor, circling the bed. Harold was in Washington trying to arrange full-time caregiving help for his mother, who had been diagnosed with Alzheimer's. It was early evening when the phone rang. The voice was that of Kenny Joyner, Pattee's former husband, who had not called me since I moved to California.

"Hi, Kenny. What's up? Are you in L.A.?" I asked.

"No," he said in a calm voice, "actually I'm at Pattee's house with your mother."

My skin begin to feel too small for my neck. My chest tightened. In that instant I knew what the word "dread" meant.

"What's going on? Why are you at Pattee's?"

"I've got some bad news. I hate to tell you this, but Jim Brown just died. I'm staying with your mother until someone else can come and be with her. She asked me to call you and Jewelle."

Regular time stops. Slow motion sets in. Understanding falters. Paralysis begins.

I could not take in the words. Something blocked them from reaching my reasoning centers.

"Who? What? What happened, what happened? When, oh, when? Where's Pattee? Are you *sure?*"

Kenny, patiently, slowly: "I came across their car on the road, not far from their house. There was a crowd. They were working on Jim when I got there. Emergency people, neighbors, friends. The ambulance was there, waiting. They think he had a heart attack in the car. Pattee was with him. They're at the hospital now, but I'm pretty sure Jim is gone. Pattee asked me to come and tell your mother. I've called my mother; she's coming over."

"Let me speak to my mother."

"Oh, God, Mother, is it true? What happened? Have you talked to Pattee? Where are the boys?"

Mother sounded dazed, far away, out of breath.

"I only know what Kenny told me. I thought it was funny to see him at the door. He brought me my dinner they had ordered for me. Fried crab, but I couldn't eat it. I can't believe it. I can't believe it. But they say it's true. Pattee and the boys are at the hospital now. I don't know when Pattee will be home. When can you get here? Will you call Jewelle?"

"I'll call her as soon as we hang up. I'll be there tomorrow."

I hung up the phone, dialed Harold at his mother's in Washington. No answer.

Tried to reach Jewelle and Jim at their beach house in Monterey Bay. No answer.

Deirdre's answering machine was on. Left a message telling her it was an emergency. Call me.

No luck in reaching Melissa, either. Left a message on her machine.

Where was everybody? I really needed to talk to them, to tell them. I wanted them to tell me it wasn't true.

Called the airlines, arranged a flight. Looked at my suitcase again. Threw everything on the floor. Repacked lightly, underwear, slacks. Needed something for the wake, the funeral. White, we liked to wear white to funerals.

Had bought a beautiful new white 1920s-style dress for some special occasion, didn't know what it would be, but had to have the dress. Packed it. Couldn't sleep much. Couldn't cry much, either. It didn't make sense. How could my sister's forty-nine-year-old husband, big Jim, happy Jim, fun Jim, be dead?

Harold, Jewelle, Deirdre, and Melissa all returned my calls the next morning. An unreasonable anger overcame me when I talked with them. Where were they when I needed them? I had to suffer by myself for too long. Jewelle and Jim had been at a movie; Harold, at a family reunion dinner with his mother. They could tell I was annoyed. They understood. I hated the news I had to give.

Deirdre adored Jim, who always cooked special dishes just for her when she went to visit: collards, spaghetti, smothered pork chops. Her reaction was like mine; she couldn't take it in. She got very quiet, whispering, "What are your plans?"

Harold and Melissa sobbed, Melissa in near hysterics, moaning, "Not Jim, not Jim." Jewelle lost her breath. "Wait, wait, I've got to sit down. 'Jim's dead,'" she uttered to her Jim. I told each one, "I'll see you in Connecticut, I'm leaving in a few minutes."

Flying home. Back where I had just been. Back to the kitchen where Jim had fixed my food, told me a joke, hiked his pants, and studied his Masons book. Still couldn't cry on the long trip. Emptiness, no tears, just anger. Feeling sorry. For whom? Jim, Pattee, me?

I looked out the window. Below, life went on. Trucks drove across fields, people went to work, salesmen made calls, children sat in school.

Cars crowded the driveway and the street for as far as I could see. An unfamiliar face opened the door. Everywhere, in the living room, the dining room, the hallways, friends and strangers sat or stood talking softly. "Shirlee's here from California," someone said loudly. Mother was sitting at the dining room table, gracious even in her grief. I felt her crumble as I hugged her to me. She looked so sad. Her spirit seemed to have left for a while.

"Where's Pattee?"

"She's in the kitchen."

Pattee came out. Pale, puffy-eyed, dressed in an unpressed T-shirt, looking as if she had not slept.

What to do next? I had no practice for this. This was my baby sister. Her husband was not supposed to die before mine. Words cannot express the inexpressible. "I'm so sorry. I'm so sorry. I'm so sorry."

In a little-girl voice, she told me what happened. By now she knew it by heart; she had told it hundreds of times. Jim had finished for the day and they had agreed it was too hot to cook. They went to Dino's, a fish place in North Haven. With Mother's dinner in hand, they left the restaurant, walking out into the three-digit heat.

"There's a car I want to take you to see. I'm going to get it for you," Jim told Pattee.

They drove to see the car, a white Mercedes. Pattee laughed. Less than five minutes from home, Jim put his head in his hands, practicing what he had learned to keep him from hyperventilating. It didn't work. "Pattee, call 911," he gasped before he slumped over.

Pattee panicked. She dialed the number but did not press the "send" button. Nothing happened. "Hold on, Jim, hold on. Don't leave me, Jim."

She stopped the car across the street from an old house where a boy sat looking out at her. "Call 911, call 911, my husband's sick." The boy smiled but did not move. The lady's words made no sense to him. For everyone in our family, life had stopped at the edge of a narrow country road, just beyond some railroad tracks, by a house where a retarded boy sat and smiled.

She began to flag down passing cars. One held some of her son's football teammates. The big young men struggled to get the bigger man out of the car and laid him on the ground. A car with a nurse in it stopped. The heavy air did not move. Someone started CPR. Within minutes an ambulance arrived and the professionals took over.

Driving by to see a friend, Kenny braked, taking in the scene: Jim on the ground and Pattee surrounded by people. Kenny went to the emergency crew. "Give me his watch and his wallet for his wife." Kenny handed the items to Pattee.

"Tell my mother what happened and take her this dinner. I'll call her from the hospital."

Not until I saw Jim's photograph on the funeral programs did I accept that he was dead. There he was, sitting at Drake's Seat, high above a majestic view of Magen's Bay in St. Thomas, happy, relaxed, grinning into the camera. He looked directly out, eyes twinkling, wearing that "I've got a great joke to tell you" smile. I couldn't help but wonder where he was. Where was his smile?

We moved the funeral site from Jim's church to a larger space, Immanuel Baptist. Several thousand people attended the wake. The girls walked behind us as we moved forward to view the body. Melissa kept saying, "I'm not ready for this, I'm not ready for this." I told her she didn't have to look if she didn't want to. Before reaching the coffin, she ran crying from the church. I hurried out after her. "Mom, I'm not ready to see Jim. I'm not ready to see Jim," she sobbed convulsively. I held her and stroked her hair. Someone tapped me on my shoulder, thrust the wake program in my face, and asked for an autograph. I was amazed at the civility of my response. "Another time," I said.

Thousands more came to the funeral. The women of the family wore white. At the altar, silver and black balloons, Masonic colors, bobbed jauntily behind the coffin. When the Masonic ritual came, hundreds of black men, all different colors, all dressed in handsome dark suits, stood, filling the center and outer aisles of the church. Their stunning presence created a thrilling moment, a humbling time.

The mayor spoke, calling New Haven "Jim Brown's city, a place made better because he cared, because he lived and worked there." During the final viewing, Harold's knees sagged. Deirdre helped me hold him up. This time, Melissa stopped at the coffin, then walked tearfully on.

To our surprise, Pattee was the last speaker. As she reviewed her life with Jim, she didn't cry. She told the mourners about their last hour. When she finished, she kissed his forehead, pulled up the funeral covering, and drew it over his face before the undertaker closed the coffin.

We buried Jim near a weeping willow tree. Taps played as silver and black balloons made their way toward white clouds and blue skies. The heat had broken. It seemed like a beautiful day. As we left the cemetery, I reached for Harold's hand. It was cold and lifeless.

More than any other death in our family, Jim's hit us like a natural disaster. That we would be without his large presence was unthinkable. That he was lying in a box under the ground was unbelievable. Even now, I have not accepted the unacceptable. Jim will be with me for a long time.

I returned to Los Angeles in a daze, sorrowing for my younger sister and my mother. I also grieved for myself, feeling vulnerable. What did it mean to plan, if it all could be taken away in three minutes in a car? I dared not consider the question of Harold's mortality.

Deirdre and Melissa got clingy. For the next several months they called with questions and instructions about our diet, our health, our work schedules. All of us were depressed.

Deeply wounded, Pattee returned to her principal's job, operating by rote. Even though I called several times a week, I did not know how to help her. It was all so unsatisfactory; nothing made anything right.

Harold seemed preoccupied. There remained a distance between us.

The Christmas after Jim's death, Melissa wrote each member of the family a letter we would have in case she died. Her rationale was that she had never told Jim how much he meant to her, and she wanted all of us to know: me, her father, her sister, her grandmother.

In my letter she wrote:

> I love the way you've allowed me to grow, and stood by me throughout the difficult times. When I was sick you were always there, and you would sing to me with the steam on for those asthma moments. How can I ever thank you for guiding me to being the artist I am today!?! Such support is hard to come by. You've nurtured my talent. . . . Sometimes I worry that I can't live up to that standard of achievement, but then I must concentrate on and believe in my path. I'd like to try to live each day as fully and well as I can, giving and loving, squeezing out time for everything. Losing Jim, at least on the physical plane, has made me slowly start to realize a lot of things. I know I couldn't bear to be without you. So I celebrate you now, while I have you. And I pledge to you a deeper, more sincere, more loving, more willing, more caring me. I'm lucky, this I know.
>
> Much love,
> Yours,
> Melissa

It took me a year to come out of my depression. Harold worked some of his off by finishing up the kitchen projects that Jim had started in North Haven. He did an exquisite job. After that he seemed somewhat relieved.

Other parts of my life are gone now. I grieve for Harold's mother, whose curtain of Alzheimer's separates her from us. And I sorrow for his sorrow. Our beautiful house on the hill in St. Thomas, the house that was supposed to be one of the sturdiest on the Island, was destroyed in Hurricane Hugo. Angry winds whipped off its tin roof, blew out its windows. Torrents soaked its naked walls and marble floors. Its hulk still stands there, I am told. I'm not sure I want to see it.

In that same storm, my television station, WBNB, was blown off the side of Mountain Top, new transmitter, new studio, and all. The station no longer exists. No one was injured, but the owners of the station folded their tents and left the island. I saw Ruben, my weekend engineer, when we went back to the islands for the first time in twenty years. Gray hair caps his head, but he still works full-time in the post office. The last time I heard, Sam was working as a key engineer for the PBS station WTJX. The islanders are not without their commercial television, though; some have cable, which hooks them up to CNN, the movie channels, and the New York news stations.

Ellis has been immortalized with a collection of his papers and *SOUL!* tapes at the Smithsonian's African American Museum. I plan to write his biography.

Most of my gay friends from our sixties days are dead now, their lights extinguished by AIDS. Most of our New York friends, our "Ellis crowd," Maurice, Malcolm, Tony, Joe, Henry, and so many others, gone. I went to many of their funerals and cried for all of them when I saw the AIDS quilt at a museum in St. Louis.

The weekend Betty Shabazz died, we attended the wedding of Sumayah Jamal, the serious little girl who had played with my daughters so many years ago. Married in a weathered brown church on Shelter Island, Sumayah was an exquisite bride. Her groom was a white Englishman whose ancestor, Robert Browning, provided the sonnets for the ceremony.

The last time I saw Betty was at her place of work, Medgar Evers College in Brooklyn. Once again we laughed and giggled together like girls, talking about Ellis and those exciting days of the sixties. Afterward she interviewed me for her cable television series. We parted laughing. That is how I will remember her.

Macedonia still stands. Although most of the congregation I knew as a child are gone, a good number of the people who have seen me through my life still survive, as do my Sunday school contemporaries and their children. My link to that church continues to provide ballast in my life. The college scholarship my sisters and I established in my father's name continues.

Taking a break from the theater, Melissa moved to St. John, where she taught dance and managed an art gallery. She said she was "home again," but it was not a lifetime move. On Mother's Day she sent me a bougainvillea cutting in a card. My eyes misted when I saw the pale pink and lavender blossoms like the ones that had covered our verandas in St. Thomas. I hated the fact that she went so far way, out of my maternal radius. But I reminded myself that I, too, had left my mother and father to go to the Caribbean. And one day when I was lonely in St. Thomas, a card arrived containing some lovely-colored autumn leaves from my mother in Connecticut. Something caught in my throat as one of those leaves drifted to my Caribbean floor.

After eighteen months on the Island, Melissa relocated to Los Angeles, where she is working her way into movies and television. I am glad that she is near.

Deirdre told us she had no heart for practicing the law she studied at Fordham Law School. We were secretly relieved. She moved out of Manhattan to Fort Greene in Brooklyn. On her first night there, her apartment was robbed. Fortunately, she wasn't hurt, just scared. It didn't deter her, though. One of her dreams is to own a Brooklyn brownstone with a garage.

Jewelle is going strong, having recently published another book and lecturing everywhere. I call her the Diva and Pundit of Northern California. Once we attended a Black Caucus weekend in Washington together. At a reception, I noticed an attractive tall black woman who was vaguely familiar. Jewelle and I said hello and introduced ourselves.

"Are you related to Harold Haizlip?" the woman asked brightly.

"I'm his wife."

Without skipping a beat, she said loudly, passionately, "You're the woman who stole my man from me so long ago."

It was Pam. We chatted uncomfortably for a few minutes, then moved on. Speechless for once, all Jewelle could say was "Ummph."

Jim has retired from his teaching post at Stanford and remains cancer free. He's working on a book he has wanted to write for a long time.

Jewelle and Jim have been married for over forty years, and both their sons make their homes in California.

Awakened from the dream of death, Pattee has emerged from her grieving ready to face life again. Now she drives a canary-yellow Mustang convertible. Her three sons in Connecticut keep their eyes on her, making sure she does not act "too young."

I think of Jim often and get angry with God every time I do.

A great job found Harold. He's doing what he loves to do. Talking and planning, just up his alley. Working for children at risk; children who need help in school, at home, and in life in general. A major drawback is he has to travel too much, and I'm not keen about that. The good news is that no desk job holds me down, and if we have the money, I can travel with him.

And so we took our first trip to Disney World. We did not take it as an omen when at the beginning of the park, near a popcorn kiosk, a large black bird let out a large gray dropping on Harold's immaculate blue blazer. There we were, two slightly older children holding hands, walking through the Enchanted Castle and the Hall of the Presidents. Just as delighted with the sights, the sounds, and the colors as any five-year-olds there. Why were there tears at the back of my eyes?

While in Orlando we visited bubbly, active friends who were in their nineties. He had a cane, she used a motorized wheelchair. They have been married for over sixty years. "What's your advice to get as far as you have?" we asked.

"Stay the course," they said, "stay the course. Sometimes marriage is like a few months of rainy Sundays. But when the sun does come out and that old pelvic pull kicks in, there's nothing that can beat it."

*H*AROLD: Whenever our telephone rang after 11:00 P.M., I knew it was Vira calling from Washington. At 2:00 A.M. her time, Ma was sound asleep and couldn't eavesdrop on Vira's anger that Mom was forgetting everything, asking the same questions over and over, and talking to her dead mother and brothers, who, she said, came to visit her at night in North Carolina. She followed Vira from room to room all day, even waiting outside the bathroom. Several mornings, she had removed her own underclothes from her chest of drawers and asked Vira whom each piece belonged to. She insisted she had never seen them before, neatly put them back, and told Vira to see a doctor soon because her mind was "slipping" real bad.

Not feeling well herself, Vira couldn't stand it. She didn't want to yell at Ma, but sometimes Ma bugged her so much that she lost her temper and couldn't help it. And she hated being followed and asked the same questions all day, so she locked herself in her room to "get a few minutes' peace," sometimes for several hours. What did I think she should do?

I once answered that question directly and told Vira to have Mom's doctor test her for dementia or Alzheimer's disease. "My mother is not crazy," she screamed. She slammed down the phone and refused to speak to me for a week.

After Ma had continually discouraged Vira from pursuing a singing career because it was "sinful," Vira had come back home. Her return to Ma's came in 1961, after Ma had married Glenn and Vira had had a series of failed marriages, several miscarriages, and false job starts. She worked as a security guard in a government building until she retired on disability.

It always troubled me that Vira could not pursue her dreams. She did have a glorious voice, and I think if I were to find any flaw in my mother, it would be that she had not been more supportive of her only daughter's career ambitions. As a result, Vira was bitter and reminded Ma every chance she got about why she was at home. I realize, though, that they were both victims of their times. Vira did whatever it took to liberate herself from our mother's expectations; Ma found it impossible to question her own religious "rules."

Vira and Ma became locked in a dance of inseparable interdependence despite a constant tug of wills, each trying to be mother to the other. They constantly fussed with each other over insignificant things but simultaneously expended great effort, time, and money on thoughtful, kind gestures toward each other. As Ma aged, Vira assumed greater responsibility for the house, managing it and Ma like a sergeant majordomo, until she said or did something that touched a sensitive nerve in Ma. Whereupon they fussed with each other for several days until they reached a resolution. Anyone who interfered or offered an opinion on their issues was immediately attacked by both of them. Each rose to the defense of the other against outsiders, including me.

When Vira called again after having hung up on me, I focused on her instead of Ma and asked about the continuous pain she was experiencing. It had become excruciating in all of her fingers and joints and kept her awake at night. Her doctor diagnosed severe arthritis, but the medication hadn't helped at all. Her hands hurt so badly that she couldn't cook, so she had given Ma Campbell's soup and saltines for lunch and dinner the last few days and had no appetite for food herself.

I asked her to tell me the name of every single medication she had taken for any reason during the last thirty days so that I could check my medical dictionary for contraindications. Near the end of her list she mentioned that she had been taking tryptophan to help sleep at night.

"L-tryptophan?" I asked.

"I just call it 'tryptophan,' honey. I've been taking it a long time for my insomnia. It really works. When I first tried it, Doctor Lee gave me a sample. Now I buy it at the health food store all the time."

"Do you take it every day?"

"Oh, yeah. Seven hundred milligrams. Otherwise, I'm awake all night."

"You know how you half-hear things on the radio when you're busy? While working at home the other night, I vaguely remember hearing something about L-tryptophan on KFWB, L.A.'s twenty-four-hour news station. I'll see if I can get more information."

Actually, I remembered quite clearly what I had heard, but I didn't want to alarm Vira before double-checking. The Food and Drug Administration (FDA) and the Centers for Disease Control (CDC) at the National Institutes for Health were investigating severe arthritis and deaths since 1989 among more than 1,500 people whose only common denominator was use of L-tryptophan, an amino acid, as an over-the-counter protein diet supplement for insomnia and stress reduction.

After two days of persistent telephone calls, I learned that the investigation was focused on impurities in the supplement that triggered a rare blood disorder called eosinophilia-myalgia syndrome, or EMS, in which the number of white blood cells (eosinophils) increased dramatically, became toxic, induced immune system weakness, and attacked muscles and other tissues. No treatment or cure had been found, and most victims died. The FDA recalled L-tryptophan, but since many people had been taking it for years, the number of EMS cases continued to rise.

From the FDA I obtained the name of the principal practitioner researching EMS and, after much pleading, convinced him to test Vira for EMS immediately. The tests results were positive. She had a severe case that would only get worse.

Vira fought valiantly against excruciating pain and physical debilitation until her death. Her swollen joints and muscle tissues defied arthritis medications and all others. Cycling on and off steroids, she gained excessive weight, dramatically lost weight and muscle tissue, and developed ulcers. Her teeth loosened and fell out. She lost her hair. It was when canes and crutches became too painful to use that she was forced to quit her job as a security guard. She was confined to a wheelchair and experienced extended bouts of depression.

As Vira's pain and physical deterioration slowly but surely incapacitated her, Ma worried and prayed, prayed and worried, seeming to identify with Vira's condition so totally that she needed medication herself. She was terrorized by Vira's illness and the fact that she was worsening, not improving. Then it started.

Ma's occasional memory lapses increased in frequency. She began asking the same questions over and over. She couldn't remember whether she'd had breakfast within ten minutes after eating it. She began rummaging through her closets for hours and hours, marveling at the nice things that belonged to somebody, asking who owned them. After twenty years of taking her telephone off the hook from 11:00 A.M. to 4:00 P.M. to avoid being disturbed while she watched her favorite TV soap operas, she stopped watching them altogether. And in the evenings, she revisited her childhood on the farm in North Carolina, reliving events and participating in conversations with dead family members and friends as if they were taking place in the present. At first, she was diagnosed with dementia, then Alzheimer's.

Vira adamantly denied that Ma had developed Alzheimer's, sometimes raging at its symptoms by refusing to answer the same question Ma had asked fifteen times previously. Unable to walk without great pain and difficulty, she arranged rides to shop for groceries and cooked meals from her wheelchair. She refused to allow anyone to help Ma or herself, adamantly ignoring her own illness by remaining as self-sufficient as possible, as long as she could.

As Vira's end came closer, Mom seemed to know it and to withdrew into a safe zone somewhere in the privacy of her mind, as if shielding herself from something too horrible to contemplate. Sometimes she sat silent and unmoving at Vira's hospital bedside, staring in stony silence at the outline of her firstborn's skeletal body, plaintively pleading over and over, "Lawd, have mercy." At other times, seemingly in a trance, she methodically combed Vira's hair, plumped her pillows, and straightened her blankets in a mother's instinctive motions to comfort her sick child. When Vira stopped breathing, Mom stared at her for a long, long time in silence. "Lawd, have mercy on you" was her last wish for Vira.

Family, neighbors, co-workers, and other friends turned out for Vira's funeral in D.C. Ma quickly forgot who had died but was glad to see so many people, even if she had to address them as "Honey" or "Sweetie" or "It's so good to see you" because she couldn't remember their names. It was as if she were responding from an instinctive but unconscious graciousness, an involuntary corroboration of the goodness and kindness at her core.

At our family's Rock of Gibraltar, the Oak Spring Baptist Church in Kernersville, North Carolina, located a mile or two down the road from Mrs. Mabe's store, throughout Vira's second funeral Ma was even more quizzical about who had died, several times nudging me and asking, "Who's in the casket?" She smiled impishly with feigned embarrassment at not knowing. At the Oak Spring Cemetery opposite the church, she was quite surprised to see her name next to Dad's on the tombstone she had purchased for both of them, above the grave she had chosen for him and herself. As Vira's casket was lowered into the ground on the far side of Dad, Mom admired the beautiful flower sprays and said they must have cost a lot of money.

A week later, as she and I drove past Oak Spring Cemetery en route to Washington, Ma again spied the wreaths piled high on Vira's fresh grave and exclaimed, "Oh, Harold, aren't those flowers simply beautiful? But why would anybody in their right mind leave them out here in the middle of nowhere?"

Several weeks later, I began to realize that my only sister was dead. I couldn't stop the tears.

Immediately after Vira had died, I, too, had gone on autopilot, arranging the autopsy, notifying family, selecting a funeral home and casket, taking care of Vira's bills and business, pulling together the funeral services in Washington and North Carolina, and, most of all, caring for Ma every second of every day. I had no time to grieve and soon understood why Vira sometimes hid in her room or overstayed in the bathroom: Ma's Alzheimer's had so robbed her of her self-confidence that she needed instant verification of her every thought or action by someone she trusted. With so much to do in so little time, I became frustrated trying to meet her needs along with doing everything else that had to be done—in coordination, more or less, with my brother Allen. And after returning from North Carolina, and after Allen had returned to California, I felt even greater pressure to keep Ma stable while interviewing candidates and exploring arrangements for her live-in care, Vira's replacement.

Staring blankly into space at my desk, I shook under the weight of one funeral and two deaths. Alzheimer's disease is no less deadly than any other killer: it slays as surely as cancer but leaves the shell to be cared for. Ma and Vira were both gone. Ma's shell, her shadow, is still here.

"Have you spoken to Mom tonight?" Melissa asked when I answered the telephone. She sounded greatly stressed.

"No. I just walked in the house from taking Ma for a bit of fresh air and dinner. What's up?"

"Call Mom in L.A., as soon as possible. It's urgent. Call her now, and I'll speak with you later." She was gone.

Melissa's urgency caused my pulse to quicken. After a short vacation on Martha's Vineyard, Shirlee stopped in Connecticut to visit with Mrs. Taylor and Pattee and had just reached California. I had come to D.C. to give Ma's caregivers a short break. The only crisis I could think of was that Shirlee had returned home to find either our apartment robbed or our friend, Helen Andrews, ill. Helen's ill, I decided. I called home.

"I have the worst news to tell you," Shirlee began, obviously very upset. "It's unbelievable. Unbelievable."

"What is it?"

"Jim Brown died today."

I heard her words, but I knew she wasn't talking about my Jim Brown, Pattee's husband, my brother-in-law and my very, very close friend. But which Jim Brown was she referring to? I knew only one.

"Who are you talking about? Who died?"

"Jim. Pattee's husband. Jim Brown died today. On his way home from dinner with Pattee." Shirlee was sobbing. "I'm taking the next flight to Connecticut."

"Jim is dead? Dead? Oh, please, Hon, please tell me that's not true. Please. Please."

During my years of battling Vira's doctors for better treatment of her EMS, I saw that she was steadily deteriorating and had time to grasp the fact that she would not improve in the long run. When she was hospitalized on an emergency basis, and unconscious, her doctor told me that her prognosis was not good; that these problems usually signaled the beginning of the body's spiraling descent toward death; that her immune system was destroyed. I fixed on keeping her comfortable and free of pain as long as she lived. Intellectually, at least, I was prepared. Jim's death was a point-blank shot in the chest.

During the drive from D.C. to North Haven, in numerous different ways I tried in vain to help Ma recall Pattee, her husband, Jim, and Mrs. Taylor, all of whom she knew well and liked a great deal. I finally changed the subject.

As soon as she saw the crowd coming toward us entering the house, her gracious instincts took over where her memory had left off, and she worked her way through the crowd like royalty, shaking hands and hugging strangers and family members alike (none of whom she could remember), offering, "Sooo nice to see you again," and "Ohh, honey, you're looking so well," or, lapsing, "I'm glad I could be here for the wedding; they're such a handsome couple."

The wave of grieving and sobbing began anew as I walked in, because everyone knew that after nearly twenty years together, Jim and I had become brothers, rather than brothers-in-law. We planned and cooked all of the holiday meals together. We also took charge of the "heavy-duty" preparations for all of our family celebrations, having our own private "party" in the process, sharing an unspoken understanding of what seasonings to use, what sequence to prepare various dishes in, how to present our concoctions beautifully, and when to roll them out—as any expert chefs would—for the family's enjoyment. And we swigged rum and Cokes in our off-limits kitchens or over barbecue grills at the Blue House, or poolside at their house in North Haven, loudly guffawing at Jim's endless jokes and ignoring the family's plaintive pleas to eat before midnight.

We also exchanged a lot of know-how about the mechanics and workings of things. Much more so than I, Jim was a genius at plumbing, electrical wiring and systems, auto mechanics, and all phases of home repair and construction. We both had collected nearly every conceivable tool sold by Sears and Home Depot and kept our garages and basements jammed with obscure parts and supplies, screws, wrenches and hammers, electrical sanders, grips and vises, window weights, saws, and other stuff that only we knew the location and use of and constantly borrowed from each other.

We both loved dressy events where we could dance recklessly with our beautiful wives, singing along with The Four Tops and Marvin Gaye, whom we both really enjoyed, recalling our teenage years and anticipating a private celebration later, at home, alone with the two sisters we loved. Dressed in brightly colored suits and along with several other good friends, we formed an impromptu singing group, "Harold and the PhD's," to lip-sync and dance several Temptation songs for a scholarship benefit that Shirlee and her sisters had organized to honor Reverend Taylor. And we spent many hours alone or at our favorite barbershop, sharing intimate "men's talk" about the similarities and differences between Shirlee and Pattee, him and me, his sons and my daughters, and about coping as family-centered black men against the subtle and overt racism we experienced—peppered with the off-color jokes that Jim felt he couldn't tell when our "girls" were with us, the ones just for "us fellas."

Jim was the brother I always wanted. We walked in each other's shoes. We understood without words. We reveled in each other's company.

My grief was so great that I could console no one, not even Shirlee, Pattee, her sons, our daughters, Mrs. Taylor, or anyone else. And I couldn't face accompanying the family to Keyes Funeral Home to approve their presentation of Jim's body. Instead, I focused on developing what I hoped would be my lasting gift of love and gratitude to him: the programs for his wake and funeral that the thousands of people would take home with them, to recall the special life of a very special man cut down in his prime.

My head swirled, my knees buckled, and I shook uncontrollably as I saw through a blur of tears the reality of Jim, resplendent in full Masonic dress, in his open casket at the front of the church, dead. Dead. My brother, Jim. Dead. So unfair. So awful. So unbelievable. From reserves greater than mine, Shirlee and Deirdre helped me to my seat in the family pew. An attendant massaged my shoulders, and handed me Kleenex and a fan as tears rolled down my face, over my lips, onto my necktie, and finally dropped into the puddle spreading on the floor in front of me.

At the cemetery, I fought in vain both the fact and the finality of Jim's death. When the Masons ended their elaborate graveside ceremony and each one began throwing a shovel of dirt onto Jim's casket at the bottom of his grave, I was horrified. I wanted to grab the shovel and beat the shit out of every one of them for doing something so unthinkable to my brother.

But I couldn't move. I couldn't speak. I could only watch in silence as Jim disappeared forever under shovel after ceremonious shovel of dirt. When a Mason offered me the shovel, I grabbed Shirlee's hand and tried to walk away. A few wobbly steps later, I looked back to make sure, once again, that Jim was really gone, that he was in that grave mounded with flowers. Dead.

After resettling Ma in Washington with her caregivers, Shirlee and I returned to L.A. completely whipped. We had no interest in much of anything and seemed to move through our routines on rote, neither able to say much for a long time as we tried to find a place for the pain and sorrow that were so raw.

I spent a lot of time on consulting projects with the L.A. school system and filled my evenings and weekends paying Ma's bills and, more important, talking almost daily with her caregivers about the progression of her Alzheimer's and its increasingly wearing demands on them. At least twice monthly I talked with Ma's primary doctors about adjustments to her medication in order to delay her spiral into mental oblivion, despite the irony of her excellent physical health at ninety-two years of age.

Allen moved to Oxnard, California, thirty-five years before we came west. For most of that time, he was a civilian employee for the navy, specializing in missile systems. Along the way, he picked up a real estate license and had some success as a broker. California has been good to him. Settled in a beautiful home about an hour from Los Angeles, with his wife and childhood sweetheart, he has two adult daughters and one grandchild and still works part-time for the navy and full-time in real estate. Over the years, a distance remained between him and me, not helped any by the fact that we lived on different coasts. I hoped that moving to California would change that. We're still working on the possibilities.

My mother also lives in California now, not too far from us. Since there's no treatment or cure for Alzheimer's yet, I watch helplessly as she disappears further behind the doors closing in front of her mind as she waves a vague, vacuous goodbye to Aunt Minnie, her only living sibling, to Dad's remaining brother and sister, to Allen, me, our wives, and her four granddaughters—all of us becoming strangers and nameless shadows in the dark, empty, mindless space where she now lives.

Of all the people I have known on the stages on which we have lived, Shirlee remains closest and most beloved to me, along with Deirdre and Melissa. Seeing, touching, and being with Shirlee, after our forty years together across so many miles, people, and events, is as exciting now as it was when I rushed around to her side of the Chrysler on our first blind date, thrilled that she preferred dining with me over studying in the library. We seem to have developed a sixth sense about each other, knowing without words being spoken what the other is experiencing and feeling. We adapt easily and comfortably between alternating roles as the chief or the Indian on our joint projects. We're each other's head cheerleader. Most of all, my faith in, trust in, and love for her have never wavered.

We team in similar alternating roles with Deirdre and Melissa, sharing their successes and standing alongside them during the bleak times of their lives. We're proud to be the parents of such good, strong, contributing, and positive young women.

I continue to wrestle with the uncertainties and unknowns of the Grand Plan. What does our past add up to? We've survived earthquakes, deaths, job loss, and unemployment—overarched by some of the most exciting and positive jobs. As ordinary people we have had some extraordinary times. What's next?

One day I will learn to enjoy the ride and not worry about the next turning. If only.

EPILOGUE

HIRLEE: The California we live in now is a more mean-spirited, fragile, insular place than it used to be. It is the land of proposition 187, a deep wound against immigration; it is the land of nonaffirmative action, a profound rejection of a level playing field; it is the land of the Northridge Earthquake, surely a preview of devastating things to come; and it is the land of post–O.J. Simpson, a place where a white female prosecuting attorney can call black women "weightless as moon rocks" without fear of censure.

We all tower over my mother now. Bone loss and arthritis have taken their toll. Nonetheless, she is still cheerful, feisty, caring, and swearing. We marvel that she is dating again, wearing a diamond heart necklace from her new beau, rejuvenating her wardrobe, rejecting "old lady dresses." She goes to most of the new movies, jazz concerts, lunches, and community events.

Her eighty-fifth birthday called for another celebration, this time a garden party tea dance. We held it on Pattee's back lawn on a Saturday afternoon in May. All week, the rains came and rushed down the sides of the large party tent we installed. Saturday morning the sun came out and stayed around for the afternoon.

All of her grandchildren came to the party, Jewelle's sons from

California, two of my brother's children from Boston, Melissa from St. John, Deirdre from New York, Pattee's sons from Connecticut. Standing in a line, they made a good-looking bunch as they toasted the life and times of their grandmother.

Wearing a pink floral chiffon dress and matching coat, Mother looked like a tiny angel floating around the tent. One of her "found family," a niece and her husband, came to the party from Ohio, their presence signaling the closure of the family circle. Swing played softly as Mother danced with her beau and the generations she had created swirled around her.

As I watched my mother watching her children and her children's children, it came to me that at the heart of any successful relationship are constancy and mutual forbearance. In her relationships with my father and then with Graham, my mother had stayed the course. As had Jewelle with Jim and Pattee with her Jim.

Harold and I have been together now for almost forty years. To me he hasn't changed much from the slender, exuberant youth ice-skating across the Boston Common. To me he is still the young man who held my hand as we waded along the edge of the waves of Lime Tree Beach in St. Thomas. The night was warm, the breeze was soft, and the ocean glimmered with phosphorescent creatures. Harold had just accepted the commissioner's job and was bursting with excitement and ideas. "Can it ever get better than this?" we wondered that night. It did.

I know now there is no happily ever after. Just happily. Death terminates all earthly romances, ends all great loves. I'd like to think that feelings go beyond the grave, though.

It is difficult for me to imagine a life radically different from the one that I've had. It's probably not the life that my parents envisioned for me, or that I envisioned for myself. But does anyone have that imaginary life?

Young people ask us what it is we look forward to, having been married for so long. What else is there? A lot. We still have dreams. Big ones. Small ones. Clichéd ones. I have other books I want to write, other stories I want to tell. Together we want to cross-country ski in Aspen, which we've done before. Go to Paris in May, walk the Appian Way. Travel to Savannah, San Antonio, and Charleston. Ride the Orient Express. Safari in Africa. See the autumn leaves in Vermont. Eat Maine lobster in Blue Hill. Help our daughters as much as we can. Mentor and save black children, uplift the race.

I don't mind aging—in fact, I don't feel older than twenty-two. Why that age, I'm not sure. Perhaps it's because I was twenty-two during our first year of marriage. I hope I will remain healthy, and every once in a while I have a few twinges about whether we'll have enough wherewithal to see us through retirement and old age. Otherwise, it's unlikely we will be blown off course. I take nothing for granted, though. I constantly check our rudder, inspect our hull, steady our wheel, and mend our sails. You never know where the next squall will appear. You have to be ready.

ABOUT THE AUTHORS

Harold C. Haizlip, Ed.D., has been a teacher and administrator in public, private, and parochial schools and school systems, a college administrator, and a frequent consultant to foundations, government agencies, professional organizations, and local and national education and youth development advocacy groups.

Shirlee Taylor Haizlip has worked in academia, social service, and the media. As a television journalist, she produced and hosted her own program. She has written essays, articles, and book reviews for magazines and newspapers. She is the author of *The Sweeter the Juice* (1994) and is the 1995 winner of the Simon Wiesenthal Center's Tolerance Award. In 1994 she received an honorary doctorate of humane letters.

The Haizlips reside in Los Angeles and have two daughters.